WEEDING AND SOWING

By the same author

Mathematics as an Educational Task

WEEDING AND SOWING

Preface to a Science of Mathematical Education

HANS FREUDENTHAL

D. REIDEL PUBLISHING COMPANY

DORDRECHT : HOLLAND / BOSTON : U.S.A.
LONDON : ENGLAND

Library of Congress Cataloging in Publication Data

Freudenthal, Hans, 1905–
Weeding and Sowing.

Bibliography: p.
Includes index.
1. Mathematics–Study and teaching. 2. Education.
3. Science. I. Title.
[QA11.F78 1980] 507'.1 79–26777
ISBN 90–277–0789–8
ISBN 90–277–1072–4 (pbk.)

Published by D. Reidel Publishing Company,
P.O. Box 17, 3300 AA Dordrecht, Holland.

Sold and distributed in the U.S.A. and Canada
by Kluwer Boston Inc., Lincoln Building,
160 Old Derby Street, Hingham, MA 02043, U.S.A.

In all other countries, sold and distributed
by Kluwer Academic Publishers Group,
P.O. Box 322, 3300 AH Dordrecht, Holland.

D. Reidel Publishing Company is a member of the Kluwer Group.

First published in 1978 in hardbound edition
Reprinted in 1980

2-0789/1072-1179-1250C

Printed in The Netherlands

FOREWORD

A title that sounds like poetry, and a subtitle that seems to contradict the title! But the subtitle is right, and originally it was just the title. A strange subtitle, isn't it? *Preface to a Science of Mathematical Education.* All sciences – in their prenatal stage – have known this kind of literature: only the term used was not 'Preface', but, for instance, 'Prolegomena', which means the same* though it sounds less provisional. In fact such works were thicker than the present one, by up to ten times. There is much more that can be said about a science before it comes into being than after; with the first results comes modesty.

This is the preface to a book that will never be written: not by me, nor by anybody else. Once a science of mathematical education exists, it will get the preface it deserves. Nevertheless this preface – or what for honesty's sake I have labelled so – must fulfil a function: the function of accelerating the birth of a science of mathematical education, which is seriously impeded by the unfounded view that such already exists. Against this view I have to argue: it rests on a wrong estimation – both over and under estimation at the same time – of what is to be considered as science. This explains the first chapter of this book, 'What is Science?', where science is delimited in various directions, against various sorts of non-science and pseudo-science, against technology, against faith. All that is expounded in that chapter – arguably out of a craving for lucidity – extends to many sciences, in particular those in the area of the social sciences. It is relevant wherever, caught between highly developed technology and rationally motivated faith, one can scarcely find an approach to a science. Among these domains education is the most prominent, and so the title of the second chapter is 'On Education', aiming at the role of education caught between technology and faith.

It is not only a science of mathematical education that we are waiting for. We need, just as badly, a science of education – with no adjective added –

* In fact, 'preface' is derived from 'praefatio', the Latin translation of 'prolegomena'.

which is for the time being even farther away. A science of education is no precondition of a science of mathematical education. It is just the other way round, as it has always been in the history of the sciences: mathematics prior to science, mechanics prior to physics, physics prior to natural science, sciences of languages prior to linguistics. This relation explains why on the way from the third to the fourth chapter, from 'On a Science of Education' to 'A Science of Mathematical Education' the tone gradually changes from criticism of that which puts on scientific airs, to a search for the silver lining. That is all and no more: there are not even the first rudiments of a science of mathematical education here; at most there are indications where to look for such rudiments. I pledge nothing; but I shall redeem all I pledge. Though it is not in order to make it easier for me to keep my promises that I do not make any, but in order to prevent anything from being raised to the level of a science when it is not one.

Someone called my *Mathematics as an Educational Task* a *Summa Contra Mathematicos*. This book could as well be called a *Summa Contra Didacticos*. They would be complements of each other, and that is alright. To everyone his due.

Right from the title onwards this Preface to a non-existent book aims at a future in the making: since the other book was dedicated to friends of my own generation, it is fair to dedicate this book to my dear collaborators from three to thirteen.

IOWO, HANS FREUDENTHAL
University of Utrecht

TABLE OF CONTENTS

CHAPTER I

WHAT IS SCIENCE?

ABSTRACT. The query 'what is science?' is not answered by a clean cut definition or by a complete set of characteristics. Science is delimited rather from other domains of human activity by criteria, some of which are made explicit in this chapter: relevance, consistency and publicity.

Truth is not mentioned among the criteria, because truth is a property of statements, whereas science as an activity is not a treasury of truth but a method of asking questions.

Relevance, as I call it, is a property not only of statements but also of problems and methods, and as such it is even more crucial than as a property of statements. Relevance can also be a property of definitions, notations, concepts, classifications, and, more globally, of problem complexes, theories, domains of knowledge. In this global sense it means being related to reality rather than floating in empty space.

As a criterion of what science is, *consistency* looks more like truth, though it seems to stress its logical component. But this is only the objective aspect of consistency. Consistency can also be intended as a property of action and of patterns of activity – as an attitude which faces consequences, asks relevant questions and pursues promising leads. For logicians the acme of consistency is the logically closed system. This, however, is an ideal picture, which is realised only in today's mathematics – even theoretical physics is a far cry from this ideal. General theory in physics is not a basis from which deduction takes place but a repository of organising devices. Physics is like a shop of mini-theories supervised by, though not dervied from, general theory. It is a pity that a wrong picture of physics, and natural science in general, has served and still is serving as a model for the social sciences, and the humanities.

Science is a public property, and in spite of the so-called secret sciences, *publicity* is one of the characteristics of true science. Nobody can be obliged to submit to initiation rites before he can study and practise science. Science is publicly accessible to everybody who agrees to learn its language, and in the long run neither schools nor prophets succeed in monopolising a domain of science, though sometimes it may be difficult to decide whether a particular science means more than the language in which it is expressed.

Relevance, consistency, and publicity are criteria by which science contrasts with its *fringe*: pseudo-science and non-science. Flying saucers, the mysteries of the Cheops pyramid, and the paragnosts are no serious problems to science but the Nazi pseudo-scientific racism was a menace to mankind and new pseudo-sciences may endanger humanity even more. Pseudo-science often sounds like a protest against public science as far as publicity means public recognition and is suspected to mean public coercion. The fringe of science is a social danger worth studying. It may also mean a danger to serious science. Pseudo-scientific infections may cause a cancer-like growth in serious science. Language borrowed from serious science may be abused in other sciences; terms like function, information, model and structure, that originated in mathematics, became meaningless fashion in many other sciences.

Science should be distinguished from *technique* and its scientific instrumentation, technology. Science is practised by scientists, and techniques by 'engineers' – a term that in our terminology includes physicians, lawyers, and teachers. If for the scientist knowledge and cognition are primary, it is action and construction that characterises the work of the engineer, though in fact his activity may be based on science. In history, technique often preceded science. For centuries medicine was a technique with some background philosophy before it became a science; and even today there are intellectual activities that call themselves science though in fact they are little more than technique with a bit of technology and a huge amount of background philosophy. Of course technique can be a good thing, and technology a valuable instrument; but both should be carefully distinguished from science; and their background philosophy has no right to behave as though it were scientifically justified.

Natural science gave us a picture of the world. We need more: a picture of man and a picture of society. They are a matter of *faith*. The rational expression of faith is a philosophy, which may be mere background, or indeed relevant in attributing values to experiences and actions and in steering technique. We cannot live without values, but we should recognise that the philosophy by which they are justified is a matter of faith rather than of science.

1. INTRODUCTION

It is not my intention to answer the question 'What is science?' by a clear sentence following the pattern 'Science is . . .', with a number of subordinate clauses. I would be disavowing all the facts of methodology which we have learned over the past century from mathematics if I attempted such a procedure. Explicit definitions may be allowed and may be effective when a well-balanced and solid stock of experience and verbal expression has been achieved, but not at the top of an imaginary system.

Nor should the reader expect a conceptual analysis, or a list of necessary criteria or of alternatives where crosses are to be put into yes and no squares, in order to decide whether something deserves the predicate of 'scientific' or 'science'. Where should I look for such an analysis or such criteria while methodology has hardly transgressed the frontiers of its prescientific stage? As an empirical science that would take existing science as a subject matter, methodology hardly exists. With eyes fixed upon some superficial features of mathematics and mathematical physics, large and pretentious methodological systems have been created, which unfortunately lack the links to the real phenomenon that is called science.

I cannot and will not list criteria that would allow us to decide whether something is science or even in a single case to corroborate that it is not science. No ready-made decision formulae may be expected when such general concepts as science are discussed. Along with any science, methodological criteria of what is scientific arise and develop.

Thus would it be correct to predict right now that ultimately the answer to our question would be 'Science is what people call so-and-so'? Why then the circumstantial preparations? Because they convey the shades of meaning. A blunt answer needs to be intelligible. Indeed, in the clause "what people call so-and-so", what is meant by 'what', by 'people', by 'call', by 'so-and-so'? Does 'what' mean one thing or a disconnected variety? Who are the 'people'? What is the 'so-and-so' aiming at? And does 'call' really read as a present tense, or should it mean a past or a future, or is its mood indicative, subjunctive or conditional?

Moreover, would it not perhaps be better to pattern the answer as 'Science is what people perform as such'? Many times I have pointed out that expressions like 'language', 'music', 'mathematics' mean not only a stock, the result of some activity, but also the activity itself. And though everybody would admit this as a triviality as far as language and music are concerned, it is not the same with mathematics. In fact, mathematics as a human activity is little known, and probably the double meaning of 'science' is not much better understood.

My question aims at elucidating some facts related to the question: is not scientific substance in science more determined by the way it is performed than by its mere being?

2. RELEVANCE

Should not the first relation to be scrutinized be that between science and truth? Is not truth the first criterion of what is scientific?

Well, truth is certainly not a *universal* criterion. Truth is faced differently in the various sciences. In mathematics truth is an easier touchstone than in the inorganic natural sciences; in the latter it is easier than in biology; and passing through the spectrum of sciences from 'hard' to 'soft' truth, the social sciences range far beyond philology and history. But this does not mean that the sciences at the hard end are more immune to non-science and pseudo-science. On the contrary, as examples will show, scientific mischief is even more rampant at the hard end. Likewise the diagnosis of what is non-scientific and pseudo-scientific need not be easier with hardness than with softness. It is worthwhile stressing this because at the hard end people are prone to deny the soft end its scientific character, whereas at the soft end people often react to this attitude with inferiority feelings and over-estimating harder sciences.

But this is not the reason why I do not feel justified in handling truth as a criterion of scientific character. What annoys me is the wrong perspective. *Truth* is a property of *propositions,* but science is not a conjunction of propositions. To start with the most obvious, a science knows *queries* too, which can often be more important than propositions. Truth as a criterion of scientificality aims at science as a stock. But scientific character or its lack can be assigned to a problem, an approach, a method, even though the results they give birth to are not true. Criteria, however, by which the scientific character of a query can be judged are of the kind: Does the query fit into our scientific activity? Is it useful? Is it promising? Is it not too easy? Is it not too difficult? And most of all: Is it correctly posed? Moreover, is not the most important feature in a query, more than the answer, the desire to pass from a badly formulated to a better formulated problem?

A query should be *relevant.* An example will show what I mean by this. In the third century B.C., we are told, Eratosthenes measured the Earth. By means of a sundial be could ascertain that the meridional arc from his dwelling place, Alexandria, to Syene, south of Alexandria, on the tropic, at the first Nile cataracts, was one fiftieth of the terrestrial circumference – indeed when on midsummer day at Syene the sun stood at the zenith, it was one fiftieth of a full circle off the zenith at Alexandria. Eratosthenes is said to have had the distance from Alexandria to Syene measured. It came out to be 5000 stadia, which meant 250 000 stadia for the whole terrestrial circumference. But what do we know about the length of the stadion (= 100 fathoms = a sprinter's distance)? The Olympic stadium was 180 metres long, but it was the longest of all stadia in Greek antiquity. In the past century philologists tried hard to find out which stadion Eratosthenes could have used, but notwithstanding all efforts the problem remained unsolved until half a century later somebody cut the Gordian knot: the query – he decided – which stadion Eratosthenes had meant, was irrelevant. The round figure of 5000 stadia indicates that even if Eratosthenes had really measured rather than estimated the distance from Alexandria to Syene, his measurement cannot have been decently accurate. The figure 5000 leads one to presume an actual result between 4500 and 5500 stadia, which means an error of 10% on either side. With a poor measuring accuracy like that, the query which stadion Eratosthenes might have used becomes irrelevant.

This does not mean that the 19th century philologists who raised the problem were non-scientists. Their investigations on the various stadia of antiquity were scientifically valuable even though they overestimated their scope. Even if the result of some investigation is wrong, its method need not be non-scientific. If, however, then or later, it had occurred to somebody to derive information about Eratosthenes' stadion from modern values for the circumference of the Earth, he could rightly be accused of unscientific methods, and this, because of the irrelevance not of the query but of the arguments. If finally somebody had taken the measures of the various stadia, expressed in metres, and had used number theory to find out which was Eratosthenes' stadion, he would have been moving in a field better characterised as pseudo-science rather than non-science. Here the irrelevance of the arguments and the lack of relevant relations are a matter of principle.

Of course *propositions,* too, can be relevant or irrelevant. The proposition $3 + 2 = 2 + 3$ is at any rate true. It depends on the context in which it is uttered whether it is relevant. As an answer to the question 'how much is $3 + 2$?' it is irrelevant though it is formally correct, and a teacher would be right to mark it as a mistake. As an example of the law of commutativity of addition it is relevant and therefore valid. The question 'why does the dog wag its tail?' can truthfully be answered by 'because the tail cannot wag the dog', but the relevant answer that would be expected is 'because the dog feels pleased'. A query is relevant if it allows a relevant answer; a statement is relevant if it introduces itself as an answer to a relevant query – this looks like a circle, and strictly formally it is, but as to the spirit it is not.

Not only statements expressing experience or knowledge can be relevant or irrelevant; relevance and irrelevance can be assigned to definitions, notations, concepts, classifications. In geometry the four quarters are irrelevant, in geography they matter. A classification of words according to their length may be relevant in the printing office, it does not mean anything in grammar. Changes introduced into the taxonomies of biology are often motivated by arguments of relevance. 'How has it become known that the name of this star is Sirius?' is an irrelevant question; 'how do you know that this is its name?' may be relevant.

Relevance is a –local– property not only of single questions and statements, but also a – global – property of entire problem complexes, theories, fields of knowledge. There 'relevant' means 'fraught with relations', that is relations to some reality rather than internal relations within the system. Irrelevance is irrelatedness, floating in mid-air, detachment from any reality. There are quite a few intellectual activities that claim scientific character though they lack any relation to any reality whatsoever – much philosophy is of this kind.

What we are left with if global relevance, relatedness to reality, is absent, is a stream of words, which under the most favourable conditions may be bridled by discipline and efforts at consistency, and under the worst conditions may mean that unchecked autonomy of language which is otherwise not unusual in poetry and prophecy. But, after all, the global relevance is often historically conditioned. Problems which once stirred up heated discussions can at a later moment in history have been disposed of as irrelevant.

The global relevance of a query or answer can be reformulated as follows: Are the worlds where the query is to be answered in one way or another, where some answer must be accepted or rejected, equal or different? If they are equal, my choice does not matter; if they are different, relevance prevails. For centuries the 'iota' in *homoiousios** has not been a matter for discussion, but there was a period when it kindled wars in Christianity. Yet I do not need theology to find examples of issues that after long discussions were not decided but tabled as irrelevant, as devoid of relations to reality. Many philosophical issues are of this kind but even in the more realistic sciences, mathematics included, such examples are not rare.

No doubt, if Einstein had not formulated relativity, others would have done so in his place, but without Immanuel Kant no *Kritik der reinen Vernunft* or any similar work would ever have been written – this shows what is the difference between theory related and unrelated (or hardly related) to reality. What became historically operational in the *Kritik* was a concretised sham version which by its concreteness was somehow related to reality.

Turning to pseudo-science one sees even clearer what irrelevance means: lack of content, or dealing with a reality created for its own sake in order to be able to claim relevance; lack of problems or dealing with a make-believe world of problems.

Mathematics seems to be a counter-example to this position. Is not mathematics by its abstractions detached from any reality? No, it is not true what

* The question whether as to his essence Christ is equal or similar to God.

outsiders often say and think about mathematics. Mathematics is not merely a language but a mental activity, and mathematical concepts are not words but realities. It is no Platonism to state this but the reflexion on actual mathematical behaviour. But there is more to it. Beside its direct relations to reality mathematics can boast numerous indirect ones, as applied and applicable mathematics, and so it happens with every science when it is applied to another one.

Every practitioner of science practises a specific science. Science specialised much later than the arts and crafts. The specialisation of science is a hard fact today. On the other hand in a continuous process of intertwining and interaction the various sciences have been brought closer together than they ever were. Innovations in one science are instantaneously applied in others. It is not easy for the individual to combine specialisation with interaction. Most often a superficial look at what happens elsewhere is not enough. One needs middlemen who live in both fields. But who can guarantee their double competence? Everybody knows the stale joke: 'According to the *X*-specialists he is a *Y*-authority, and according to the *Y*-specialists he is an *X*-authority'. If, however, *X*- and *Y*-specialists do not communicate with each other, the rumour of this symmetry can take a long time to spread abroad. If not, meanwhile one dog has eaten the other. Sometimes it looks as though the frontiers between sciences are not nobody's but everybody's land.

It is the land where pseudo-science, charlatanism, and quackery are flourishing – they cannot be passed over if science is discussed. Experiences, classifications, concepts, theories do not seep into other domains of scientific activity by mere diffusion; it costs effort to transfer them, and sometimes this transfer can be a first rate scientific achievement. Where it is too easily done, superficiality can be the cause, and ineffectualness the consequence. Though a great splendour of relations is exhibited, its relevance can be an illusion. The 'universality of nature's forces and energies' or some similar principle is superficially invoked as a generalising argument; sham theories are built from a hotchpotch of fragments of science; scientific languages and style are parroted. This is the way quackeries came, and still come, into being. From the 18th century onwards magnetic and electric phenomena were 'universalised' according to this pattern to bring forth animal magnetism and electric quackeries. From the law of conservation of force – today it is called energy – which was immediately seized upon by quacks to apply to the conservation of masculine sexual force, up to the fabrication of vitamin and hormone enriched soaps and creams, every new scientific discovery has been universalised by pseudo-scientists. Condensors, induction, insulation, rays, waves, and last but not least, the atom have quickly and efficiently been misused. Nothing is safe.

Scientifically adorned ignorance and stupidity, learned charlatanism, pompous and scientific sounding language, imitation of scientific attitudes are all unmistakable symptoms, but the motives behind them cover a broad spectrum: from sincere belief in a scientific jargon repeated by people who do not guess that the terms they repeat rather than being beautiful sounding metaphors do mean something in the science that is imitated, up to the manifest fraud of scientific advertising by money-grabbing charlatans, there are many shades of irrelevant pseudo-science.

But also in the intercourse between disciplines, what is taken over from one into the other is often restricted to the jargon, devoid of any content – this holds not only for pseudo-science and quackery but also in the normal scientific activity. This is seriously to be deplored, not because jargons could endanger real science but because, by their mere existence, sham relations can delay creating genuine ones. As a mathematician I deplore such distortions as have a stress on mathematics. If I exclude fields where mathematics has been applied from olden times, and economics, I should say that the transfer of mathematics is often superficial and its application irrelevant. Taking possession of mathematical jargon devoid of content is the rule of charalatans, but even genuine science is not immune against it. O. Spengler's *Untergang des Abendlandes,* a hotchpotch of badly understood mathematics, was a milestone in this development. At that time, in the twenties, the slogan 'functional' was borrowed from mathematics, in the midcentury it was 'information' and 'entropy', now it is 'model', and in a few years all will be 'structure'.

The most instructive case is that of 'information'. High esteem for mathematics does not always prove deep knowledge of it. If people less acquainted with mathematics are repeatedly confronted with the 'information' and the formula which is said to measure it, they will finally believe that something might be in it, and where one sheep goes, the others follow. Fortunately it does not last long. Clean science quickly scotches focuses of infection.

With cybernetics, which was borne after its name had been invented and was nursed with the assistance of charlatans, the infection did not last long. It was just the impressive formula for information – which would never be applied – that neutralised 'information' as pseudo-science. One can understand that mathematicians were amused or shrugged. It is to be deplored that they did not act more forcefully. Where mathematics is abused, they wash their hands of it, not in innocence but in ignorance.

So it happened with 'model'. A term was borrowed from mathematics, and as usual nobody cared whether this word meant anything in mathematics, and if so what. Unfortunately in mathematics and neighbouring sciences the term has two – almost opposite – meanings, one within mathematics, and one in the relation of mathematics with other sciences, and this fact may have contributed to the misuse and the success of 'model'. Today the pseudoscientific congenital defect of the term 'model' is forgiven and forgotten. 'Model' has become a pompous term, evoking scientific associations, which may mean nothing, or as it happens everything: agenda, contract, division, formula, holiday trip (vacationing model), menu (meals model), pattern, rule, schedule, theory (in alphabetical order).

Much worse is the misuse of 'mathematical model', which most often means an abuse of mathematics itself. At this point, where mathematics is only cited as one example of an irrelevant interscience application, I will not elaborate on this abuse of mathematics and similar abuses, but in due time I will come back to this point.

3. CONSISTENCY

A while ago I dropped, perhaps too casually, truth as a criterion of scientificality in order to turn to the criterion of relevance, which to my view looks more relevant. I recall this fact, not because I am sorry about it but because the new criterion I will consider now is more closely related to truth: *consistency.* The absolutist, metaphysical undertone that may be heard in 'truth', does not sound in 'consistency', which instead seems to be fraught with logic. Yet I do not mean consistency in an exclusively logical setting. Consistency should be interpreted not only in an objective sense, as a property of a system, but also from the viewpoint of the acting subject, as a characteristic of acts and patterns of acts. In a crude way the consistency of a system means that the system does not affirm a proposition along with its negation. A man is consistent if having said A he remembers it where relevant in order to restate it, and adds B to it where it is a necessary consequence, or rejects it deliberately where it seriously impedes consistency. But there is again more to it. It is meaningful to require consistency not only in making statements but also in asking questions and posing problems. There is, or there should be, a coercion not only of answers but also of questions. Evading pressing questions can mean subjective inconsistency; while consistency urges that they are intentionally searched for, that suspicion is cultivated and shaped into criticism, and that flaws and gaps in the stock of experience and knowledge are located and mended. The greater wealth that a concept acquires if it is detached from the ready-made system and tied to the system being made, becomes again apparent.

The acme of consistency is, according to some people, the logically closed system; methodologists who took their bearings in mathematics and natural sciences understand consistency in this restricted sense. Unfortunately the closed system is at most possible in mathematics; even in the most rigorous sciences it is an ideal picture which can charm the eye as long as the reality is disregarded or not noticed. It is not true that sciences like theoretical physics are governed by, or derived from, a general theory. Instead the general theories are tools of organisation and bearings, stocks of concepts and methods, a background and means of epistemological validation. The Newton-Lagrange equations answer the questions that may be asked in mechanics as little as do the Maxwell equations in electromagnetism. Most often problems are solved by *ad hoc* approaches rather than by deductions from the general theory. It is a spirited occupation to derive purely mathematical consequences from the general theory, but it is not the only task the physicist is charged with, nor is it his most important one. He is expected to mathematically translate problems as they are posed in the realm of reality, and in this undertaking the general theory functions methodologically but not like a major premise from which, with an appropriate minor added, conclusions are drawn. No-one has ever derived from Maxwell's equations how electricity propagates in insulated conductors – in such a case one is glad to apply Ohm's law. Among the numerous applications of quantum theory, for instance to explain chemical valences, there is hardly one that appears as a logical conclusion from quantum theory. It cannot even be taken for granted that quantum theory is able to explain mathematically the atomic spectra apart from the simplest. In fact, every real problem is approached by *ad hoc* methods, and there can be no doubt that physicists are entitled to act according to this policy.

It is not my intention to denigrate the achievements of the exact natural sciences by stating this fact, but it *is* my intention to warn against the overestimation of the deductive element in these sciences. History tells how difficult it was to impose a more than locally deductive structure upon mathematics. So it is not to be wondered at that at present the so-called exact sciences lack almost all the preconditions in which such an ideal state could be achieved. If the view is fixed on reality rather than on the ideal picture, a science is a fair of mini-theories under the supervision of a general theory. Every history of science can tell you how in the era of Aristotle or of Descartes, science bore only a slight resemblance to the philosophers' description of it. It is less known that even today the relation between science and its methodology is not much better. And if this is the state of affairs in the hardest sciences, what can be expected at this point from the softer ones? Or wouldn't the lack of general theories be an advantage for genuine methodology?

I have dwelled upon this point because the exact sciences are often considered as a paragon. It is not unusual that in the socio-cultural disciplines methods are advertised as characteristic of the natural sciences, though what is offered agrees more with what methodologists think about the natural sciences than what happens in practice. It is not to be wondered at that these caricatures father only caricatures. Much in the future development of the socio-cultural sciences will depend on whether the high esteem in which the so-called scientific method is wrongly held gives way to a more critical appreciation.

This warning is intended to prevent objective consistency from being identified with deductivity. To be sure, deductions take place when consistency is attempted, but though a few deductions do not suffice to generate a deductive system, consistency need not be in danger. And conversely, in the personal sphere systematic deductivity can characterize dogmatists and wranglers rather than consistent scientists. Products of methodical madness such as offered by schizophrenic minds can be striking examples of thorough systematism and strange deductivity. Every era has known – famous and less famous – examples of systematic maltreatment of languages, distinguished by the most extreme consistency. The authors of these products live in a world where language has become a reality, the only reality – which makes consistency easier – and a mock reality because it is language devoid of its normal contents. Chewing words, as is the habit of some existentialists, and more generally, the tendency in some philosophy towards autonomy of language from contents, is a feeble reflection of pathological phenomena.

4. PUBLICITY

Starting from relevance and consistency I have arrived at the third feature of science, though, as it happened, from its negative side: publicity. Science is a social fact, something that is publicly exercised and accessible, subjected to public praise or blame, a common estate, a catholicity. From olden times there existed so-called secret sciences, science eschewing publicity, magic art and mysteries, secret teachings of the master and sacred covenants of secret fraternities. If it happened that this secret covered genuine science, then secrecy did not last. Once upon a time it occurred that the secret mathematics of the Pythagoreans was publicised.

There are people, even in the grove of Academe, who seriously believe that physicists from Einstein onwards, should have been aware of their responsibility and kept secret the scientific discoveries that were due to lead to the nuclear bomb. Shaking one's head is the least reaction that this deep-rooted lack of understanding deserves. If Kant had kept his *Kritik der reinen Vernunft* secret, to be published after a century's delay from his decease, nobody would have paid any heed to it (and meanwhile neither Hegel nor Marx could have elaborated on it); but had de Ventris withheld his decoding of Linear B, some other man would have invented and published it; the same can be stated with even greater certainty about discoveries in natural sciences.

But I do not mean just this when I introduce the criterion of the publicity of science. It includes much more, and more essential, features. Today nobody needs to undergo initiation rites when he wishes to study some science, he need not fulfil personal preconditions, take oaths and make vows of faith, in order to be admitted to the knowledge and exercise of some scientific activity.

These are no trifles, because by stating these facts, I describe a state of affairs that science has not been able to boast of for very long, and I have disregarded relics that contradict my statement. Every science knows schools. In former times schools had to spread the master's doctrine, today they are more or less closely knitted groups of cooperation. But 'school' can also mean – and there are enough examples to prove it – that a group or a faction is distributing offices and subventions among the obedient ones and refusing them to non-conformists. In the long run, however, it is not that easy to determine by such means what science is.

More often schools are more innocent. It is true they like to cultivate their private languages, and whoever does not know the watch-word, whoever cannot pronounce the shibboleth, is excluded. Does this exclude publicity? Is not everybody entitled to learn the language concerned?

Yes, but this is more easily said than done. If a psychologist explained to me what is a 'basically determined multi-discriminatory response', it would undoubtedly last a while until he had finished, and it is not certain whether I would have stopped listening before that. I might have understood that it is quite a simple concept which is only complicated by a lot of pretentious words, but then he would have explained to me that all of them are as badly needed in the structure of the system as the Latin names of plants in the system of the biologist. If, however, a scholar from the humanities would like to know what entropy is in physics, the etymology of the word would be of no use to him, and a definition as it is found in a dictionary would be of little use. He is obliged to learn a substantial piece of thermodynamics to understand the concept, and in order to formulate this piece of thermodynamics quite a bit of mathematical training is required, which is not learned in a jiffy.

As a matter of fact it is not true that a science can be identified with its language, and that it is enough to know this language in order to master the science. Language is a tool with which to express contents, scientific ones included; if there is nothing to be expressed, language is just a stream of words, and if there is nothing understood, it is idle talk.

But deciding whether something is idle talk asks for a responsibility outsiders will shrink from, though it need not be that difficult. It may happen that somebody is speaking his own language and communicating with no one, not even with himself, that his discourse is incoherent. It can happen that he is communicating with himself but with nobody else. It can be a small group who pretend to communicate with each other, though in fact everybody produces his own stream of words or idle talk.

All these cases can be disregarded. The real problem are the cases of partial communication. For instance, in some discipline a Master has published obscurities along with plain speech; or, let us say, things of a kind which at their first appearance are greeted with incredulity and remarks like 'I have read it up to this point, but from there onwards I could not understand a bit and I gave up'. Perhaps there are some courageous people who try it, and among them a few who finally explain they grasped the meaning, and who will lecture and write about what they had grasped. They are joined by some more people who, as they claim, also succeeded in understanding the obscurities – hesitatingly in the beginning and more courageously as time went by. There exists a critical number for such evolutions. If a certain percentage, say 10% or 20% of the people concerned, say they have understood the matter, growth does not stop until the 100% mark is reached; in fact, whoever refuses to join the crowd would make a fool of himself or dig his own grave. The way to find out whether they had really understood it is the same as that which works very well in oral examinations. One asks 'please apply the matter here or there', or if it is something that is not easy to be applied, 'please, formulate it in your own words'. In fact it is a striking feature of many such suspect obscurities that those who claim to have understood them do not dare to apply them, or parrot them literally, or almost literally, with the wordings of the Master or his authorized interpreter, lest with the slightest deviations they risk demonstrating that they did not genuinely understand it. For this reason undigested quotations are a bad omen.

For a certain time it was the fashion to put the blame on language if people did not 'understand' each other personally, socially, philosophically, politically: it was said they speak different languages without knowing it. If somebody complained about an insult the alleged offender explained it as a misunderstanding – today they call it 'a communication break'. The deepest misunderstandings are liable to arise in social environments where such terminology is cultivated as soon as people dare to express their thoughts and feelings lucidly. This can be an attitude so unheard of that others are led to suspect it as irony or a dirty trick.

Even in the trade of science it can be unwise to express one's thoughts in plain and clear talk – the in-crowd will say 'he writes for the public'. Obscurity of expression can be a symptom of laborious thought birth – what has been acquired with great effort is delivered with even greater effort. This can be the background but it need not be. Stammering can as well indicate that the speaker has not mastered the subject matter.

The latter is certainly the preferred explanation in mathematics. A mathematician who says or writes incomprehensible stuff is asked to give more particulars. If he does not or if his explanations are insufficient, the matter is closed. Never in mathematics has anyone become famous by an idea that nobody understood, and obscurities are not accepted even if they are advanced by the greatest mathematician. I perfectly agree that in this respect mathematics is a particularly simple case, but something could be learned from mathematicians, by imitating not their language but their style of self-command.

But once more, it is not the language that matters basically and finally. What I called the publicity of science is not determined by linguistic possibilities. What deserves to become a public possesion will eventually be accepted as such, and most often without much delay. Today this distinguishes science from art, which needs a generation or generations to become public possession. But around science a wreath of deposits has been, and still is, formed which is not public property – at least not as science. On one occasion I called it the fringe of science.

5. THE FRINGE OF SCIENCE

Around every nucleus of human experience, activity, comprehension, there exists such a fringe. That of art is artistic trash, that of faith is called superstition, and science has its pseudo-science. The relation between nucleus and fringe is a different one in each of these examples. Pseudo-science has already been discussed in connection with its irrelevance. What matters now is that as to content as well as method pseudo-science does not communicate with public science. Both the irrelevance and the incompatibility with public science can assume pathological expression. In this respect the fringe of science would not be so important were it not for the existence, in healthy science, of deviations from the main road which one would like to distinguish from pseudo-scientific pathologies, and forms of pseudo-scientific infections which one would like to signalise.

There are no eternal criteria to distinguish nucleus and fringe. Tastes are changing. Yesterday's art can be to-morrow's trash, and conversely. Faith of past centuries is now ranking as superstition. This seems to apply to sciences too, for instance, as regards astrology. But astrology is not a good example of pseudo-science. Today's astrology is a pseudo-science by its lack of communication with public science. But what happened with astrology in history is that it has been recognised as a superstition, and likewise much presently flourishing pseudo-science is sophisticated superstition – the so-called parapsychology as far as it has succeeded the belief in ghosts, the quackery as far as it continues thaumaturgy. But beyond this there is enough pseudo-science which cannot be explained by superstition.

What is thriving at the fringe of science is sometimes a strange mixture of fragments of science, a hotchpotch of language borrowed from science. Sometimes it is a consequential structure with characteristic features. Even mathematics is not spared the pseudo-scientific fringe. The evidence is abundant: a host of people who claim to have solved famous problems – squaring the circle, angle trisection, Fermat's theorem. They succeed in a twinkle where skilled mathematicians have proved the logical impossibility or experienced the tremendous difficulty of the problem, since they are not hampered by any logic or have invented one of their own. Jugglery with the numbers of the apocalypse or the measures of the Cheops pyramid with the aim of decoding hidden secrets, is another example – in a way an applied mathematics, at the fringe of the public one.

Most often pseudo-scientists are acting as individuals, but others are united in extensive, influential, fanatical sects. Between the world wars, Hörbiger's 'Worldice Theory', a protest against the official astronomy, counted many enthusiastic followers in Europe. According to this theory the moon consisted of ice – a doctrine that could not be checked by direct inspection and could be refuted only by arguments derived from public science and consequently thought invalid. I do not know whether this theory still enjoys partisanship now man has stepped upon the moon. It is not at all impossible. The most modest defence of the worldice theorists would be to admit they had erred as far as the moon is concerned, but to maintain the theory in principle. Yet it would be more in the spirit of this pseudo-science to accuse the astronauts of having suppressed or falsified evidence under the pressure of public science, or to dispose of the lunar journeys as fraud. This was indeed the way supporters of the Flat Earth did it: pictures of the rotundity of the Earth and of the South Pole as well as the flights of satellites were ignored or disposed of as fakes. To a scientist the identical descriptions of flying saucers and their crews are suspect enough if he notices that they come straight from a novel of Wells, but what does this argument amount to? Arguments are valid within a science but not to refute pseudo-science.

Alongside mainstream science an undergrowth science is cultivated and secured by an *a priori* nullification of all adverse arguments ascending from that official science, which jealously and malevolently hushes up all contradictory evidence, in full command of the state-machinery of repression. Isolated systems develop at the fringe of science, some of an impressive consistency, since their authors decree their own logic and by their own authority decide which facts they accept or reject. As it happens, the pathological, schizophrenic features of those systems are matched by corresponding personal features of their authors.

Their influence is undeniable and it would be better not to underestimate it. These underdogs at the fringe of science enjoy much sympathy. Political and social resentments favour them where public science is identified with the state and the prevailing social system. In the view of quite a few people science is seated upon an icy Olympus whereas the fringe below is accessible to everybody. There he is addressed in a language he can understand, and told things he likes to hear. No entropy and no basically determined multi-discriminatory response, but flying saucers and the beyond. There he learns all things public science is withholding to the advantage of dark powers or to its own security. One need not turn a great many pages back in history to remember how dangerous the mass impact of pseudo-science can be. Pseudo-scientific bestsellers have been the mile-stones along the fatal road that led to the victory of nazism – from the *Rembrandtdeutsche* to the *Minutes of the Sages of Zion* to the pseudo-scientific novel *The Sin Against the Blood.* Up to now Dänicken cannot boast similar success, and as long as the influence of pseudo-science is expressed in royalties rather than in polls, no political consequences need be feared.

Nevertheless it disturbs me that after so many experiences with the mass success of schizophrenic pseudo-science, the phenomenon has not yet got the status of a socio-psychological problem that deserves to be studied. Is this fringe of science as indispensable as it is said the asocial fringe of society is? Or which incongruence in our instructional and educational system could explain the mass success of pseudo-science? Eventually in the course of history the ghosts did not yield to the radiance of enlightenment but of electric light, but perhaps without enlightenment electric light would never have been invented. Would better scientific instruction exterminate these pseudo-sciences that adorn themselves with the prefix 'para'? How should we teach young people to find their bearings in their own world, to become resistant against attempts to beguile them with pseudo-worlds? And how can we ensure that the public character of public science is felt as public freedom rather than repression? Or can we not succeed as long as the state itself is felt as repression?

Why is it necessary to stay so long on the consideration of the fringe, if science is the subject? As symptoms of genuine science relevance and consistency are less worrying than its publicity. Who or what is moulding the common countenance of science? Every catholicity asks for a heterodoxy – is this as true of science as it is of faith? Has the common face evolved in liberty, or was it moulded under magisterial pressure, like the Lysenko dominated biology of the Soviet Union in the fifties? And if it is not governmental pressure, aren't there levers – offices and subventions – and gentle ways to have them manipulated if not by pseudo-scientists, then by incompetent people who are allowed and authorised to settle what is public science? As everybody knows these are not merely rhetorical questions.

Moreover, if a discipline grows powerful schools which are competing but hardly communicating with each other, who then truly represents public and who pseudo-science? And if it is taken for granted that a variety of legitimate tenants are allowed on the plot, why should it be a mere two or three? Why cannot everybody claim the true tenure? Why is there a Marxist sociology beside that which it stamps bourgeois or capitalistic, but for itself declines such adjectives? What, beyond the genius of its creator, distinguishes psychoanalysis from creations of less gifted or less successful brains?

I pose these questions only to delay their discussion. I will not leave them entirely unanswered. Anticipating I can say: much of what has been mentioned, or alluded to, in the last paragraph, is not science or can hardly rank as science. How then can it be classified?

6. SCIENCE AND TECHNOLOGY

On the last few pages I delimited science from its fringe, pseudo-science. It took me more words than it deserved. It is more to the point to delimit science against other nuclei of experience, activity, and comprehension. I mentioned faith and art; while art does not need attention in this context, faith cannot entirely be disregarded. But now I turn to that vast domain that I like to call technology though sometimes I prefer 'practice'. Years ago when I attempted analyses like the present and included as technology the activities of the physician, the psychologist, the educator, the justice, and the pastor, along with those of the bridge-builder and electrical engineer, I was assailed as though I had committed a capital crime. Never before was I hounded as bitterly, in a discussion where I had not meant to harm anybody. But obviously they had felt harmed. Words like 'engineer' and 'technology' can evoke unpleasant associations. An engineer reminds some people of a plumber, and technology seems to them like plumbing, though in fact 'technology' derives from the same old word 'technè' that means 'art'; but art sounds like something of high standing, at least the peer of science. The worst sin I committed against European tradition probably was that I tied university studies to a term that reminded people of polytechnics. The reason why in the past century separate colleges were created all over Europe for engineering, veterinary medicine, economics, was the fossilisation of the faculties of the universities, or simply reluctance to recognise younger sisters. Only gynaecology succeeded in making a breach, but its representatives were still for years scoffed at as male midwives. A quarter of a century ago the inclination to exalt university subjects above those of other schools of higher learning was still strong. Things have changed meanwhile and so I hope I may venture more successfully to extend the term 'technology' to all that deserve it rightly by analogy to the technology of engineering.

Yet sometimes I will say practice instead. This is a term familiar to physicians and lawyers, and the greatest fault they would be able to find with me would be that I grant their activities the same name as activities like that of the engineer so as to deal with them on the same footing. It is still a venture.

If knowledge, understanding, cognition are primary to the scientist, acting and creating are primary to the engineer, even if he is a physician, justice or teacher. It is the scientific background that brings someone nearer to science than others, or the scientific equipment of his stock of procedures and of his workshop, the methodological qualifications of his activity in general and in particular. People would not accept that the professions taught at a university belong to technology because it seems an undervaluation if 'science' is replaced with 'technology'. But a professional man who diagnoses or cures a patient, who as a judge or a lawyer argues in support of a sentence or a plaint, who educates or teaches, does not in this activity embody a science any more than an engineer does who builds a bridge or designs a switching circuit. He applies science, and nobody is entitled to consider this as an inferior activity – if this were my intention, I would never have been able to write this chapter. There are sciences where the practicians by far surpass the theoreticians.

In Dutch there is a – not too consequential – terminology that assigns the word component *kunde* (knowledge) to a science and *kunst* (art) to a technique; in medicine, for instance, one speaks of *geneeskunst* along with *geneeskunde*; the physician who learnt *geneeskunde* at the university, will exercise *geneeskunst* in his practice; *geneeskunde* is the technology of the technique *geneeskunst*.

As a matter of fact there is an unceasing interaction between a technique and its technology, there is no sharp border-line between them. The practitioner noting down and analysing his experiences or the theoretician advising and briefing the practician, do not do science; on the other hand so much fundamental and paradigmatic knowledge can arise in the course of practice that everybody gladly recognises it as science. The road from scientific knowledge to practical activity is articulated by relays which are the more numerous the more fundamental the knowledge is. Chemistry knows a large density of such relays; where a product is synthesised to understand the process of synthesis, this is different from producing it as a final product, which perhaps is used as an intermediate component in other syntheses or in analyses – it is a highly complicated pattern. Applied science can also be a science, and it is not easily decided at which link of this chain technology comes in. Why then do I insist upon the distinction? I will answer that shortly.

To be sure scientific activity can also be interpreted as – theoretical – action; the acting persons can have been influenced – consciously or unconsciously – by practical objectives. Yet practice, even in preparatory action, does not start until the objectives are consciously aimed at. It is not difficult to identify everyday rote as technique. With big designs it is more difficult to tell where the theory ends and practice sets in.

In history many of our techniques preceded the corresponding science. Techniques which are today known as agriculture belong to the most ancient mankind has developed; notwithstanding all precursors agriculture as a science did not come of age before Liebig. It is, however, not a proper distinction to stress that the farmer proceeds empirically whereas the scientist bases himself upon theories. The wealth of empirical facts was even after Liebig, and still is today, accepted as relevant knowledge, including facts that fit into no theory. On the other hand from olden times artful men devised all kinds of theories for understanding growth and fertility that passed beyond the scope of animistic and magic explanation. The true distinction between present agricultural techniques and those of the past is that the modern version is supported by a technology, which in turn is decisively influenced by non-technical sciences like physics, chemistry, biology. It is a long chain of applications which in increasing degree aim at the practice that leads from the sciences in which knowledge, understanding and cognition is primary to the techniques of stable and field.

The crafts form another source of our present techniques; after millenia of continued development they are carried on by manufacturers and industry. Crafts, and initially even industry, lacked a technology – industrial technology is not much older than the oldest of our polytechnic institutions. The rise of science from the 16th century onwards was prepared by three centuries of inventions and discoveries, but even after science had come of age it lasted centuries until natural sciences essentially influenced techniques of natural sciences.

Genuine science is no recent invention. Some sciences can boast a time-honoured lineage. The first was mathematics, which quickly outgrew its applications; then astronomy, which as astrology was of eminent practical importance – both of them sciences which reveal to the modern investigator the origin of modern science.

Medicine is a different case. Though historically hardly younger than agricultural and craftsman's techniques, medicine was practised from Greek antiquity, or even already in old Babylon and Egypt, as a kind of science, which in this traditional form maintained itself up to the end of the 18th century. But a closer look at this science is most disappointing. The relation between theory and practice widely differed in that medicine from what is the case in ours. No doubt, from time immemorial there have been excellent practitioners in medicine, men who made good for the lack of relevant theory by keen observation and immense experience. But this impressive technique was supplemented and supported by a science no more than in agriculture and crafts, or rather – and this distinguishes medicine from agriculture and crafts – a wide gulf yawned between so-called medical science and medical technique, a gulf across which a bridge was under construction from the 16th century to the 19th century by a true developing medical science. Up to the end of the 18th century the *collegium medicum* consisted in a philological interpretation of Hippocrates and other classics. This classroom erudition and a few theses sufficed for a man to graduate as a doctor of medicine who then learned the practice of his trade at home from his father or uncle or from barbers and herb-women. The traces of his university study were an academic title, a philosophy for Sundays, and a learned jargon. Why do I tell this thus circumstantially? The reader knows academic professions which are at present as far advanced as medicine was two centuries ago.

Greek medicine was a collection of empirical rules, bordered with a background philosophy: according to the pattern of cosmic physics with its four elements earth, water, air, and fire, the humours of the human body were divided into black bile, phlegm (lymph), yellow bile, blood, and the temperaments in melancholics, phlegmatics, cholerics, sanguinics, in order to fit pathology and therapy in that physical cosmic frame. Even as late as the beginning of the 16th century little was known about human anatomy, not to mention physiology. A fundamental fact like the double circulation of blood became known as late as the 17th century. Only after the invention of the microscope could spermatozoids and ova be identified as components of generation; the origin of infectious diseases has been known for no longer than a century. We have come a long way.

How far have others of today's techniques progressed from craftmanship to scientific consolidation? There have been social techniques of government, production and distribution as long as *homo sapiens* has lived in social agglomerations. Of these techniques the best developed today is probably so-called military science, that is the technology of warfare, which is based upon numerous sciences and techniques – not only on those of nature. (I do

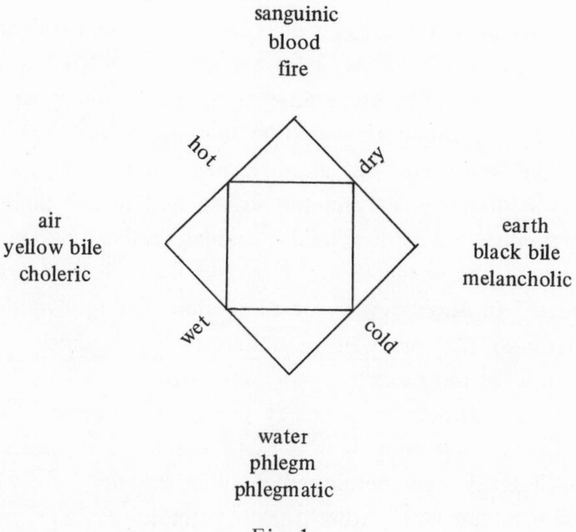

Fig. 1.

not discuss the question whether the more theoretically oriented political military science and the so-called polemology is to be considered as a science or rather a background philosophy.)

In the sequel when I discuss social techniques, I will disregard the techniques of warfare, which is a quite special case. Social techniques are effective on different size levels, which are today distinguished by the prefixes 'micro', 'meso', 'macro'. In particular in the macro structure the social techniques are characterised by a trend to regulate, transform, and control the social process. Traffic regulations and time-tables are impressive examples of what in some perspicuous sectors somehow succeeds, and what in less perspicuous ones as national economy and social stratification is attempted. Nobody will regard a traffic regulation or a time-table as a scientific product nor the designing of it as a scientific achievement. They are, rather, quite characteristic instances of techniques and engineering activities. The same certainly holds everywhere where interventions into the social process are carried out or prepared.

Micro-economy, as an example, is a primeval technique, and traces of macro-economy date back as far as the oldest kingdoms. Theoretical attempts at economics in modern times show a full scientific character according to each of our criteria, relevance, consistence, publicity. I think the reason is that in economics all values can be measured with *one* measure, money – or rather, this holds as far as economics is restricted to questions where this is possible. Difficulties arise as soon as economical systems are compared, which communicate so little with each other that their value measures are incomparable. But another question is urgent: is economics really a science, or rather a technique with a background philosophy, and then not with one, but with several – decidely active – background philosophies, depending upon the technical system they are expected to explain and consolidate? In other words: Are not actions and intervention so much in the foreground that knowledge, understanding, cognition do not get decent opportunities to be exercised and aimed at?

The genesis and growth of sociology has little in common with that of economics. In the beginning it was restricted to mere philosophy, then numerous techniques were developed, genuine theories, too, which I have the impression supplement rather than contradict each other, but these theories serve the *a posteriori* exculpation of techniques rather than their development.

If there is one discipline whose adepts are shocked if their field is called a technology, it is law. I certainly know, and admit, that what is called jurisprudence contains a full share of genuine science even if philosophy and the history of law are disregarded, but I would look for this share where it is not usually localised. The tradition that students of law are the right people in administration and organisation is not only to be belittled. In the social sector knowledge of law and legal procedures has up to now fulfilled a task that in that of natural sciences was reserved for mathematics: the task of exemplary conceptual analysis and paradigmatic formalising. Though the depth of deduction with such concepts as characteristic of mathematics is rarely, if at all, attained in law, the object of that conceptual analysis, as pursued by the lawyer, is richer and more varied and for this reason less accessible to the kind of formalisation that characterises mathematics, at least up to now. But what will happen in the long run? By way of an aside, I guess that mathematical skills in conceptual analysis and formalisation will outstrip those based on law, thanks to mathematicians travelling in the wake of computers. Anyhow, what I wished to stress are not these restrictions but rather jurisprudence as a technology. I think this view also agrees with more recent, easily distinguishable developments in the selfconsciousness of the judicature towards social engineering – a development that took place somewhat earlier in other social professions.

What is the purpose of these examples? The issue this time is to display the tremendous variety of relations between science and technology in various domains. In the natural sciences, in spite of what is still left to be desired, there is a close connection and even interaction between science and techniques, reinforced by mediating technologies; in the social sector, there are domains where science is separated from technique and technology by a broad gulf, or where nothing like science proper exists – domains with a uniform technology like economics and with a large collection of techniques like sociology.

Science and techniques – a third comparison should not be overlooked. A few pages ago I dropped the word 'faith' and promised to come back to it. I will do so though not straightforwardly.

7. SCIENCE AND FAITH

For some time I could not make up my mind whether it should be 'faith' that joined 'science' in this subheading. People who read subheadings only would think of new efforts at confronting dogmas and creeds with science. By mere accident the scale was turned. It was by reading a treatise on economics where after 270 pages of scarcely digestible mathematics the author asked, and at the same time answered, the question: what is true of all this? He said: "This is a matter of faith".

In fact the author did not fear that his formulae were wrong. It was his intention to ask whether the magnitudes involved in, and the relations stated by, the formulae corresponded to some reality – a reality, of course, as viewed by himself. He did not *know* whether this was fulfilled; he believed it was so, and this was not simply a belief as if I say: 'I believe he is 37 years old' or 'I believe I have met him before'.

To the first shepherds and hunters the world was just as large as they could drive their flocks and hunt their game; to the settled farmer it looked still smaller; though to all of them it appeared unlimited all around and only closed from above by the blue sky, which one fine morning – one can never tell – would crash down on the Earth. Seafaring extended the Earth; stargazing the skies. The ocean and the celestial sphere became new frontiers.

Then what is called the Copernican revolution happened. The Sun replaced the Earth as the cosmic centre, but as though this was not enough, our sun was sentenced to be only one among many; later, our galaxay did not fare any better. Among many – this did not mean thousands or millions, but milliards and billions. In similar proportions scales of distances and of the age of the world increased. Then, with the same powers of ten as human dimensions, they had been cosmically transcended, and dwindled away in the microcosmos of molecules, atoms, nuclei, electrons.

Only to the scientist does it matter how precise such numbers are; nobody else will worry about one power of ten more or less. But such scientific facts do mean something to him. They constitute his world picture, a picture that is not remembered too often but somehow influences his everyday, or at least his every Sunday, thought and mood.

Science pretends to know something about the evolution of the universe, and even more about that of our planet, and there is strong evidence in favour of the evolution of life, though little is known about its mechanism. All this, simplified and extrapolated in space and time, belongs to our world picture, in which we seem to be the last link and the summit of evolution.

Extrapolating is an old game. Technical and cosmic imagination have made strange flowers sprout forth from the world picture. Space travel and moon visits have become a reality but technical and cosmical imagination roam further and further, and evolutionary visionaries like Teilhard de Chardin do not lag far behind.

All this is part of our world picture, the expression of a faith, rooted in science, but still a faith. Saying that the universe measures 10^{10} light years is science; it is faith if this size gives me the creeps or pleasure, or if I expect my equals on other planets. Only in the realm of faith can I ask questions about the meaning of the whole.

But faith asks for more than a world picture: it also asks for pictures of man and of society. These are certainly not scientifically 'proved' or provable as is the world picture: they are no extrapolations of scientific facts, not even if they have been strongly influenced by evolving science. Once Aristotle interpreted biologically the difference between the sexes as a difference of quality and value, between the passive material feminine principle and the active spiritual masculine principle, and surrounded this dualism with a philosophy of potence and act; today we know that the activity of the male and passivity of the female in sexual intercourse and even in the active rush of the sperms to the waiting ovum are misleading if understood as symbols of fundamentals; they do not indicate what properly happens in the fertilisation, which is a union of equivalent components contributing equal shares to the coming into being of a new creature.

Has this scientific discovery contributed to shaping our picture of man? I think so – at least in the respect that at present no philosopher would dare to prove the inferiority of the female by Aristotelian arguments. It is true that Aristotle's philosophy of female inferiority was not a cause but a consequence of social discrimination, but afterwards it served well in justifying discrimination theoretically, and for this reason it may rightly be argued that the eventual failure of the justification was detrimental to continuing discrimination.

I will not try to estimate how much the natural sciences contributed in general to the struggle against slavery, exploitation, racial and social discrimination. In former times such discrimination was justified by arguments of biological technique, the technique of the farmer and cattle breeder. Nobility and one's own clan were better and more valuable by the same principle as one breed of horses or corn may surpass the other, that is because of the privilege of heredity. Natural science has refuted this sort of argument long ago and natural scientists will view it more critically than others in every particular case. Nevertheless these cattle breeder arguments are tenacious, and though today nobody would muster the courage to usher them in by the front-door, it is easy enough by back-door statistics. A quarter of a century ago I worked through the whole literature where people attempted to prove that as far as intellectual qualities are concerned heredity as compared with environment is by far the more influential factor, that children stick to their parents' environment not because of environment but of heredity. All the material I scrutinised was tremendously poor and tendentiously arranged.* In the last few years sensational new statistical research has been published to prove the genetic inferiority of the American black – 80% heredity and 20% environment, was the cut. I cannot guess how such figures can be defined, not to mention proved; and after the experience of a quarter of a century ago I do not trust them. Astonishingly such investigations are cited and used as arguments in European countries while it is assumed as a matter of course

* See also pp. 47–48.

that our 'negroes' are distinguished from our 'whites' not by the colours of their skins but by the social position of their parents and their living quarters.

Is it not against science to mistrust statistical surveys *a priori,* people would ask. I have *no faith* in what such surveys try to prove, just as I do not trust the statistical attempts of parapsychologists. This attitude is rooted in natural science, but more firmly somewhere else.

There is much that contributes to our picture of man and society – first of all social intercourse with people and membership of a society. Education, sermons, and propaganda influence our pictures of man and society and are influenced by them. Certainly what is contributed by psychological and sociological theories is no trifle, but most of it is just not science but the reflection of a picture of man and society.

I have used the term 'background philosophy' several times. By this I mean the rational expression of what I have been describing as a world picture and a picture of man and society. Faith has moulded these pictures at least partially, and the need to justify them rationally gave birth to more or less explicit background philosophy. I could have extended this concept of background philosophy even farther: Maxwell's theory, which is hardly ever properly applied, and quantum theory, which fares no better, are indeed background philosophies – in fact very active and mathematically expressed ones; and theoretical economics seems to me of the same calibre. But these – scientifically based – background philosophies will be explicitly excluded in what follows. I mean those background philosophies that rationalise the pictures of world, man and society.

Background philosophies serve many aims though they are uniformly motivated: to justify technical and scientific activities and the way they are performed, in our own eyes and in the eyes of others. One can pursue natural sciences with no world picture because the world picture is inherent to, and grows out of, natural science. The technique of natural science is already another case, and many engineers' phantastic natural philosophies may have arisen under the psychological pressure of a technology lacking a world picture. But pursuing natural science with no *world* picture does not imply that pictures of *man* and *society* can be dispensed with. Just because they are not inherent to natural science, they obtrude themselves on the pursuer, not as objective but as subjective preconditions. To guarantee the personal engagement they are indispensable in natural science and the technology of natural science, because the pursuer feels obliged to justify his activity before himself as well as before others.

I labelled background philosophy all that centres on the pictures of world, man, and society, while neither belonging to science nor to technology. This philosophy can be an adornment, but it can also be active and influential, and in the sector of natural sciences and their techniques it is so as soon as it is relevant. For a long time it has been a romantic fashion to condemn technical progress, as far as it is due to the natural sciences, as contrary to nature; some people wished to return to old world manners in nurture and dress or at least said they wished to. Meanwhile it has turned out that milk is more healthy without typhoid germs; that butter is perhaps not so much more healthy than oil as people used to believe; and that in general substitutes surpass the 'natural' equivalents by far. Natural scientists themselves discovered and uncovered what is dangerous in natural science, and they did not keep it secret; and no doubt natural sciences, as far as they are concerned, will also eliminate these sources of danger. Relevant criticism can be met in a relevant way.

All this is so much more difficult in the social sector. There the pictures of man and of society are not restricted to a more or less corrective function, as they are in natural sciences. Already in medicine they interfere in a more decisive fashion. In the social sciences it should be the same. Perhaps it is the same; but if the philosophy developed around different pictures of man and society is exerting influences – and who would deny that it is – it happens straightforwardly, not through a science, a technology, a technique, but from mouth to mouth; from the social philosopher in the chair and at the desk to the auditor and reader, who as a citizen is a fellow-creator of the social reality – a most impressive example is the propagation of Marxism. The counterpart of the gulf that cleaves sociology is the possibility of short cuts that can bridge the isolating gulf. Obviously this can be a virtue as well as a vice. It is no depreciation of philosophy to state, which is trivial, that philosophy alone cannot move weaving-looms nor teach children the multiplication tables; neither can it run a society, which seems to be not so trivial. I prefer a philosophy that operates along pertinent techniques but this seems hard to realise in the social sector.

8. VALUES

I cannot avoid touching upon the controversy on freedom from values before ending this chapter. If sociologists discuss it, we outsiders are easily led to believe that all sociology turns around the question whether science is free from values. They always say 'science' rather than 'sociology'. If one asks which one, they look at as if you should be ashamed to believe there is any other.

This is not in fun; it is in bitter earnest. If sociologists consider their own professional discontent – for what else is it? – as exemplary, they prove they have not properly understood their own situation among those of others.

'Freedom from values' and its opposite are not an invention of sociology. 'True' and 'false' are also values, but nobody would claim that science was not subjected to them. Well, let us disregard these particular values. The validity of the Pythagorean theorem and Newton's law of gravitation is neither negotiable nor redeemable, it cannot be denounced to please some religious or political convictions, it cannot be watched over by police nor patented. They are propositions and laws that do not change with the world picture – which, rather, they may determine – and certainly not by pictures of man and society. One can appreciate such scientific facts as relevant, interesting, applicable, and in this respect they may be valuable – or for that matter valueless – and consequently not free from values, but this is inconsequential as regards the scientific facts. I would say: science is not value conditioned.

Technique, however, is *a priori* another thing. An engineer does not design a bridge in order to pronounce a scientific fact, but in order to build it, and if he has designed a 50 km long bridge and there is nowhere to place it nor a man to pay for it, then it was an intellectual game. Among thousands of patents only a few are ever exploited; in spite of the artful inventors, the remainder is considered as worthless.

Values matter in science when problems are set out – something may be interesting, relevant, easy or difficult, promising, accessible to techniques; they matter in scientific method too – a method can be useful, artful, comfortable, one which can seduce the explorer to dare a try. Beyond these values technique knows utility of the product as a value.

Up to this point the concept of value in science and technique does not look problematic. It is a new question to ask whether values can be assigned with a scientific right to the objects of science. Is it scientific to state that 'the circle is a beautiful figure', 'sulphuretted hydrogen smells bad', 'Hitler was a criminal'?

These examples are so ridiculous that it looks like joking. But if in the last sentence I would read 'asocial' instead of 'criminal' and realise that this allegedly asocial man represented a society, the question becomes more serious.

How can something be asocial? If 'society' is a descriptive concept, then its asocial fringe is part of it and 'asocial' is a *contradictio in terminis.* 'Asocial' is meaningful only if 'society' is normative. But according to which norms? If invariability is part of the norms of 'society', any trend towards renewal is asocial. It depends on the definition of repression what is repressive.

The social norms are only partially codified, and what is actually codified are executive and repressive regulations rather than the norms themselves. The norms are determined by the pictures of man and society and perhaps rationalised in some background philosophy. This has little to do with science but it is not the point where I will leave the question. I will not retire upon the argument that this is social *technique* which as technique of natural science cannot dispense with norms. I would not simply say: Society must be organised somehow and the use of technical means to perform it is decided by utility arguments.

It is indeed not that simple. It is true that if values intervene decisively, it is technique rather than science that is discussed, but the proper reason for this is that background philosophy plays a larger part in technique than in the sciences.

Why is the problem of freedom from values posed ever anew in sociology? It seems to me that sociology is essentially background philosophy, and then, to be more precise, one with no adequate foreground. There is an abundance of social techniques; techniques, however, that are hardly affected by the background philosophy. What they call sociology is a strange spectacle to the outsider: they see a large number of sociologists, who undoubtedly qualify as remarkable, but no sociology. The reason is obvious: sociologists are remarkable in that they are the creators of a background philosophy, which according to the picture of society is differentiated into more or less related philosophies. I do not say contradictory philosophies because the differentiation is caused rather by different stresses and aspects.

Where then does the sociological hangover come from? An ecomomist knows levers and switches to more or less control the economy – unfortunately not enough. He knows, for instance, how the economy will react to increasing and decreasing the bank-rates. Sociological techniques have not progressed as far as that, one would think. Or should one? I remember the war-time, when we lived under occupation. One day, in order to inhibit allied broadcasting propaganda, the Germans decreed the surrender of all radio receiving sets; non-delivery would be punished with "five years penitentiary to be served in a German *Zuchthaus*". To no avail – almost nothing was delivered. A few days later a supplementary penalty was announced, "confiscation of furniture", and this warning did it. If not 100%, the surrender of radios was not far from it.

Obviously an authoritarian or terrorised society reacts quite dependably if only one knows the right levers. Knowing the levers is something like science, and being able to operate them a technique; but background philosophies are not forces that can operate levers.

What then is the use of background philosophy? Earlier I mentioned the short cut: it is in being taught. It is taught in order for the philosopher to act upon the students as fellow-creators of society. One tries to change society by propagating the way it should be. To be sure, this has always been done and has sometimes proved successful. Revolutionary laws were adopted when the society was mature enough to accept them, and maturity was attained by propaganda, which was answered by counter propaganda: mentality, too, is influenced by propaganda.

Nevertheless teaching background philosophy is not the same as propagandising, because teaching includes testing its consequences, through 'examinations'. Although I once underwent an examination in philosophy – a reasonable one – I cannot imagine any more dreary happening than a philosophy examination, and for this reason I am utterly sceptical about the efficiency of this 'short-cut'. Philosophy examined, ideology examined – is it not a boomerang? And if it does not work, what then? Even more background philosophy?

However it may be, what sociologists call the problem of freedom from values is in my view the problem of background philosophy with insufficient foreground. Sociologists with a weak background philosophy will maintain freedom from values, whereas those for whom background philosophy means much or all, will deny it.

CHAPTER II

ON EDUCATION

ABSTRACT. The German language knows a well-defined triad of terms 'Unterricht, Erziehung, Bildung', which is vaguely reflected by the English 'instruction, education, culture'. Instruction and education are the ways to acquire *culture*, to become an educated man; but from the point of view of culture, no particular topics are indispensable, because for the individual man culture means the way in which he personally has integrated the instruction and education he received.

Education depends on one's picture of man and society. One can try to find out scientifically the optimal distribution of rewards and penalties for teaching the tables of multiplication, but it is a matter of faith and one's picture of man whether one accepts or rejects any particular educational system of reward and penalty. It is a matter of faith whether or not one believes that results of instruction can be measured, notwithstanding the scientific pretensions of educational measurement. Educational technique needs a philosophy, which is a matter of faith rather than of science.

How education is influenced by *society*, is shown by a sketch of the Dutch educational system, which to a certain degree is paradigmatic. Efforts are made to change the system, to replace it by a system of *equal opportunity*. All over the world there are people who believe equal opportunity can be attained by administrative measures, by a superficial integration of various types of schools, or school populations. Genuine integration is being circumvented by more or less sophisticated *systems of differentiation* such as Mastery Learning, developed by general educationists. The effect of all these systems is that "for whosoever hath, to him shall be given, and he shall have more abundance: but whosoever hath not, from him shall be taken away even that he hath." Many systems of differentiation forget about the social context of learning, which cannot be restored by teaching social sciences as some people seem to believe.

I advocate the *heterogeneous learning group*. My analysis of the mathematical learning process has unveiled levels in the learning process where the mathematics acted out on one level becomes mathematics observed on the next. In the group, and in particular in the heterogeneous group, this relation of acting out and observing is stressed to the benefit of the learning process itself.

Innovation in education is a great learning process on the part of society, which cannot be programmed in advance. As I see it, it starts in the classroom, in a rapid cycle of design, tryout, evaluation and adaptation; its first result is a curriculum presented for discussion – an example of democratic innovation.

Part of the innovation is a fundamental change in *teacher training*, an integration of its subject area and its didactical components on the one hand, while on the other hand stressing classroom experience and consciousness in observing learning processes, both of the learner and the observer.

All this is part of a *philosophy of education* in which every single topic is worth as much as its suitability for integration into education as a whole.

1. WHAT DOES 'EDUCATION' MEAN?

My English style is far from perfect and I can only agree with reviewers of my book *Mathematics as an Educational Task* who found fault with it. Most of them granted me the privilege of trespassing against a language which is not my own – a privilege which I thankfully accept. One of them felt so offended that it prevented him from paying attention to the contents of the book, which I can fully understand.

That book was originally written in German, because when I started writing it I was living in the United States of America, and for good practical reasons I avoid as far as possible writing papers and books in the language of the country where I am staying. When the German manuscript was ready, I translated it into English. Editing texts is an annoying business. It is not to be wondered at that some transgressions escaped the eye of the English speaking copy-editor.

Likewise the present work was first written in German and then translated by myself into English. In spite of my past failures I repeated the old procedure. The only alternative would have been to start with the English text. I do not believe that books like my previous or present one can be efficiently and meaningfully translated by anybody other than the author himself, apart from a few persons who, however, have more serious business in mind.

Actually the English versions are no translations. With the text before my eyes I write the book anew in another language. This procedure takes about a fifth to a third of the time a professional translator would need, as he feels obliged to take the text as it stands. This is one reason why I prefer my own method. The other is that translating books like the present one requires full understanding not only of the objective contents but also of the subjective intentions of the author, which are difficult things to combine with each other and with full mastery of the two languages.

I mention this because to make sure whether my theory is correct, I asked somebody, whom I consider to be competent, to translate the first pages of the second chapter of the German text into English. I admit it was a crucial test. He did not succeed, or rather he did not try. The dissemination of science extends beyond geographical, political, and linguistic borders. If something is untranslatable, one may suspect that it is no science. Philosophy is different. Kant's *Kritik der reinen Vernunft* has been translated into several languages. Are the equivalents chosen for terms like 'Vorstellung', Anschauung', 'Empfindung' – and also the 'Vernunft' of the title – good equivalents? I would not know how to test it, but I do not believe that it would matter much.

Puns and plays upon words are often untranslatable, but nothing is lost if they are dropped or replaced with others. 'Gymnasium', 'lycée', 'grammar school', 'highschool' have no simple equivalents in other languages: they are 'translated' by putting them into italics. If you want to know what they cover, you have to collect information about foreign school systems, just as in order to find out what the name 'Shakespeare' really means, you have to read his works, perhaps in a translation (where the name 'Shakespeare' is translated by 'Shakespeare').

In the German version the title of the present chapter was '*Vom Unterricht*', which literally translated would be 'On Instruction'. In the English version I chose 'On Education', because this was what I meant, even in the German version. But the literal translation of 'education' is '*Erziehung*', which I could not put into the title, because 'erziehen' is primarily what parents do when they bring up their children, and an *Erzieher* is not an educator but somebody who, legally or morally, acts *in loco parentis*. So when I put 'Unterricht' into the title of the present chapter, my first task was to explain that I did not mean it, and this attempt took me a few pages. But did I really mean 'education', instead, when I put 'education' into the English title of the present chapter?

I have introduced the present chapter with an explanation of my policy on translations. I trust it has become clear why I did so. There is a fundamental incongruence between various languages in the terminology concerning 'education' which betrays differences in national philosophies, influencing, and influenced by, the appropriate terminology. Some languages sharply separate '*Unterricht*' from '*Erziehung*' (instruction as distinct from upbringing). The first aims at teaching by formal instruction, the second at shaping attitudes of all kinds – moral, social, emotional, religious. Of all kinds: this includes cognitive attitudes too. So it can happen that an author speaks about *mathematische Erziehung*, which aims at higher goals than multiplication tables or solving quadratic equations – goals of evolving mathematical attitudes, whatever these may be. So when I put 'Unterricht' into the title, I had to explain that I wished to include such higher objectives, or rather, that in my view any teaching would include them *a priori*.

Both terminologies have their own merits, and their drawbacks, the one separating sharply 'Unterricht' and 'Erziehung' as well as the other which allows us to use one word 'education'. The first reminds one of different kinds of educational objectives, and in particular of the existence and paramount importance of involving global attitudes, but it suggests that there are separate educational processes of *Unterricht* (teaching) and *Erziehung* (upbringing). The second terminology, of one single term 'education', suggests a unity of educational process, but forgets about differentiating its goals and about stressing global attitudes versus particular behaviour as an educational goal. The first terminology provides a better description of the objectives, the second is more adapted to the educational process.

I am first of all going to adduce examples and arguments in favour of the unity of the educational process. This unity is a natural feature of the education children receive at home and even in the kindergarten. Gradually *Unterricht* is stressed and separated from *Erziehung*. A problem I give one of my grandchildren or a walk I take with him, is it teaching or is it bringing up? One of my grandsons, proud of his (first male) teacher, reports that "if one of the children is naughty, the whole class gets sums in arithmetic". That teacher certainly believes in the moral value of arithmetic lessons as did generations of teachers before him. Nobody would deny the pedagogical consequences of teaching arithmetic, although a few people would express this conviction in less positive terms. I think it has never been claimed that teaching can be detached from its general educational context, but there is still a need to understand and interpret it within this context.

If after a few years of formal education in the primary school one has succeeded in grading the children according to their ability to learn arithmetic and spelling – at one end those who know they are stupid and accept this knowledge indifferently or hate to acknowledge the fact, and at the other end those who know they are clever and perhaps pride themselves on this gift – one has achieved a result of enormous pedagogical consequences, whether one likes it or not; if then the school population is divided according to these principles in order to continue its path of training at schools corresponding to their abilities, as happens in many countries, an act of educational organisation with decisive consequences has been performed; and if after a few more years of schooling they are discharged from educational constraints, instruction has stamped them for their whole life. I do not know whether somewhere someone has undertaken to interview a group of adults who had always been the poorest of their class, in order to discover the moral and character consequences of this experience, but probably it would not be too difficult to bring their antipodes, the ever cleverest, to such a self scrutiny. I cannot predict the results of such an investigation for pedagogical influences but nobody will seriously deny their existence.

Nor can I tell whether the instructional system to which I alluded in the last paragraph is the right one and whether it is unavoidable. There are tendencies to get away from it, but I do not know whether the attempts at doing so are the right ones, or whether with the best intentions in the world one does not get ever deeper into the swamps one would avoid. How could I know it, indeed, as there is no knowledge about it in the sense of scientific awareness. All the same I am entitled to believe this or that, to philosophically justify my faith concerning instruction and its educational consequences and to contrast it or to distinguish it by degress from that of other people.

It is a fashion today to stipulate the formulation of educational objectives, general and operational. Though I shall discuss this tendency later on, I will anticipate right now one particular theme: instructional objectives which may be classified as educational objectives in the sense of 'Erziehung'.

In German terminology, *Unterricht* and *Erziehung* form a hierarchy with *Bildung*, which is the highest of the three. Literally *Bildung* means 'formation', but its true translation is 'culture' though this latter term lacks the specialisation on education that is the most notable feature of *Bildung*. A key term in German pedagogy, *Bildung* occurs in such combinations as *Bildungsideal* (the cultural objective of education); *Bildungsromane* (novels describing the cultural education of an individual) have been a recurring feature in the literature of many countries, but the term is characteristically German. All translation problems around the noun *Bildung* vanish if one passes to the adjective *gebildet* which is faithfully rendered by the English 'educated' and the French '*instruit*' in the combinations 'an educated man', *un homme instruit*. Well, in our civilisation, everybody gets an education, *chaque homme reçoit une instruction*, but only a small minority are *gebildet*, educated people, *gens instruits*.

What do we mean by *Bildung*, by culture as an educational goal, what distinguishes it from *Unterricht* and *Erziehung*? The difference is in what the educated man *did* with the education he *received*. Experience and knowledge, physical and mental abilities that a man has acquired by learning and training, become his cultural possession as an educated man, if he is impressing them with his own stamp, if he is integrating their variety by his own personality.

Culture as a goal of education sounds old-fashioned today. Is it adventurous to demand it? Fashions are changing and old fashions will return. Some day it will happen to *Bildung* too. Then at a stroke people will draw up decimal classifications and operationalise the cultural aspects of an educated man without realising the self-contradiction in what they are undertaking.

How could one enumerate what is comprised by the culture of an educated man? The multiplication tables up to 10 or 20, the spelling of words up to the 3000th or the 6000th in the frequency list, the wars of the Red and White Roses, the 50 united states of America, Chaucer or Ezra Pound, the difference between pop-art and op-art, the Gilgamesh epos or *The Lord of the Rings*, Samuel Johnson or Virginia Woolf, how many symphonies of Beethoven or Bruckner, how many concerts and museums, that which every educated man should have read, a journey through Italy as in the 19th century, or to Mexico, the names of the last Nobel prize laureates or of all of them, the last joke, or the smile if it is told, reluctance or frankness – somehow all this and somehow none of it belongs to culture as a goal of education. It is not the content that matters but its individual assimilation, elaboration and dressing, and this cannot be caught by dissecting classifications and simplistic operationalisations. All the same one should believe, one should urge that *Bildung*, culture, is one of the objectives of education, the objective that education obliterates its own trails and traces.

Certainly culture is not the only goal of instruction and education. But perhaps it is not so difficult to agree about one thing: that education should avoid obstructing culture, or furthering pseudo-culture or barbarism. From this standpoint, the postulate of culture as an educational goal, more precise postulates on education can be derived: for instance, that integrating experiences and knowledge should be undertaken early, that offering disconnected matter should be avoided as long as the integrating power cannot assimilate it, and that intrinsically connected matter should not be offered in a disconnected way.

Today's theory and practice are full of tendencies to present subject matter in a logically thoroughly analysed form, as it were in an atomistically pulverized condition – later on we will illustrate it by a few horrifying specimens. Mighty efforts are made to adapt instruction to the objective of measuring precisely all its consequences – I mean the short term consequences, up to the next test, since evaluation and responsibility do not extend to what would still stick three days or years after that date. Will anything stick? Yes, I think so, and this could be *Bildung*, culture.

I have always nurtured a keen interest in history, and for some time I even hesitated whether I should not study history rather than mathematics. As a university student I attended courses in history and repeatedly afterwards I have made serious studies of history, for instance, in all details of the period from 1670 to 1750. Once I knew a lot of historical dates. Though I forgot most of them I look over history as over my own life. Were they useless, the dates, kings, dukes, popes, wars and peaces? No, they were the scaffold upon which I erected my structure of history. The lofty building stands there in my imagination, but the scaffold has been cleared away; I do not need it any more – I have acquired more organic means of structuring. Would it have been possible without years and dates? Probably it would. Instead of dates it could have been coins or coats or arms or pedigrees or armours. Eventually much of what one has learned turns out to be superfluous – more than what is lasting; but this, too, is an essential feature of acquiring culture, that little is retained by the sieve, but it is one's own sieve which one has created oneself.

This makes it difficult, if not impossible, to motivate even a single subject by culture as an educational goal. Each particular subject may be dispensable but the whole must be a whole. Yet there is one thing that can be motivated by culture as an educational goal: the way subject matter is offered and acquired. It should not be in an atomistic way, nor with a view to measurement. 'The atomistic way': that is lists of historical dates, spelling booklets to be learned by heart, the atomic weights. 'With a view to measurement': this means disregarding what the measurement specialists are not able to measure.

This is not yet the worst. The worst is that this kind of programming essentially restricts the options of the learner. Of course, nobody is free to select what he likes from all that exists. There are restrictions – enormous restrictions – in the freedom of choice. But it is this freedom of choice that makes culture feasible as an educational goal: people are instructed, they are educated, but by their own activity they become educated people. Freedom of choice, however, does not mean that one may pick one out of several options as, for example, after a sentence of death one might choose between hanging, strangling and drowning. Choosing, too, is a thing that must be learned; it starts locally before it can be practised globally. It is farcical to have first beginners discussing about how they would like to learn the three R's, and university freshmen about which courses and exercises should be given: and it is more so if the decision is taken in advance and the argument reached by manipulation, and if the learning process is sharply rationalised and straightforwardly steered. A freshman in the exercise class or a candidate in the oral examination who asks 'May I call this x?', or 'May I draw a figure for this problem?' or 'May I apply the mean value theorem?' proves that – helpless as a firstgrader – he has not learned to choose even at the local level, and this devalues the global choice of the study he has selected. To be sure, an adult who still likes to be tied to leading-strings or who thinks he is pleasing other people if he pretends to like leading-strings, cannot complain. It is his own fault, but would he do it if leading-strings did not exist? Of course they are no new invention, they have always been used in education. The modern educator says he holds them in abhorrence; but quite a few would rationalise the educational procedure as a business and steer it as an industrial process such that rather than leading-strings they look like harnesses the learners are put to in order to pull the education carriage.

Freedom of choice is freedom for responsibility. Accepting and bearing responsibility must start in a small way. Feeling responsible for great ideals of humanity, for war and peace, for the struggle against exploitation, hunger, repression can mean that one shrinks from the responsibility of calling something 'x', reading a property to be proved from a figure, or applying the mean value theorem, if the examiner could demand something else. Or with a more contemporary illustration: conservation starts at home.

Is it right to belittle such high moral values as the sense of responsibility by divesting it of its moral component? I do it intentionlly. Responsibility is primarily the reverse of freedom of choice, and only at a far distance has it anything to do with morals. Anyhow moralising is not my intention. I have used words like culture, freedom of choice, responsibility, because I am discussing education. Someone who believes they do not belong to the order of the day may have truth on his side. It is my right to believe they are indispensable. It is my choice that I pronounce them and my faith that I have to do so. To be sure it is no merit of mine that I may pronounce them as I am not the first, not even the thousandth, who dares to do so.

2. SCIENCE AND THE PICTURE OF MAN

The only thing this work has in common with science is that its author is a scientist. One could investigate scientifically with how much constraint a man can best be drilled to recite and apply the multiplication tables and to write his native language flawlessly, and likewise how sweets and whippings can most efficiently be distributed to obtain an educational optimum. It is a pity that, say 70 years ago, educational research with χ^2 and the analysis of variance had not yet come into being. Just imagine an investigation of, say 1903, about whether fractions can be better instilled with or without the cane – differentiated, of course, according to the length and to the country of origin of the bamboo, and perhaps subsidised by some cane industry. It is a pity such a contribution to the literature is lacking. Yet, whoever reads the present pages 70 years from now will not be in a position to complain: today, research with χ^2 and variance analysis is done as to whether the transitivity of a relation or the structure of a group table is better learned with rewards or without. (From the literature I do not know about differentiation according to the size of the reward and as little about the application of the minimax principle – the pursuit of maximal output with minimal expenditure – but this only proves my ignorance.) *Of course* education with rewards is more effective, as was education with the cane 70 years ago, and probably this could be proved beyond doubt. But what is the use of it if education with sweets and whippings is repudiated?

At any period in history the state of educational technology depends on that of society. Well, 70 years ago there were people who were against the cane. What would they have said about an investigation on the expediency of the cane in teaching the multiplication tables? That it was no science? With all those χ^2 and variances? And – I am sorry I forgot to mention it – the report was not about the cane but about a 'castigation medium', which sounds most scientific indeed. And even if one feels that such investigations could not possibly be scientific, how could one prove such vague feelings scientifically? It is not relevant, one would say in the terminology of the first chapter. Not relevant? But seventy years ago it *was* relevant whether a better educational output could be obtained with or without a cane, and investigations on this question – whether they are termed scientific or technological – would have been as relevant as the question.

At any rate there were adversaries to beating. They have succeeded (though as appears from the literature, here and there beating is still in use). We do not know for sure how multiplication tables and fractions are best learned and yet they succeeded. Why did they? Because parents said 'My children should not experience being beaten for poor arithmetic'. But others would have said 'I had the tables drubbed into me with a whip, why should my children fare better?' Or did the parents say 'it is my exclusive right to thrash my children'.

It might be considered a pity that we can no longer investigate 'scientifically' whether lickings are bracing to character, or whether big sticks produce better soldiers and citizens, but the results would not be relevant any more. In the view of the opponents of corporal punishment, they have never been relevant, whatever such investigations would have proved. Cane pedagogy does not fit anymore into our picture of man. The picture of man is the decisive factor, and it will remain so even if one fine morning a science of education existed which would solve all problems in detail. Instruction and education are techniques; it depends on my picture of man how I practise them and which technology I adhere to, and all my writing about them are what, in the first chapter, I called background philosophy. Perhaps it has become clearer why I must linger in side-tracks – or what look like side-tracks – before I reach mathematical education. There may be things I cannot prove with scientific force; but I refuse to obtain them surreptitiously by pseudoscience. I intend to present them with reasonable arguments as consequences of a reasonable faith. Nobody is compelled to accept my picture of man, but it is not patented either. I did not invent terms like cultural ideals, freedom of choice, responsibility. What I am saying now has been said a hundred times before, not for seventy years, but for seven times seventy: it is still topical and perhaps after seventy years it will still be so. Thanks to those who did not believe in the pedagogy of the cane, beating fell into disuse. Well – sceptics say – it has been substituted by other kinds of terror to which whole classes are reacting with belly-ache. Even if they are not used to terrorise, one should not forget about multiple choice tests. They are more dangerous since they are not creations of bad temper or wickedness, but products of a benevolent, scientifically behaving technology. Strangely enough, so many things are tested, but not the test itself. I admit there have been tests made of whether quadruple choice is better than sextuple choice, whether 50% difficulty is an ideal discriminator, whether and to which end misleading cues should be built in, whether and how and under which conditions time restriction is suitable. But whether education should be adapted to the possibilities and means of testing it has not been investigated, nor, if not, how it can be avoided. As a matter of fact, this negligence is also rooted in a faith, the belief in the measurability of educational devices, which is hardly compatible with my belief in culture as an educational goal, freedom of choice in the educational process and sense of responsibility in applying what one has learned. It is just a faith like mine; and the reason why I call the other one a dogma is that it strides along with a scientific swagger in order to accuse my faith of being unscientific.

I characterised my book *Mathematics as an Educational Task* as a philosophy of mathematical education. Its basic statements are indeed motivated by a background philosophy. I there explained the Socratic method and the method of reinvention: but I had no evidence to justify them other than pictures of man. I condemned the dogma of systematism as a wrong faith because it contradicted my picture of man. If the adult mathematician is entitled to invent his own concepts and to reinvent those of others, to practise mathematics not as a stock of knowledge but as an activity, to explore fields, to make mistakes and to learn from his mistakes, then the same privileges should be granted the learners from early childhood onwards. I said this, and I condemned the arrogant *Quod licet Iovi, non licet bovi* of the adult mathematician, who as a didactician prescribes for the learner not only what he should learn, but also precisely on which path, and forbids him all side-leaps which could lead him into error. I have not proved that what I aspire to is better, as little as one really knows whether teaching is more effective without beating – possibly it is not better. I am advocating another method because I believe in it, because I believe in the right of the learning child* to

* My earlier book dealt with learning mathematics, which in a certain way differs from learning other subjects – a little known fact, which I hope to discuss later on.

be treated as a learning human being. This is my view on education; defending it I call philosophy; but do not ask me for scientific proofs.

Is it not arrogant to reproach others with the fact that they will not deal with children as human beings? I did not reproach anyone. I spoke about the learning child, which in my view is a learning human being. Learning is just the point where in the theory and practice of many people the humanity of the child ends. Developmental psychology is lavishly cited and quoted to justify such theory and practice. But if I am not mistaken, developmental psychologists have never analysed learning processes. They have only stated that children at this or that age do not make use of certain mental structures and abilities, and that when they are older they do make use of them. It was neither investigated nor argued how – by which learning processes – the new faculty was acquired. It is a quite characteristic feature that it was never investigated whether development means only gains and no losses – I think that this question has not even yet been posed.

Moreover I do not claim that the child's learning is the same as that of an adult. I only stated the right of the child to the same freedom in learning which is claimed by the adult, the same freedom of trying and experimenting, of analysing before synthesising, the same right to integrate material, to make mistakes, to think provisionally and to acquire one's verbal expression by one's own efforts.

I repeated this from my earlier book as an example of a philosophy that interprets a picture of man. But I have dwelt long enough on the picture of man. I now pass to another component of faith – the picture of society.

3. A CASE IN POINT

The child should be able to use in society what it has learned at school; and in order to determine what it should learn one has to know what the society looks like for which it is being prepared – this is an old demand though not the one I mean when I speak of the picture of society. I do not mean the picture of an ideal society either. Those who clamoured against beating also pictured a new society but no Utopia.

Membership in the society means participation; the wishes and expectations of a society's members are mental pictures which influence future structures. Ideas in many minds are voiced by a few, often in a pointed manner, and the utterances of the few influence the ideas of the taciturn. Society's picture of itself influences education; and conversely education produces changes in the society. But don't misunderstand me: schools, as part of society, influence it. They do so by the subject matter, by the way the subject matter is taught, and also by their social environment. I don't believe, however, that society can be changed by teaching theories about society at school; but this is a point I will discuss later on.

When I wrote *Mathematics as an Educational Task*, I viewed the social problems of education too narrowly. It is true that several times I voiced my discontent with traditional European *élite* education*. But discontent as a guide is untrustworthy. I ought to confess that within the framework of my knowledge of secondary education – say in my own country – the most academic part of the system was unduly stressed. To make clear what I mean I am going to explain a few of the features of our school system in the Netherlands - European readers will transpose them by analogy to their own systems, and those whose countries enjoy a more democratic looking system may still wonder whether their social problems of education are much different from ours.

Our primary school (1st–6th grade; age 6–12) is general in the sense that children are not separated from each other on intellectual criteria (though not in the sense of publicity, as the majority of our primary school children attend denominational schools). From the 7th grade onwards the system branches into AVO (general secondary education) and L.B.O. (lower vocational education), and this happens in the ratio of about 60% for AVO to 40% for L.B.O. In L.B.O. five main streams are distinguished, whereas after one or two 'bridge years' AVO divides into three branches, a six years course leading to university studies, a five years course leading to higher vocational studies (such as colleges of education and higher technical schools), and a four years course, which is more or less terminal. The terminology L.B.O. lower vocational education, suggests other than intellectual criteria for the branching off; it suggests that L.B.O.-pupils enter this type of school in virtue of a positive choice, that is, with a view to a future trade or profession, and that AVO-pupils are those who at the end of the primary school have not yet made any decision or have excluded vocations accessible through L.B.O. It is

* Strangely enough to some reviewers this statement was the most controversial of my earlier book.

indeed correct, in general, that eventually L.B.O. pupils will find themselves in vocations which they seem to have favoured when they made their choice, whereas AVO pupils will be found in vocations of another character; but this does not prove that the prospect of a certain trade had been the decisive factor. The term L.B.O. is a historical reminiscence, but from day to day L.B.O. has less and less in common with vocational schooling, general subjects are more and more stressed, vocational subjects are now delayed to the third and fourth year. Why then is the branching off not shifted by two years?

Well, today L.B.O. has quite another function than orienting toward an early choice of vocation, and with respect to this function many other countries know types of education which may be compared with our L.B.O. It is the task of L.B.O. to accommodate those pupils who cannot fulfill the demands of AVO – more precisely those which, on account of their achievements at primary school and in tests, are believed not to be able to follow the AVO programmes. They enter L.B.O. because AVO does not admit them. Rather than an early choice of vocation, it is a negative selection – based upon achievements in arithmetic and spelling – that leads children into L.B.O.

In former times it was a fashion to describe the difference between AVO and L.B.O. pupils by the terms 'theoretical' and 'practical intelligence'. Today 'practical intelligence' is not much more than a euphemism. It has been shown that L.B.O. children are much inferior to AVO children, not only intellectually but over the whole line – with regard to character, creativity, artistic gifts, social behaviour. As everyone may expect, this lag is only increased by the accumulation of ill-motivated pupils in the same type of school; in an educationally inferior environment these children receive qualitatively reduced instruction.

Properly speaking my case description was still too simplistic. L.B.O. is not a homogeneous system. There are five main streams in it, which can be arranged according to the intellectual abilities of the pupils – at the top the lower technical schools and below the lower domestic economy and trade schools (for girls), and the lower husbandry schools; along with our division of AVO in three streams our educational system is certainly the most ramified in the world. This refinement – water to the mill of educationists – is historically rooted and was elaborated and reinforced by the – quite reactionary – education act of 1960, which was passed at a time when, all over Europe, the tendency was towards unification.

On the other hand the theoretical uniformity of our *primary* education is not as well matched by the practice as it would seem. The primary schools themselves are already divided according to the future destination of their pupils: schools from which the majority of the pupils pass to AVO and where the pupils are systematically prepared for the decisive tests, and schools that deliver only a small percentage of pupils to AVO. Moreover for simplicity's sake the so-called 'bridge' classes in AVO where the decision should be taken on the separation into the 6 years, 5 years, 4 years streams, are often 'homogenised', which means that the pupils are sorted out right at the entrance of secondary education.

The separation of primary school children according to their intellectual abilities, of course, comes about through their living environment: differences between urban, suburban, cottage rural, farmhouse rural environment, and within the cities between quarters, are stamping the populations of the particular schools. The living environment again is socially determined, and so it is not to be wondered at that the eventually decisive factor in what seems a choice at the end of the primary school is the social extraction of the pupil. This is somewhat corrected by his intellectual abilities but both are closely tied to each other as they are to the attitude factors.

Readers elsewhere will certainly recognise familiar features in what I have said about the situation in my own country. Though a case study in the sense of sociological investigations, it is in a way paradigmatic, and so it may be expected that its theoretical interpretations and practical conclusions in our country are similar to what is uttered elsewhere on this theme.

4. ENVIRONMENT AND HEREDITY

Since the child is by heredity connected to its environment, namely through its parents, some people ascertain that eventually it is the whole of hereditary factors that decides the child's path through the educational system. It is an old query whether man is determined by 'nature or nurture', by heredity or environment, and quite a few people assert that heredity is dominating to such a degree that environment is no match for it. A quarter of a century ago, I plunged into the literature and scrutinised the evidence and arguments in favour of that thesis; the material I found was tendentiously collected and unscientifically worked out. Recently the query has been resumed and answered in sensational publications. I did not study the new material, but the mathematical formulation of the alleged result is a warning to be prepared for the worst; for instance, the author is said to have proved that the influences of environment and heredity are in the ratio 20:80 – it passes beyond my mathematical understanding how to define and figure out such ratios*. The material has been collected in the United States of America, where white and black people were compared; the results were readily adopted in Europe where – I mentioned it earlier – nobody seems to notice that our negroes must distinguish themselves from our whites not by the colour of their skins but by the type of school. In Japan there is a kind of caste, the buraku-min, three millions, living in 5000 Ghetto-villages, the burakus; as late as in the 16th century this caste branched off from the main stream, when flayers, tanners, and other 'unclean' people were excluded from the society. Though this caste system has been abolished a century ago, discrimination is still vigorous, albeit not based on race differences, which cannot have developed in three centuries, but on the evidence of the birth place. In intelligence tests the buraku children average 15 points less than other Japanese children, which is about the same difference as that between white and black in America; juvenile criminality of the burakus is $3\frac{1}{2}$ times that in the remainder of the population, which is also similar to what is experienced in America; and the percentage of people living on relief is double what it is in the remainder of the population. Since these divergences cannot be explained by racial difference, it is not farfetched in this case to estimate the influence of environment on intellectual and social achievements as rather high, perhaps higher than that of heredity. Other examples are the intelligence difference between anglophones and francophones in Canada a generation ago, and similar cases of cultural lag: it is too ridiculous even to ask the question whether this is due to heredity.

No doubt heredity is an important factor in the spectrum of mental ability of an individual, but it is not simply a statistical computation problem to figure out the ratio of heredity and environment in this spectrum. Right from birth the influences of environment are effective. I cannot manage to underestimate them. The most important thing a child is learning in its first years, is its mother-tongue, which it acquires in its domestic environment;

* I wrote this before the revelation that the basic data were a fake.

there it also learns its social reactions. It has been stamped by the far-reaching influences of environment when it enters school. This new environment can exert correcting influences, but the domestic environment – or its lack – remains a paramount factor.

Today endeavours are made everywhere to counteract the prejudice caused by environment and to offer equal chances to all. In my country, plans are studied to keep children together in one type of school – *middenschool* – during the three or four years after primary school. England knows its Comprehensive School, which has not, however, superseded the old Grammar School. In Sweden a uniform school system has been introduced; in the Federal Republic of Germany *Gesamtschule* experiments are being undertaken. It is a recurring argument against this 'democratisation' that the age of 12–13 years is much too late to give equal chances to all. The objection is right. One should start with primary education (only to hear the same objection that it is too late because the true solution would be equal chances from birth onwards). In the United States of America school children of different city quarters are artificially being mixed to counteract discrimination by race. In Europe nobody would propose such a thing. Obviously discrimination by social environment is felt to be less cruel than discrimination by *race*, and therefore there is no proper inducement for imitating the American example, if living conditions account only for a *social*, rather than *racial*, discrimination.

After six or twelve years of life it does not matter too much where the lead of the one and the lag of the other comes from, from environment or heredity. It exists and the school does not seem able to do anything about it but gradually reduce the chances of the underprivileged ones more and more.

5. EQUAL CHANCES FOR ALL

The situation I have sketched here is well-known all over the world. Everywhere efforts are made to change it, everywhere people struggle with enormous difficulties, and everywhere people are divided into progressives at one end and conservatives at the other, between optimists and pessimists, between planners and indolent spectators. In favour of the progressive doctrine there is always one argument, a historical one: progression in the past, which in spite of temporary reactions has been lasting. 'No', the others say, 'the summit has already been crossed, we are now on the descending branch.'

'This is what the conservatives of each generation in the past declared anew, and they erred', the optimists say. 'That is true', is the answer, 'but today things are different.'

This is the pattern of discussions, not only in questions of education, which drag on everyday. Who is right? It is right, I think, to believe in the future, only it is often a wrong future people believe in.

There was an era when the three R's were an art mastered by a few, and still at the end of the 18th century it was the general principle that the children of the poor should learn reading (and singing), while writing and arithmetic were superfluous. Perhaps they were superfluous in the society of that time, but those who under the influence of the enlightenment did learn them contributed by this fact to changing society, so that for some among those who had learned them and for many of the next generation they became things that were no longer superfluous.

Should it continue this way? At any rate it continues. More children get more and more differentiated education (but quality is decreasing correspondingly, the sceptics say). At our four years course AVO schools the number of pupils taking mathematics in the 3rd and 4th years has quintupled after a modernisation of the programme six years ago (but they no longer know Heron's formula, the teachers of continuing vocational schools complain). I took it as an expert judgment how fast things are deteriorating today when I heard a fourth year university student, who as a part time assistant in the physics laboratory worked with the freshmen, complain about present-day youth.

However this may be, the call for more and better education for more children sounds to quite a few as a challenge which is readily accepted. It is believed – though even this is doubted – that the quality of education depends on the educational environment. Equality of chances then requires that they are not separated from each other at the time they enter secondary education. But if it turns out that rather than favouring the less gifted pupils the community with them would be detrimental to the gifted ones, what then? When, now long ago, the general school in many countries was propagated and eventually introduced at the primary level, the counter argument was that the future spiritual, economic, political leaders of the nation could not possibly be educated in one classroom along with the future masses. Though not explicitly uttered this argument may still hold in the views of many. But it can also be reversed: it is a necessity that the prospective occupants of high professions and offices do not walk their educational path in isolation – a social necessity for the society and a characterological one for those concerned. This is the way the integrated secondary school can provide social education along with intellectual, artistic and technical education, not, as some people propose, by stuffing the students' brains with social science (or so they call it), but by preparing them for a society where people with qualitatively and quantitatively diverging talents must cooperate.

Is it not asking too much if, moreover, it is required that intellectual, artistic, and technical education are not impaired by the demand of social education? Well, in education, asking always means asking too much. If, in grading, *C* means passing, why do we ask for *B* or *A*?

Yet I am fully aware of the size of that task and I would wish there were more awareness of it wherever people discuss this kind of problem. If this sounds arrogant to the reader, he will in a few minutes understand what I mean.

Though I do not wish to belittle the systematic thinking activity and power of innovators, I do not believe that the apparently fundamental problems they tackled and the solutions they offer can effect more than bureaucratic transformations, which are just rippling the surface of an ocean of problems. The profound-looking solutions are simplistic; they betray that those who offered them were not aware of the real problems. They are not to blame for it as it is not their domain. We do not blame a zoologist if he cannot milk a cow, or do we? Innovation projects in education are designed by general educationists, and in many countries it has become quite the exception if such people have got acquainted with education in another way but by digesting theoretical literature – I mean education here not as an abstraction or a bureaucratic structure, but as the educational process, which takes place at school and in other educational environments. On the watchtower of what it is now the fashion to call the macro-structure, and even in the meso-structure, the proper educational problems are far away, but unfortunately this is the safe harbour where theoretical innovators like to linger. There the effect of bureaucratic measures is overestimated and the really important kernel, the pedagogical and didactical situation, is disregarded. One believes that instruction can be reformed by laws, decrees, ordinances and organising measures and is surprised if it does not work. The recent failures of innovation projects and policies in several countries are due to the same ideology: education dealt with as a bureaucratic concern. It is even worse if – as in the Federal Republic of Germany – innovation is dominated by sociologists – the fatal consequence of a thinking error. I do not at all underestimate the weight of possible contributions of sociology and sociologists in the process of innovation – as little as I do with general educationists. On the contrary, I would set great hopes on them, I would consider them as indispensable provided one knows the right spot to place them. The great mistake – a mistaken principle as we will see – is the belief that one can descend from generality and abstractness (the macro-structure) by deductions through a hierarchy of levels to the topical and concrete actuality (the micro-structure) – this deduction, or what they call such, is no deduction at all but progressive trivialisation. Though obviously wrong, the deductive perspective is so frequent in educational theory that I cannot but waste much time on discussing it.

(My theme is still 'equal chances'; I digressed only to warn against simplistic solutions.)

If I cannot trust sociologists and general educationists I am under the obligation of thinking afresh about the problems. There is first the unfortunate slogan of the equal chances that reminds one of the roulette table. Where does such a thing exist? Each of all the spermatozoids in the uterus that hasten to fertilise the ovum has perhaps the same chance, but as soon as the ovum is fertilised, the deal is made – let us not discuss now to which percentage. The new-born infant cannot choose his parents and their social environment; they start with equal chances as little as the sprinters on the cinder path. If blind fate is meant, I would rather think of the blindfolded goddess that weighs according to right and justice, if only I knew what right and justice were. 'Equity' is more to the point than 'equal chances', which promises what nobody can fulfill. 'Fighting discrimination' is perhaps the best term though it sounds less positive. Should not disadvantage be removed by granting special advantages? It can hardly be avoided just as more care is bestowed on a sick person than on a healthy one.

An effective means of discrimination is segregation. So it is quite natural that discrimination is fought by desegregation – I explained earlier why it is not far-fetched to state this in terms of the American racial issue. In terms of instructional policy desegregation would mean the integrated secondary school. But this is not a patent medicine. Much more must be done than lumping together what is separated. This is generally agreed on, but the modalities are controversial. The modalities, or what they call such, are the details of organisation and the political frame.

But this is shirking the problems we ought to consider: is the integrated school environment of the general secondary school better than the divided ones of, say, our Dutch L.B.O. and AVO? Does it improve education? Would it not be better to protect the more able pupils against 'dullness' and not to expose the 'dull' pupils day by day to confrontations with higher intelligence? Well, if the new integrated secondary school is expected to continue the old instruction as to subject matter and method, the answer may be: yes, it is better not to integrate; the 'dull' pupils have sufficiently proved that they cannot keep pace, that they hate that kind of instruction. Mere organisation is not the way to change this. To know what really should be done one has to start reasoning from contents and methods of instruction. I will shortly return to this point.

The integrated school environment should be a positive factor. But how to account in it for the diversity of its members? The answer is by differentiation. Under the common roof – not only of the school, but perhaps even of the classroom – they receive differentiated instruction. Differentiation is the newest fashion now in Europe – an easy prey to general educationists. Subdividing, schematising, drawing schemes is their delight – the same delight that bred and nursed the fine ramifications of our Dutch system of secondary education. Several models of differentiation have been invented in the last few years, with no regard to and no responsibility for actual instruction, but whatever you choose it is the same principle of empty boxes fabricated by general educationists and to be filled by people who are considered as competent in instruction and subject matter, and who are called upon to cut the traditional instruction into slices that fit into the prescribed compartments of the system. Moreover the result is always differentiation according to subject matter, never according to method (which I do not advocate either). If things go wrong, if the system intensifies the social diversity, sociologists are grudging – against each other. They plead guilty since all of them believe that sociology holds the key to instructional reform though they disagree on the whereabouts of the keyhole. I told you there is no reformed instruction in an unreformed society, one party says, whereas their adversaries try to stop the 'unwanted' social differentiation by new finesses in organising the differentiation of instruction.

The alleged paradox of 'reformed education in an unreformed society' by which German sociologists try to prove their indispensability in educational innovation, can be answered by another that is more to the point: reformed instruction with unreformed curricula and unreformed teachers. This is indeed what has been tried – unsuccessfully – in many experiments. 'Reformed instruction', that is Comprehensive School, *Gesamtschule*, *Middenschool* in monumental letters above the entrance, where behind the front door, now under one roof and along a ramified system of galleries the sheep are separated from the goats. Is it necessarily that? Yes, it certainly is if our choice is reformed instruction with unreformed curricula and unreformed teachers. Then the 'unwanted' differentiation, or what the German sociologists call so, is unavoidable. Differentiation is a euphemism indeed. They say 'differentiating' and they mean 'dividing'. It is their destiny, because integration is only feasible if you start from the teaching contents and methods, but this is not the concern of the schematisers.

Differentiation is unavoidable. Pupils are differentiated and they react to the instruction which is offered them in a differentiated way. The newly proposed systems respond to this natural differentiation not with as natural an integration, but they stress it by separation, by a sharper separation than the traditional school did. The result is that the 'good pupils' get better (as to intellectual achievement rather than to social integration). And what happens with the lower half of the integrated age class? Its bright pupils are now condemned to mediocrity and inferiority. Julius Caesar preferred to be the first man in a provincial town rather than the second in Rome, but such preference is not a Caesarian peculiarity. These are the unavoidable consequences of any system that knows first, second, and last ranks, or it should be a string quartet, where the second violin need not be second rate. The increasing distance between bright and poor pupils, the Olympic exaltation of the bright and the downfall of the poor into a deeper Orcus – this is the real problem of the integrated age class; and whoever forgets to think about it had better not indulge in experiments.

We cannot avoid the burning question: how should we respond to the natural differentiation in the learning process? I can only repeat my answer: such questions can only be discussed on the basis of teaching contents and methods. Endless quarrels about fundamental educational problems come to a happy end as soon as the wranglers decide to talk about real business instead of abstract theory. Afterwards the view can be broadened and sophisticated – and it should be – on the solid basis of competence. Deductions from generalities are possible if they have been preceded by induction towards the general: from education in general to competence, if the path from competence to education in general has been travelled before.

6. EDUCATION BOTTLED AND FUNNELED

Equal chances for all, yes. But of course there is no use mixing up sheep and goats, 'black' and 'white'. Eventually all that counts is heredity rather than environment. 'Equal chances' means that everybody gets the education he is created or prepared for, how much or how little it might be. With the good of the underprivileged at heart give him an education he can get on with, teach him the trick how to do it, routine skills he can master, but do not overcharge him and his teachers with the demand that he can understand what he learns – such ideas are cited as final conclusions of the reports where it should have been proved that the shares of heredity and environment in the measured intelligence are as 80 to 20. So thoughtlessly conclusions are drawn, which as a matter of fact would be wrong even if the assertion about the ratio of 80:20 could be given some meaning.

No doubt they have the good of the underprivileged at heart if they wish to spare him intelligent learning and make him happy with tricks how to do it and routine skills he can master, but it is too bad that they nurse perverse, albeit quite popular, ideas about what is learning and what is its use. Indeed what use is it to teach an anyhow underprivileged child, say, arithmetical skills it will never apply? The problem, how far a car comes with 60 liters gasoline if its goes 12 kilometers on one liter, is answered by half of the pupils in the first L.B.O. year (12–13 years) with a division, and since the underprivileged children cannot even do this, the school responds with the effort to raise their achievements in long division. It is the same old tune: 'They cannot grasp it anyhow, so I teach them arithmetic by rote, which is a solid thing for them to learn.'

The best intentions cannot make good for superficial ideas on learning. Superficial – this means creating schemes and structures for learning which should be filled by others with learning contents and processes. An instructive example is *Mastery Learning**. Everybody can learn everything if time

*Footnote on p. 63.

permits, they say, and for safety they instantaneously explain that this is an aphorism. Well, a true aphorism legitimates itself; whoever feels the need to legitimate an aphorism, admits that it is illegal. The surface of an aphorism should conceal profound truth. The claim that everybody can learn everything is superficial, but is as wrong as it can be. As a matter of fact, it is no aphorism but an advertising slogan, and the excuse that it is an aphorism, is a mere wink: in advertising you cannot do without exaggerating. But even as a wink it does not become more true. The thesis everybody can learn everything if time permits is fundamentally wrong because again it is based on a perverse idea of what learning is.

It is no new idea that one can pump as much water as one wants through a pipe that is as thin as one wants, if time permits (though they might have died with thirst at the other end) and the basic idea of mastery learning is as little original. It is only a new edition of what is called in Germany the Nuremberg funnel, illustrated by a blockhead which by a funnel on his head gets knowledge poured in.

Learning is not a continuous process as taught by the behaviourists. The essence of all learning processes are the discontinuities, the jumps – I have stressed it often enough, and I will return to this point. Learning by rote, in fact, gets on in small steps, but once the technique has been acquired, small steps do not help any further. There are thresholds in learning which are too high for a few, others which are not surmounted by many learners, and again others which are insurmountable to the great majority even if they are allowed all the time they want – this everybody knows who has understood what learning is.

Well, well, it is old wisdom: industry gains the day, and diligence conquers all. I need neither proverbs nor counterexamples, I know a lot of them. For instance, a mathematics student who during four years was regularly and urgently advised to give up his attempts (though his father was convinced he would become an excellent mathematics teacher), who after four more years at another university passed the intermediate examination, and after six more years the final one – altogether 14 years for what a good student manages in four years – I do not know whether he ever got a job and, if so, how he performed. Well, this is a model of Mastery Learning: he has accomplished it but do not ask me how, or, still less, for what purpose. There are plenty of such proofs of mastery learning in practice, and even theoretically the fundamental idea of mastery learning can be proved whether you like it or not: for everybody there is a positive probability that he passes a certain examination, and even if this is as low as 1%, in 500 trials the probability of passing becomes as high as 99%.

It seems to be a sound proof, but it is wrong. Not because the trials are not independent, but because the problem has been shifted. It was claimed that everybody could *learn* everything if time permitted, but, if anything, it has been proved that everybody can *pass any examination* if arbitrary repetitions are allowed. 'Being able to learn a thing' has been identified with 'being able to pass a test'. It is an identification I shall dissect later on, but in order to anticipate a well-known behaviouristic objection, I touch upon it right now. It is the objection: having learned something is expressed in a behavioural change, which is revealed by comparing reactions in pre-test and post-test. No, I say, if I wish to know whether somebody has learned something, pre-tests and post-tests are as much worth as pictures in advertisements for a fat reducer 'before and after the cure'; it reminds me of the race of the hedgehog and the hare, where the heads are counted only at the start and the finish and Mrs Hedgehog stands in for her husband at the roll call. In order to know whether, and if so, what somebody has learned, one has to ascertain which learning process took place, and if the process itself is not directly observable, ascertaining this requires much more complex evidence than pre-test and post-test can provide.

Several times I used the word advertising. Is it a malevolent exaggeration? I do not think so. Whether you like it or not, education can be a business, and there is no business without advertising. Even people who are now respected as classics of education, were not averse to it – I am not going to adduce examples, which can in fact be traced out easily by everybody who is interested in it. Writing, editing, publishing textbooks can be big business, and there is nobody I would blame for it or grudge it, in particular if it is good work. But there is one thing to be observed: the difference between advertising blurb and scientifically sound claims. So-called research papers on Mastery Learning read and sound as television advertising for the one detergent that extracts all dirt not removed by other detergents. Today there seem to be industries that by contract take over the school system of a whole district; they sell a completely standardised instruction and are fair enough to ask payment for the successes only; what is a success and how much it is worth, is figured out from the difference between pre-tests and post-tests and accordingly recompensed; pre-tests and post-tests are of course supplied by the manufacturer himself and included in the bargain. Nobody is going to buy a pig in a poke anymore. Up to now half of these industries seem to have failed, but these are unavoidable childhood diseases, and the other half that still flourish prove that it is sound business.

Do not expect a cry of abomination. It is not that I fear to cover myself with the same ridicule as did the people who believed the end of the world had come when they saw the first railroad. No, it is a logical development. If one can compute from the difference between pre-test and post-test how much somebody has learned and if one knows how many points are required for Mastery, then education has become a commodity like anything else and subject to the same economic laws. If education is a business, an industry, then production should take place in as rational and rationalised a way as in other economic fields.

Have I strayed? I came from 'equal chances for all' to the attempt to meet the challenge. One of them is Mastery Learning. There 'equal chances' means that all are given a fundamental instruction package and the time to master it. Whether it has been mastered, the test will show. There are many variants – 'the A.B.C. model', 'basis and addition', 'the I.M.U. model', 'I.P.I.', and all the others, but it is ever and ever the same story. Later on examples will reveal the incredible naïveté of assiduous workers who cut and squeeze traditional teaching matter into these schemes, competent people scared by the whip of the general educationist. Today the methods are more sophisticated than they used to be. It is not any more the funnel of Nuremberg but the hypodermic syringe with weighing before and after the shot. It is also more sophisticated as regards the equal chances. For instance, if the pupil must learn to multiply fractions, the basis includes the objective 'being able to find the composition result of two given fraction operators' – which is a euphemistic circumscription of the old algorithmic rule 'numerator times numerator, denominator times denominator' – and the first test of this ability consists in solving correctly three problems, after which the learning processes ramify and the unsuccessful ones are trained with 20 more problems, whereas the successful ones may read a proof of that rule. Or, in a more sophisticated tripartition, where the middle group marks time, the others are given remedial or supplementary matter.

Such a method can be excellently organised and quite successful, in particular if the competent people disavow the schemes of the educationalists wherever it is recommendable. The whole can also be programmed and – futuristic ideal – the children can be kept working at home and receiving the problems and reading the solutions by telecommunication or be connected to a computer with which they communicate in the working process. Then the problem whether and how to bring together all children of the same age in the same school type will have faded away. All have the same chances, but of course everybody on his own level. It is the summit of fairness.

7. THE SOCIAL CONTEXT

Still there is something wrong. How to use the ardently desired integrated school environment if the funnel of Nuremberg makes that something we can dispose of? Well, the sociologist says, the funnel of Nuremberg requires a sociological counterweight: solid sociology in the teaching programme or at least as an impregnation of all instruction. This is perhaps an extreme position but it fairly well describes present tendencies, in particular in the Federal Republic of Germany. I cannot blame those sociologists. If the decision has been taken in favour of some funnel of Nuremberg detached from the social learning process, this context must be found elsewhere. Only the fundamental decision was wrong, but even the identification of instruction with the funnel of Nuremberg cannot be blamed on the sociologist who is unacquainted with education and who is hardly shown anything else by the general educationist.

On one count the sociologist is right. The funnel of Nuremberg, however perfect it may be, cannot be the aim of our desires. It is no gain that it allows us to dispense with the school environment. The school should prepare for society, or rather be a limb of society, but then not the picture of a workshop where workers communicate, if at all, along an assembly or signal line. Nor should school activity be the sum of isolated achievements, but rather a collectively organised learning process. 'Equal chances' means not only that all may try their powers with the same material and may claim equivalent guidance, but also that this happens in equivalent environments. Subject matter, material, and guidance are replaceable, but not so the environment.

I discuss this not to prepare the reader for a simple solution of the problems but to stress how difficult they are. The school class such as we know it at present, is for the pupil in the first line the society of his friends (and for the little ones a large family), and only in the second line a workshop. This should remain so. Yet the working methods could be improved. Pupils there work together, but more often only side by side. The togetherness should be reinforced rather than abolished as is prescribed by the most extremely individualising methods, or weakened as happens in almost all innovation projects. Moreover, collaboration should become more deeply rooted.

I believe in the social learning process as a carrier of social innovation, and take exception to an educational sociology, estranged from education – in particular in the Federal Republic of Germany – which finds the appropriate means in a social science pervading the instruction, in teaching social theory rather than social life. I think they will be heavily disappointed; and even more the more they trust indoctrination. Religious confirmation lessons are gone and one does not get them back by replacing their 1–2 hours a week by ten hours of indoctrination. The worst in this method is its overtly unsocial character. The pupils with the best initial conditions get the valuable opportunity to exercise themselves in criticism – criticism of indoctrination – whereas the less privileged ones are abandoned to dullness.

And then the remainder of the curriculum is at the mercy of the educationist; he may contrive schemes that should give everybody what he is worth. But it seems to be fatal destiny, however the system is named, A.B.C., or X.Y.Z., or I.M.U., or I.P.I., whether it is one political system or another: "For whosoever hath, to him shall be given, and he shall have more abundance; but whosoever hath not, from him shall be taken away, even that he hath." Is it a cause for despair? No, but I believe that profound problems can only be approached in a profound way.

Profound, that means at the roots, in the instruction, in what is disdainfully called the micro-structure. Another word for what I mean is 'radical', at the roots. Not with general schemes contrived in the armchair.

8. THE HETEROGENEOUS LEARNING GROUP

I believe in the social learning process and on the strength of this belief I advocate the heterogeneous learning group. My own ideas concerning the heterogeneous learning group, my appreciating it, and my arguments in favour of it, have arisen in observing mathematical learning processes and thinking about my observations; the chapter on mathematics education would be the right context to consider it, but I cannot avoid discussing it right now. The heterogeneous learning group comprises pupils of different levels collaborating on one task, each on his own level – a common task such as is often undertaken in society by heterogeneous working groups of people collaborating on different levels, each on his own. In my book *Mathematics as an Educational Task* I explained what in my terminology 'level' means in the learning process; I do not know whether and how this applies to other learning work, and for this reason my propagating the heterogeneous learning group is restricted to learning mathematics.

According to some people the heterogeneous working group can be motivated only by political arguments; there are no educational arguments in favour of it, they say, on the contrary, educationally the odds are against the heterogeneous learning group. This might be true as long as one thinks in terms of general education theory. It looks quite different if seen from the point of view of competence, and then I mean mathematical competence. I think I am able to show that the structure of the mathematical learning process I called levels invites learning in heterogeneous groups. This seems to me a fundamental idea, and moreover a good example for the genesis of such educational cognition as is only possible if starting from the standpoint of competence.

For the level structure of mathematical learning processes it is, if not a characteristic, then at least a frequent attendant phenomenon that mathematics *exercised* on a lower level becomes mathematics *observed* on the higher level. Often this happens unconsciously, but it reinforces itself, if it enters into consciousness, to become an Aha-experience, such as certainly every mathematician knows from himself and others. The cognition of the level can mean much in the learning process; then the accomplished learning process becomes subject matter in new learning processes. Now, it is easier to observe learning processes with *others* than with *oneself*, and therefore one should not preclude the learner from the opportunity to make such observations. One more thing, and an important one, is learned if one observes others learning a subject matter that one has learned to master before; one understands how another learns, guesses how oneself managed it, objectifies this lower level activity in order to repeat it consciously even if meanwhile one has mechanised and algorithmised it.

I have anticipated this aspect, the profit gained by the higher level pupil in the collaboration; in fact this is not the only source of gain, because in detail, too, he can learn mathematical substance by observing the solving methods of his collaborators. The gain on the lower level seems to be more obvious, but after a more profound analysis one notices that it is not so. If this gain should be realised, it does not suffice to understand the functioning of the heterogeneous learning group from this point of view as an educational totality. It is necessary to direct it intentionally *a priori* to this aim or *a posteriori* to guide and to steer it. In the heterogeneous learning group all kinds of educational relations can be formed; its members learn to lead and be led didactically – this is the lowest level of didactics, which in fact is not transcended by all, or even the majority of, active teachers. On a higher level – as in the mathematical learning process – one will reflect on the acted out didactics, one's own or that of others – it is the least that in my opinion future teachers should be taught. It is, however, not unthinkable, and I have even observed it, that members of a school learning group subjected the didactics of their own learning and that of the others to reflection. 'Directing intentionally and *a priori*', as postulated above, meant erecting road signs in the learning programme which necessarily lead to these didactic observations; and '*a posteriori* guiding and steering' meant interventions that make the didactic relations within the group conscious.

Does this sound fantastic? It is based on experience. In fact the normal class is such a – much too large – heterogeneous learning group. Its main construction error is the existence of a central member, the teacher, who like a telephone operator intercedes and interprets the conversation and impedes the direct intercourse. There are, however, quite a few teachers who know how to reduce their activity to that of a computerised telephone office to such a degree that the result is almost direct traffic between the pupils. Yet the intentionally heterogeneously composed *small* learning group requires more. I readily admit that after quite a number of experiments we know too little about the functioning of such a group to make prescriptions or even to give advice.

In courses and conferences for teacher trainers, teacher guides, teachers, and parents we account for the postulates I formulated. What matters there is the acquisition and the consciousness of not only mathematical but also didactical abilities; there not only the subject matter but also its didactics do count. If there, in heterogeneous learning groups, our material is worked on, the members of such a group must observe the individual learning processes – of their own and of the others – and they must judge whether and how our programming of the learning processes works. In particular they must become aware of what in this functioning the heterogeneity of the learning group means, and whether and how it contributes to intensifying the learning process.

In such experiments we experience how difficult it is in the learning process to view side by side with the aspect of subject matter that of didactics and to accustom others to the same attitude. Certainly it will require much effort to create appropriate material for heterogeneous learning groups and prepare the teachers for working with such material. But the main question that is still open, is whether the great diversity of *motivation* of pupils – a variability both in character and intensity – would not be a more serious stumbling block than the difference of levels. Up to now we only faced groups with a rather uniform motivation: adults with the same interests, and pupils who in the singular situation of the experiment are extraordinarily motivated. My experiences in the primary school indicate much greater variations in motivation than in intelligence but also the means to overcome them. Nevertheless I still fear diversity of motivation in the integrated school environment as the rock on which the undertaking may be stranded.

Why do I stick to the idea of the heterogeneous learning group in spite of all uncertainties? Why do I stress such sophisticated looking features of the heterogeneous learning group as collaboration on different levels where the level is understood not only as a characteristic of learning content but also of didactic activity? Why do I wish to grasp and stimulate the social learning process in all its peculiarities? I do so because the tendency towards individualisation is so intense, so justified, so natural that it should not artificially be frustrated but in just as natural a way be inserted into the socialisation of the learning process. I have little illusions as regards the result. Even then whoever has, to him shall be given (albeit another kind of gift), but perhaps it is a way to treat the have nots more decorously than to take away from them all they do have.

* (Page 55.) Reports on 'sensational successes' obtained by Mastery strategies refer to a series of unpublished dissertations. Referring to unpublished research is not unusual in education; it is, however, rather unusual to check such references. When this happened in the case of Mastery Learning, it appeared that the quotations were wrong and the research quoted did not prove any superiority of Mastery Learning. Cf. Bibliography [94].

9. THE STRATEGY OF INNOVATION

The title of the present chapter contains the word 'education', and if this book belonged to the kind that begs for scientific respectability, the chapter would have started with a definition of what education is. Often enough before, and on the first pages of the present book again, I have explained why I disapprove of this approach in the work of others and proscribe it for myself. As in the case of 'science' I chose another approach: analysing the semantics, even by comparing different languages. The English word 'education' has so broad a spectrum of meanings that this analysis was necessary. Nobody would expect a history of literature to deal mainly with publishers and printers, or a history of landscape-painting with aniline production, but it is not unusual to identify education with a complex administrative structure ranging over acts on education, governmental decrees, educational systems, school organisation, size of classes, timetables, objectives of instruction, programmes, regulations on appointments and salaries. Efforts of innovation are commonly understood in this 'macro structure', where such cumbersome details as competence, subject matter, or teaching methods can easily be disregarded.

Even without any further explication it would have been clear what I mean by education and instruction. But I stressed it then and now, where I thought it was necessary: I underlined the importance of the didactic process in the classroom. This does not at all imply that other aspects can be neglected. On the contrary, there is no instruction without school buildings; without architects who design them; without textbooks which are written, published, approved; without teachers that are paid; without timetables which are introduced and observed; without preparatory and continuing schools; without ministers of education and janitors – this is no joking matter. Yet, in order to express my philosophy of education and educational innovation I have fixed my view on that spot where this philosophy can act the most efficiently and where according to this philosophy innovation should strike. It is understood there is much around this stage that may in no way be disregarded. Take our Dutch AVO-L.B.O. problem I sketched above. Whatever will happen, whether L.B.O. is independently improved, or whether integration in a *Middenschool* is aspired to, it cannot but require fundamental decisions under the veil of organising measures. For instance, a quite prosaic one: if by integrating different types of school, and by assembling teachers with different kinds of training and different diplomas under one roof, equality of salary becomes an issue, then there is no way to shirk the decision whose rank determines the amount paid, and whether in-service training should make good for lack of diplomas. I mention this, not as an oddity, which it certainly is, but as a paradigm. Educational innovations, which everybody would favour, can be delayed for years on the grounds that they might impair a precious social equilibrium which manifests itself in salary and rank levels. I am glad you confess that, says the sociologist who doubts the possibility of educational reform in an unreformed society. Yes, you are right, if you mean a reform of society that would abolish bureaucracy*. But as far as I know, reforms in society show the inverse tendency, don't they?

On the macro-level innovators are hampered by bureaucracy as it is the task of bureaucracy to assure stability. There are exceptions, progressive behaving bureaucracies – an example is that of the Federal Republic of Germany causing an educational catastrophe by introducing New Maths by governmental edicts**. Though it fits very well into such a system that some fine morning in October 1968 the conference of ministers of education of the Federal Republic of Germany, with no visible expert background or backing, could 'recommend' how arithmetic should be taught in the future, nevertheless it is hard to understand. Clearly nobody cared about how such a measure should be carried out. It is clear as daylight, and today a common place, that any innovative measure, even if it does not involve brand-new subject matter, requires an introduction strategy: that new textbooks ought to be written, new teaching methods developed and teachers prepared as to content and methods. In fact, even this is much too weak a formulation, which was already obsolete in the sixties. Today it is an opinion shared by the majority of those concerned that from curriculum development, via the establishment of new programmes and the elaboration of subject matter, to the retraining of teachers, all innovative activities should take place in a continuous interplay

* I do not mean 'bureaucracy' pejoratively. Bureaucracy is red tape accidentally, but essentially it is observing fixed rules which assure social equilibrium.

** As far as I know the F.R.G. is the only country where high government officials decide what mathematics is and how it shall be taught, though such 'recommendations' are not worth the paper on which they are written. In fact this is an old tradition, and it is not to be wondered at that sociologists and general educationists try to take over from government officials.

between centre and periphery: this is what people understand by democracy today.

If I look at macro- and meso-structure in education, my attention is drawn by the features which are overlooked in the bureaucratic view. Till now, when discussing education, I restricted myself to the didactic process in the classroom. But we have now reached the point where we should look at the didactic process in the classroom as embedded in the meso- and macro-structure, and innovation as a whole as a big social learning process, with many of the characteristics (in particular that of level structure) of the learning process in the micro-structure.

This realisation has also been the result of a learning process. Till recently, all educational innovation in the Netherlands was established by acts and edicts (as they did similarly in other countries): the bridge class in general secondary education (AVO), the fourth year in lower vocational education (L.B.O.) and its reprogramming, the reprogramming of teacher training, to adduce recent examples. But the preparation of new mathematics programmes by means of a kind of experiment, and by retraining and further training, was a cautious attempt at involving the educational field in the innovation. In France the prescription of new mathematics programmes for secondary education with no preparation and as little participation of the grass roots has excited serious discontent and indignation. Similar symptoms have indicated failures in the innovation process in other countries.

Meanwhile voluminous textbooks on innovation have been published, where armchair educationists indulge in void schemes. Inventing and prescribing such schemes in order that others may squeeze something into them is no learning process: the learning process does not start until others are confident enough to use the schemes, only to be stranded in the end in utmost despair. Learning processes in the classroom are programmed, guided, steered; and they can be so because the learners are assisted by teachers who are more experienced and more judicious. The process is programmed, guided, steered by experience and judgement. Innovation, in order to be a learning process, should be more flexible, as the experiences and judgements which lead to programming only emerge and condense within the learning process; since there are no guides and helmsmen from outside, the learning process must be guided and steered from inside.

Such ideas are as eyesores to general educationists. Flexibility is considered as amateurism. They wish to be technologists, but they are technocrats; they do not allow themselves and others even the flexibility of the bridge-builder who adapts his technique to the soil, although they would need a thousand times that flexibility. The numerous innovation projects that were initiated in the last decade in the Netherlands can hardly be accused of amateuristic flexibility; they were mounted in agreement with the strictest rules of the innovation art as laid down in the holy books of education. Alas, it was not there written that they would inevitably be stranded.

Whoever teaches or innovates, teaches or innovates *something*, and it is this something that prescribes laws and rules. There is no content free instruction or innovation, and no useful theory and technology of instruction and innovation detached from content. Since I know that this goes directly against all tacit teaching axiomatics and innovation theory, I will continue this argument later on.

If I say that content may not be disregarded, it is obvious I do not mean the bare subject matter but the actual learning process, not only in the classroom, but in the broader arena, which includes curriculum developers, test producers, teachers, those who guide teachers, evaluators and parents. Restricting myself again to learning and teaching, *mathematics* is my heuristic and, as I hope, paradigmatic starting point.

It could be worthwhile to expound how we, at the IOWO, arrived at viewing, accepting and starting this broad learning process as a whole; but this would be too long a story to be told here. After two years of exploring how a small group of primary school teachers would work out the subject matter of retraining courses in their classroom, and how larger groups could be trained and retrained with this material, we have been running an integrated primary school experiment, where operational objectives are not advanced *a priori*, but derived *a posteriori*, where subject matter and method are continuously adapted to experience, and where design, try-out, evaluation and adaptation follow each other in short, quick cycles. The same collaborator who designs the material guides the try-out, evaluates it, and adapts the design, which is tried out anew in a parallel class one or two weeks later, or even in a third; only after it has been discovered what the pupils can learn with the material are the learning objectives isolated; then the whole is again arranged and commented upon in order to serve at the same time in teacher training, retraining, and parents education, where the same cycle is repeated, albeit with a longer period. Evaluation material is developed in the course of the operation which would reveal the traces of learning processes rather than acquired knowledge. This is the way our primary school mathematics curriculum comes into being. It will be followed up by an epitomising adaptation for discussion among others in the field, the *discussion curriculum*, the nucleus of a democratic innovation strategy.

This is a brief sketch; there is no way to go into detail but through exemplary learning processes. Moreover, since there is nothing in it that could be claimed as definitive, I could only show a collection of instantaneous pictures in a big learning process where at every spot ramifications invite choices which ought to be made as consciously as possible. These are indeed not patent solutions.

10. TEACHER TRAINING

Teacher training, too, is instruction. The reason why I detach it from the integrated learning process is that it is institutionalised instruction such as schooling rather than innovation such as, nowadays, teacher retraining. In my book *Mathematics as an Educational Task* I stressed the training of secondary school teachers too heavily as compared with that of primary school teachers, which led to a distorted view of the relation between competence and pedagogics in the education of teachers. Nevertheless I maintain my conclusion with all its consequences for further training:

> Obviously teaching also belongs to the activities people learn by doing, and obviously in pedagogics, too, it is no good staying on this bottom level. This implies that the first study at university can contribute only to a modest extent to pedagogical-didactical training. (p. 167)

I believe, however, and I did so even then, that the first training should comprise more and better didactics than it does nowadays.

In all national educational systems there are two trends in the character of teacher training visible if one follows the line from kindergarten to university:

> a progressive specialisation of the teachers corresponding to the age of the pupils;
> a shift of stress from pedagogics to subject matter.

Though the first tendency looks well-founded, one may doubt whether the second is as easily justified. Clearly the pedagogical situation and requirements are different according to the age of the pupil, but is it really true that the higher age brackets can be satisfied with a less intensive educational training than the lower ones? But at this moment I do not feel the need to answer this question as I have serious reasons to question the value of today's pedagogical training as far as I am acquainted with it, and in this broader context the first question loses its particular character. Roughly speaking our teacher training knows three levels:

> primary school teachers;
> secondary school teachers of low competence;
> secondary school teachers of high competence (academic high school teachers).

The earlier mentioned L.B.O. schools (lower vocational schools) are manned by primary and low competence secondary school teachers. Only the third of these groups has received a proper mathematical education, and that on a level far above the school level. By a reform in the fifties mathematics has been cancelled as a subject matter in the training of primary school teachers – a windfall which allows us to fill the disagreeable and conspicuously gaping hole, which should be filled anyhow, with vigorous mathematics instead of the dead one of the past. Up to now mathematical training of the middle group was scanty, both as regards quantity and quality, which was miserable. I said "up to now", because in the last few years new institutions for training this quite numerous kind of teacher have come into being. The creation of these new institutions may prove highly significant, as their programmes and methods are, as it were, written on a *tabula rasa*, which might be imprinted by innovative ideas on instruction in general, and in particular, in mathematical instruction. No doubt the training of academic high-school teachers will be influenced by these innovations. Meanwhile the training of primary school teachers awaits radical reforms. Which requirements should teacher training be expected to fulfill, in our case and beyond?

In my earlier book I urged that the mathematics we teach should be *fraught with relations* – I explained this term in many pages. The same demand could be formulated for instruction in every subject matter, but in order to discover and formulate this demand one might need mathematics, where the inclination towards instruction lacking all relatedness is indulged in with more pleasure than elsewhere.

I would like to extend this demand to teacher training and in the course of this to illustrate it by its impact on teaching mathematics, without repeating the arguments I adduced in my earlier book. *Fraught with relations*, this includes first of all the relationships between the training and the goal the training aims at, the relatedness of the instruction the student receives with the instruction the student is expected to give in the future, its contents, its methods, its incorporation into a larger unit of education. Second, the internal relations, that is, between the various pieces of which the training of the future teacher is composed. Thirdly, the extra-instructional relations of the instruction the student receives and is expected to administer, that is, the social relevance of what he learns and teaches. (Of course, 'first', 'second', and 'third' do not indicate rankings.) It might be useful to examine programmes of teacher training – prescribed and actual ones – in order to know whether they can stand the test of these criteria.

I wish to prevent a serious misunderstanding I warned against repeatedly in my earlier book: urging the existence of some relations does not necessarily mean consciousness about them. Unconscious relations can be particularly efficient, and making all things explicit can be poor pedagogy. But this statement should not be misused, it is not meant as an excuse to evoke mysterious unconscious relations where no trace can be proved. Indeed, relations unconscious to the learner should be known to the teacher who can avail himself of this knowledge in the organisation of his teaching.

In fact, the things that remain implicit in teacher training may be fewer than in the past. It is claimed that students are critical nowadays and inclined to ask why and to what purpose they must learn this or that. I think they are quite right, and I cannot understand teachers who would prefer students who learn because they must. Often it may be hard to answer such questions 'why' and 'to what purpose', but at the same time it can be an advantage that they invite scrutiny.

The future low competence secondary school teachers are more immediately directed towards the profession they aspire to than the future academic high-school teachers. It is remarkable that often they reject teaching theory and similar abstractions if detached from actual instruction. But how do they face the mathematics they are obliged to *learn*, while their own school experience tells them that they will never *teach* it?

I cannot answer this because, in the commissions where I meet them and where their trainers struggle with mathematicians from outside the teacher training institutions about the mathematics they should learn, it is a struggle above their heads as they know little if anything about the mathematics that is discussed. Is it therefore meaningless that they attend these meetings and listen? I do not think so. It may be useful provided that the subject of such discussions is the kind of relations I urged teacher training should abound with. Even if they are not familiar with the one end of these relations – higher mathematics – there still exists the other end that they are reasonably acquainted with.

There is more to it. The relations between subject matter of school and of university can be more effectively understood in mathematics than in any other domain. It is not so simple in mathematics that at the university a certain quantity of subject matter is added to that of the school. Of course, neither is it so in other domains; but thanks to what I called the level structure, the "high" in higher mathematics means raising the level, or at least should mean it, and if something should be made conscious in the learning process at university, it is this raising of level. Where does this actually happen? It is just what was lacking in F. Klein's *Elementarmathematik vom höheren Standpunkt*. I once proposed to write a textbook dealing with a particular mathematical domain on two levels: left and right the same subject matter; left such as is grasped by one's own first learning process, and right such as is formalised after it has been grasped. This idea can be arbitrarily refined – one can add two more pages: one that shows how the person I teach achieves his grasp, and the other deals with the formalisation of the manner of his achievement – there are indeed many more levels. Why, a textbook like that would be a great risk. I would be concerned not about the publisher but the author who may risk his scientific reputation, as others might doubt his mental health. But why should students not be taught this way? If duplicated on stencil paper much is allowed that is protested at if it is from a printing press.

Beyond algorithmisation I stressed mathematising as a mathematical activity: by this I meant organising raw material, whether it is mathematical or not, by mathematical means. Analogies and isomorphisms of problems are important tools of mathematising; tactics and strategies of mathematising are the nucleus of what a teacher should learn to teach. Yet where can students, and where can their trainers, find an exposition of mathematising, its tactics and strategies, neatly divided into chapters, sections and subsections? The answer is simple: Nowhere. Indeed nowhere, because all this is implicit, included in our mathematical activity, and this lack of explicitness is its strength. It is our habit and second nature, and therefore it is hard to analyse it by introspection.

But there is a mighty method to discover it: the observation and intelligent analysis of the learning processes of others. All that is a pedestrian habit in ourselves becomes a fundamental discovery as soon as we see it arising in the activity of younger, less skilled persons; one must have witnessed and undergone it in order to be struck by it; a written or printed report does not suffice.

I will illustrate this later on by examples, but right now I anticipate what I consider as its consequnces for teacher training (the training of mathematics teachers, I mean; for I do not know what is transferable to other disciplines; and even in natural sciences, which I can survey a bit, much is entirely different.) The future teacher should learn to observe and analyse learning processes, not only those of his pupils, but also his own, those of his fellows, and his trainers. For the trainer this means that he leads and guides his students to the places where the learning processes take place, that he opens their eyes and minds to observation and analysis. It is a not so new but still rarely fulfilled requirement that mathematics is taught not as a created subject but as a subject to be created. For the same reason, armchair pedagogy in a standard package should yield to those pedagogies which are created by pupil, student, and trainer in a common experience.

This learning does not end when the student becomes a teacher, as is the traditional assumption. Observation and intelligent analysis of learning processes in service is itself a learning process in further training, which is again reinforced by being analysed. Formal further training should not only serve the teacher's spiritual enrichment but should by means of the discussion of experiences also increase the profundity and the refinement of observation and analysis.

I know very well, and I admit, that these are high demands. Since 1962 we have done quite a lot for the further training of mathematics teachers, first for the high competence secondary school teachers, then for the low competence ones, and finally for the primary school teachers, though in the latter group we reached a small fraction only, and their further training was no end in itself but part of the preparation of curriculum development for the primary school. As regards the secondary school teachers it was originally only further training with mathematical subject matter. We restricted it in this way, not because we underestimated the didactical component but because we did not consider ourselves competent enough to teach the teachers in their own domain of competence. Our hope that the teachers would be experienced enough to process the mathematical subject matter, and adapt its essence to the classroom situation, was disappointed; textbook authors filled up the gap, and whether they did it better or worse, it was in no case a translation of the mathematics we had intended, into didactics. Hesitatingly with the high competence secondary teachers and more vigorously with the low competence secondary teachers we tackled the problem of the didactic component. Mathematics and didactics firmly integrated is what we offered to the primary school teachers – integrated also with regard to the guidance of the courses which in every particular case consisted of a mathematics and a pedagogics trainer, colleagues at a teacher training institution. With further training of low competence secondary school teachers the same would be more difficult, though progress *is* being made; with that of high competence, it would be almost impossible. Teachers who help us train their colleagues in the knowledge of subject matter cannot be persuaded to pay attention in the refresher courses to the didactics of the subject matter (which they act out in their own classroom teaching) – nobody has trained us to do so, they reply. They are right, it is a different thing to perform an activity and to observe it. Is it really too high a demand to ask that the teacher observes the didactics he acts out, and that the future teacher is taught this level raising activity?

I alluded to numerous relations when I demanded that teacher training should abound with relations. Which teacher trainer can survey all these relations, one will ask me, frightened by the burden he is charged with. Relations between school and university mathematics? Are they not two difference subjects taught by different people, who suspect each other to be charlatans or a highbrow, respectively. Relations between the teaching methods of both of these mathematicians, where for the one the method is implicit to the subject matter, whereas the other understands and offers it detached from its content? Relations involving the incorporation of subject matter instruction into a larger body at school and at university level, while this incorporation, if it is at all taken seriously, is trusted to integration specialists who do not know what they must incorporate and integrate? Relations between the different pieces that together constitute the teacher training – well, this would be the easiest thing if one could at least get those who teach these pieces around one table. Relations that establish the social relevance of the subject; while thinking about social relevance is left to sociologists, who are not interested in the subject the relevance of which they should establish?

How could we do it? How can we pay regard to relations beyond our specialism, the trainers would complain, considering it as self-evident that the trained ones will succeed in something the trainers are not able to: integrating patchwork. Often teaching patchwork cannot be avoided. If it is unavoidable in non-vocational secondary education, it should at least be restricted as much as possible. The patchwork medical students are offered in classrooms and laboratories becomes integrated in the hospital, but nowadays efforts are made to start integrated instruction earlier; many other courses of academic training are still far from this point. Certainly, integration is a life long process – its result is culture – but just for this reason it should start early, and so should the efforts to make its necessity conscious to the student.

My goal is integrated teacher training, where in particular the subject matter and the didactical component should penetrate each other; individualistic lecturing, unrelatedness of subject matter, and didactical formalism do not fit into such a system. In such a training team pedagogues and didacticians should know the subject matter, and the man who teaches the subject matter should not shrug his shoulders if didactics is discussed. I know this is a hard thing for mathematicians. They should move from a field where everything can be proved into one where nobody can tell you what proving is. Of course, one of the reasons for this reluctance may be that they are used to restricting themselves to that mathematics where all can be proved, to a mathematics put into parentheses within reality. On the other hand one can understand their fear of a slippery road and of the jargon of educationists and their – often not unfounded – suspicion that it might be a language with no content involved, and invented for its own's sake.

Innovating teacher training is not a simple thing. I notice hopeful approaches where bureaucratic measures do not block the way and where nothing is expected from such measures either, where the thought is radical, that is, uncovering the roots, the learning process.

11. EDUCATIONAL PHILOSOPHY

It is obvious that the present chapter has not been conceived independently of the first. Nevertheless I wish to stress some connections. I did not conceal that the statements of this chapter do not represent science – though I hope it is not non-science either – but I do not wish to adduce this as an excuse. I discussed the techniques of teaching, and in spite of all friendly advice how it could be improved, lack of systematism is one of the reasons why this discussion is not even technology. On almost every page one reads words like "I believe" and "I think"; and demands and wishes were pronounced – I disapproved, I approved, I feared, I hoped. The bridge-builder is expected to do more than fearing and hoping. He has got the task of computing the requirements of the bridge such that it holds out. Of course he may still hope that he gets the commission to build it, and fear that something happens to obstruct it.

Faith and hope spring from a philosophy: their opposites do likewise. I have tried to keep this philosophy in its place as a sounding board rather than as the melody. I feel at home in the philosophy of mathematical education; I characterised *Mathematics as an Educational Task* as such. A philosophy of education and instruction, a systematic exposition of the general ideas – where can one find it? In the past, this, or something like this, might have existed; or were the more essential ideas even then more implicit than explicit? I do not know the contemporary literature well enough and even less the minds that shape it. A total view on education and instruction of all branches, ages, for each temperament and intelligence – is it not too high a demand? I do not demand it for myself nor for lawgivers and administrators of education, but for the benefit of the one who is in charge of it, the teacher. Does it suffice to tell him he is trained to be a cog-wheel in a big machine, called education, where he knows only his closest surroundings? Asking this question means answering in the negative.

Where are we heading? Our educational system used to be well defined. If mathematicians, for instance, discussed education, we meant in the first place, or exclusively, an elitist minority, which themselves looked forward to higher education as their next goal, at universities where mathematics was taught by an elite of professors, who were devoted to the highest mathematics. Was there more in the world beyond these elites? Was there a mathematics for the masses? Yes, it existed and was known from hearsay.

Did this change or is it going to change? Yes, because all is moving. I cannot see where we are heading. If I take a closer look at what happens in law-making concerning education, what is done in innovation, which problems are discussed, I notice an undercurrent opposite to that visible on the surface. Are we going to reinforce the elitist character of our elitist education, by refining it, by creating a hierarchy of elites; and if so, who conceals or who sells us the philosophy that should justify it? Is it right to ask this question and then to retire like a snail into the shell of a well-defined topic for a particular age level and a well-defined range of intelligence?

I view mathematics education, which occurs in the subtitle of the present book, differently; and I stress it right now in anticipation. I believe that in all didactical undertakings a specialism such as mathematics – moreover concretised in every respect – is a valuable and indispensable starting point, provided that at every step the postulate is recalled that education is one and indivisible, and that every piece – for instance of mathematics instruction – is worth only as much as can be integrated in the total picture of education.

CHAPTER III

ON A SCIENCE OF EDUCATION

ABSTRACT. Is there a science of education? There are marvellous techniques of education, there are excellent educational engineers, there is a more or less developed technology, there are serious publications on many topics, there is much philosophy of education and finally there is a tremendous amount of production that puts on scientific airs, but there is little that lives up to these pretensions. There is a terrifying lack of criticism. Instead the rules are fashion and ritual, which have to be rigorously observed, and are observed, by anybody who wants to be respected as an educational scientist.

For many years one of these grand fashions has been *educational objectives*. There is a tremendous theoretical literature on how to find out educational objectives, how to formulate them, how to classify them, how to test them and how to assign levels to educational objectives. They consist of abstract ideas contrived in the armchair by general educationists – using a tremendous amount of irrelevant theory, which has never been put into practice in any reasonable way. In fact, educational theories cannot be figured out behind a desk.

Another fashion is *curriculum theories*, which tell curriculum developers how to develop curricula, but the miserable people who in good faith embarked on curriculum development according to such theories, have been severely punished for their blind trust and lack of criticism.

Opinion polls is a popular device in educational technology. There is a lot of theory about how to statistically collect opinions on educational objectives, on subject matter, on teaching methods, on attitudes – opinions of the interviewed subject on his own attitudes or on those of other people – much theory and little common sense. Practice based on such theory is a poor showing, untrustworthy and irrelevant.

Evaluation is the most developed branch of educational technology, but as to theory it is an underdeveloped area, irrelevant or hypocritical. There are complete theories on formative evaluation and diagnostic tests, but efforts to fill out these patterns have been failures.

Theories developed by general educationists are *empty boxes*. Subject area specialists are admonished to provide contents for its wrong philosophy of separating form and content. Relevance of a theory can be provided by one single instance. Producers of empty boxes will excuse themselves for their incompetence as generalists with respect to any subject area. There is, however, one subject area in which they should be competent, that is, in teaching general educational theory. The attempts of general educationists, however, to design instruction in general education theory according to their own demands for formulating and testing educational objectives and for curriculum development, have resulted in collections of logical and educational blunders.

The production of empty boxes is the consequence of a philosophy that separates form from content. Many *rituals* in 'education' originated from a shallow behaviourism, from atomistic philosophies of knowledge, from interpreting knowledge as a disconnected set of concepts, from interpreting learning as the attainment of concepts. I call them wrong philosophies, because they are the expression of a picture of man and society that conflicts with my own. The products dominated by this philosophy have had a discouraging and frustrating influence on able educational engineering, which fortunately still exists.

Much harm has been done to the social sciences by uncritically adopting terms, ideas, and methods from natural science. Among the more recent cases the most striking is that of the terms '*model*' and '*mathematical model*', which are misused to cover either empty boxes or dogmatic theories. The most serious abuse, however, is *statistics*, as applied in educational technology. Mathematical statistics was invented as a device for organising criticism; it is taught to future educators as an uncritically used collection of mathematical recipes. People who seriously believe that blindly and carelessly collected statistical data can be improved by mathematical processing may be a minority, but mathematical statistics *is* widely adopted in educational technology as a means of creating or enhancing scientific respectability. For serious researchers this must be a frustrating ritual. Most of the applications of mathematics in education are irrelevant, and quite a few are wrong.

Education is a vast field and even that part which displays a scientific attitude is too vast to be watched by one pair of eyes. It is probable or even certain that jewels lie hidden under the mountains of irrelevant material. The harsh judgments of the present chapter are illustrated by a small choice of examples, which could be extended *ad lib*.

How could educational theory develop in such a way in the course of, say, half a century? There was, and still is, a need for relevant educational theory. People cannot live with mere technique and technology. Teacher trainers need something they can teach future teachers whether it be relevant or not. Half a century ago there was nothing they could use; now it is too much to make a reasonable choice between. Fashions and rituals are a heavy yoke. It is a bitter choice: submit to the yoke or perish.

Is there any hope left? Yes, if the awkward separation of form and content is abrogated. Teaching means teaching a specific subject, and any theory of teaching can only arise from a particular theory of teaching a particular subject. Moreover a theory of teaching should be the complement of a theory of learning. Learning is a *process* and should be observed and studied as a process. Observing a process is more than taking a few snapshots. Learning is an *individual process* but statistics can at most provide average learning processes.

Learning is essentially a discontinuous process. If a learning process is to be observed, the moments that count are its *discontinuities*, the jumps in the learning process. This I learned from observing mathematical learning processes. I put my thesis forward in *Mathematics as an Educational Task* and it will be illustrated by many examples in the next chapter.

1. DOES IT EXIST?

How many pages can be produced about the empty set? Well, books. A whole book was written to prove that the set of non-cyclic simple groups of odd order is empty. I will not go as far as to prove the non-existence of educational science. Yet up to now I avoided terms like educational science and here and there availed myself of circumscriptions, which in fact is no elegant procedure. I even hesitated for a while to put it into the title of the present chapter. From the first chapter onwards where I asked, and somehow tried to answer, the question what is science, the reader could have suspected that I aimed at the scientific status of educational research, but he could also have learned that by this I meant no harm. An engineer, who builds a bridge across a river, or a dentist who fixes one in the jaw of the patient, practices no science but a – scientifically based – technique and likewise I have classified much in the sector of humanities and society under technology rather than science, though some people will take it amiss that I assigned them to engineers. Repeatedly I characterised the work we do in our curriculum development institute as engineering. We build something and to do this we need to know a lot of things, and if time permitted we would like to know numerous things that we cannot use, or cannot use now, in the building process. There is, however, more than time alone that is lacking for proceeding in that way – later on I will discuss it.

There is an excellent literature on education – in particular on education in the narrow sense of pedagogy. (Of course there is rubbish too.) It is no disgrace to the author if a book is not only good but even a public bestseller. There are excellent books that tell parents how to educate their children, kindergarten teachers how to play with children, teachers how to teach, to educate, to develop creative gifts. It is not because it is popular reading that I do not call it science – there exists popular science indeed. It is technique with a bit of technology, not unlike Do It Yourself manuals.

There exist technological manuals for use in instruction and education – for instance, on the technique of evaluation, from the development to the use of tests, on educational media, on school buildings, on statistical methods of comparing gifts and attitudes, and each of them may serve many useful aims. There are excellent investigations – and worthless ones – about how to teach this or that, and whether it is teachable; and there is a sophisticated technique for designing such investigations.

And between these extremes there is so much, of which I know little and can appreciate even less. From mathematics as my starting point my view is limited anyhow. But as far as I can see, all I notice is technique and technology, or philosophy – good or bad – and I do not need even the yardsticks of relevance, consistency, and publicity I cut out in the first chapter, to decide that it does not allow me to dispense lavishly the predicate 'science'. Once more, this is no criticism; what I call technology is indispensable, necessary to life, and at present still more important than science.

Every era has known good pedagogues, excellent teachers and outstanding interpreters of educational ideas, and still, to my opinion, the state of pedagogy and didactics does not differ much from that of medicine a few centuries ago, with gifted and even genial doctors, whose rich experience and unfailing intuition made good for the lack of a scientific basis – and of course, with quacks. In spite of enormous efforts 'educational science' is still a pile of empirical knowledge useful in educational activity though lacking interior connections and lacking a theoretical and at the same time operational basis. I do not want to depreciate it: I only assert it is not the way science comes into being. Science requires leisure and renunciation of the topical techniques.

It is true: there is much in this field that behaves, and even more that is regarded, as if it were science. This is what my criticism should hit and where the criteria of the first chapter, implicitly or explicitly, should prove their force. I offer my apologies before I censure two or three specimen products while not even mentioning hundreds that would have deserved to be censured at least as radically, and while keeping silent about praiseworthy counterparts of what I have sharply criticised. I know only a small section of this field, and I cannot even tell to what degree it is representative; even if I did not do anything else other than studying this kind of work, I could not survey much more. I have engaged myself in studying what draws the attention of somebody who comes from a background of mathematics education, and in this perspective I am able to, and I will, evaluate it. A second restriction: My view attached itself to what is topical, what is echoed by every wall, and what everybody should have read. Certainly the hidden bloom of violets escaped my attention, which may be my most serious failure. A third restriction: my criticism is pragmatic, aimed at developments that jeopardise decent mathematical instruction, undermine its foundations, or make it impossible. It is a pity that too many mathematicians are frightened by the jargon used in this field so that they do not plunge into this matter; among the few who have dared it, there is certainly no one who is not deeply concerned about what he was confronted with.

2. IN FULL BLOOM

For a few years I, and everybody busy in education, have been so deeply buried and drowned by quotations from, and applications of, Bloom's *Taxonomy* that I did not feel blessed any more. When I decided to try to make my acquaintance with the book itself*, I found it was not so simple, because in all the libraries where I am a customer it was permanently out. Eventually I succeeded, but who can describe my surprise? I felt thunderstruck! Rather than the charlatanism I expected on the strength of quotations and applications, so-called, I found a serious, decent booklet, though of a quite different kind from what I had expected – in literature one always has to track down the sources.

The authors of the *Taxonomy* were examiners at U.S. colleges, and this determined its tendency: a general tool to coordinate the evaluation of examination results; not as in the Netherlands new examination norms each year, but a general pattern from which the needed norms could be derived in every particular case. It hardly needs to be mentioned that this club of examiners had considered that kind of instruction which was dispensed in the early fifties at American colleges, or more precisely, the instruction in literary and social subjects, which played the principal part. This is explicitly and implicitly quite clear. Terms and values used in the *Taxonomy* betray their origin in an instruction the nucleus of which is the mother tongue and civic education. Though the authors advance suggestions for more extended uses of this taxonomy beyond the evaluation of the special kind of examination from which it arose, they warn against such extensions, though not without playing down the warnings immediately in order not to cut off future developments. At any rate this taxonomy can only be understood with the background knowledge of a homogeneous instruction and strict instructional norms created by a strong *communis opinio*; whoever applies these patterns of norms is thoroughly acquainted with what students know, the kind of courses they attend, the instructional methods which are the general custom, but he is also indoctrinated with a sharply defined educational philosophy strongly depending on culture, time and country. Only with such a background are the valuations of the *Taxonomy* meaningful.

* B. S. Bloom *et al.*, *Taxonomy of Educational Objectives. The Classification of Educational Goals*. Handbook I: *Cognitive Domain*, New York 1956, many editions.

The most striking feature is the complete absence of fundamental cognitive objectives which are typical for natural sciences, technology and medicine. In the catalogue of objectives – which we will roughly reproduce after a few more pages – one looks in vain for such expressions as *observation*; higher level expressions such as *experimenting* and *designing experiments* are also lacking. The authors were entirely absorbed by a certain kind of instruction in humanities – they were not very likely to know anything else – which is instilled by books and other printed or duplicated material, perhaps also by audio-visual media. They did not notice at all what an enormous part – certainly in the teens and twenties – is played by intelligent observation and intelligent experiment in cognitive development, and how strong the component of educating intelligent observation and intelligent experiment is in school and university instruction of the natural sciences. This lack of comprehension, wherever observing and experimental sciences are concerned, is no news for anybody who practises a science, or even mathematics. Before the final publication the authors of the *Taxonomy* had issued a proof print and submitted a thousand copies of it to the educational world, in order to gather suggestions from the field with the intention of taking them into account. I cannot believe that nobody alerted them to this gap: though I can imagine how they would have reacted to such a suggestion: with a charitable smile one shelves the objection and answers the critic by saying that observing and experimenting are not cognitive, but, say, psychomotor objectives, which of course is a serious distortion of what observation and experiment really mean.

It would not, in fact, be farfetched to remark that even in some so-called humanities intelligent observation and intelligent experiment play a part, or at least, should do so. Would it not be meaningful in teacher training to have students observing learning processes and experimenting with them? But I am not very likely to be far off the mark if I suppose that this kind of instruction was not too well-known at American colleges in the fifties (and is probably still not); among the numerous examples of test items in the taxonomy no one has anything to do with the educational component of teacher training. There is one more factor to be indicated here: the educational philosophy prevailing in the United States, which claims to use the method of natural sciences, does not know, or rather, does not acknowledge, the concept of observation that is typical for natural sciences. Educationists are blocked by the idea that in natural sciences measuring prevails and they imitate this without noticing that in the natural sciences measuring is preceded by observing, that non-measuring observation is the bulk of the method of natural sciences and measuring is its finishing touch. Not only measuring but also experimenting fare badly if they are not preceded by phases of observation.

Of course the lack of observation, experimentation, and design of experiments in the classification of objectives of instruction is not felt as a deficiency unless the applications transgress the original bounds. The original target of the *Taxonomy* was to examine an extensive but nevertheless well-defined sector of instruction, such as was customary in the United States of the fifties: it should facilitate the grading of examination results. Applying this pattern of norms to curriculum development and the preparation of classroom teaching is a dangerous transgression. It reinforces the tendency to identify the objectives of instruction with examinations and to teach only what can be examined; if finally the contents of examinations are also determined by the pattern of norms, the vicious circle is firmly closed.

The *Taxonomy* recognises the following main levels:

1.00 Knowledge
2.00 Comprehension
3.00 Application
4.00 Analysis
5.00 Synthesis
6.00 Evaluation

By this order the students' achievements are weighed numerically according to whether they are judged to fall in one of these classes (of course it need not be a grade system 1, 2, 3, 4, 5, 6). These levels are refined: for instance, with Knowledge one distinguishes

1.10 Knowledge of specifics
1.20 Knowledge of ways and means
1.30 Knowledge of universals and abstractions in a field

which are differentiated in the second decimal digit. The differentiation of Comprehension* into

* In the applications of the *Taxonomy*, 'Comprehension' is sometimes replaced with 'Communication'. Clearly uneasiness was felt about the passive character of 'comprehension' and they looked for an expresssion which included the active aspect. If one reads the *Taxonomy* carefully one can only judge that this is a gross misunderstanding. Indeed, communication in an active sense can never be ascertained by choice tests, but only by active linguistic expressions, say, by essays, and is for this reason automatically classified as synthesis.

2.10 Translation
2.20 Interpretation
2.30 Extrapolation

is particularly important.

Notwithstanding lengthy descriptions in the *Taxonomy* the meaning of the terms is difficult to grasp. The easiest way is to view one well-defined piece of instruction with traditionally well-defined valuations and to reason not from the level of the description to the valuations, but conversely.

I once explained in a lecture what the levels of the *Taxonomy* are supposed to look like with an isolated fictional example. Take the expression 'an incarnate vegetarian':

1.00 *Knowledge*: knowing what 'incarnate' and 'vegetarian' mean;
2.00 *Comprehension*: grasping the pun (the stylistic figure);
3.00 *Application*: telling the pun at the right opportunity;
4.00 *Analysis*: being able to find out whereupon it rests;
5.00 *Synthesis*: inventing similar examples;
6.00 *Evaluation*: being able to compare the values of such examples. (Evaluation is in general a task of the teacher.)

It strikes immediately that once the pun has been indicated as such, *Comprehension* is devalued into *Knowledge*; once the pun has been explained, *Analysis* is devalued into *Knowledge*; if finally similar examples can be quoted from a book, even *Synthesis* is devalued into *Knowledge* – a typical phenomenon that will occupy us more profoundly.

I already indicated that such important aspects as *observation*, *experimentation*, design of experiments are lacking in the *Taxonomy*. It is most astonishing, however, that in the classification something is lacking and in no way to be placed, which could be called the

ability to pass tests,

that is, reacting adequately on them, a complex ability in which partial abilities can be distinguished such as

insight into test structures;
ability to disentangle test structures;
ability to weigh evidence;
insight into the psychology of test producers.

Has no-one ever indicated this serious lack to the authors of the *Taxonomy*, or has it never been noticed? The ability to react adequately to tests is – certainly in the American society – one of the socially most important abilities, notwithstanding taboos that inhibit pronouncing the fact and that even prevent its diffusion from the unconscious of those who should be able and obliged to know it, into their consciousness.

If the authors of the *Taxonomy* had their attention drawn to this gap, they would without doubt reply that test achievements are no objectives of instruction but means to evaluate their attainment. A malevolent answer to this would be that in the philosophy of the *Taxonomy* this means has long ago become the main end, and in this way the discussion could be continued with much quarrelling and without resolution.

It can, however, objectively be shown that the ability to react adequately to tests plays such an influential part in passing them that it must be appreciated as one of the most important factors and cannot possibly be skipped. As corroboration I quote the *Taxonomy*:

1.25 *Knowledge of methodology*

43. A scientist discovers new facts by
1. consulting the writings of Aristotle
2. thinking about the probabilities
3. making careful observations and conducting experiments
4. debating questions with friends
5. referring to the works of Darwin.

Of course this has nothing to do with methodology. The only thing the student can be expected to do is to consider whether the obvious answer might be a trap.

An entirely different example from 2.20 (*Interpretation* p. 113): A text the details of which do not matter, is followed by the instruction

After the item number on the answer sheet, blacken space

A– if the item is *true* and its *truth is supported* by information given in the paragraph.

B– if the item is *true*, but its *truth is not supported* by information given in the paragraph.

C– if the item is *false* and its *falsity is supported* by information given in the paragraph.

D– if the item is *false*, but its *falsity is not supported* by information given in the paragraph.

This is followed by items the contents of which do not matter either, because what is tested here first and foremost is the ability to read the instruction – a useful ability which in fact is difficult to place in any class of the *Taxonomy* and certainly not in the one that is intended here.

Anyone acquainted with the test literature – in America and abroad – will be able to adduce even more striking examples than these.* Although the authors of the *Taxonomy* have been astonishingly moderate, quite a number of examples for the various taxonomic classes partially or entirely test the ability to cope with tests, an ability about which as deep a silence is observed in this book as about the rope in the house of the hanged man.

I will return later on to the question what purpose the *Taxonomy* properly serves. Meanwhile I turn to the question how in theory and in practice objectives of instruction, exemplified by test items, are placed into the classification of the *Taxonomy*. I restrict myself to mathematics in order to be sure that my possible inability to allot places to certain items in the *Taxonomy* or to understand a proposed allotment is not due to a lack of competence, though I have checked taxonomic attempts in other fields and noticed the same deficiencies as I did in mathematics.

I pass over the mathematical examples of the *Taxonomy* itself, which by their smell remind me of dead stock of the arithmetic department in the college department store of 1900. Rather than this I chose the best I found and kept after an extensive exploration of the literature, a contribution of Th. Romberg and J. Kilpatrick to a School Mathematics Study Group publication**. Divided according to the grades K-3, 4-6, 7-8, 9, 10, 11-12 it contains test items from various mathematical domains, labelled with the *Taxonomy* classification, albeit without any indication by which criteria the placement was achieved. The contents are decent mathematics, and sometimes even the criteria of classification can be found out. A word problem in arithemetic, however simple or complicated it might be, is *Application*; but *Application*

* In an arithmetic test for our primary school which helps to determine the pupils' subsequent type of education, I found misleading cues in one third of the items. Pupils of that age are easily misled. As soon as an answer contains a misleading cue, it is chosen by about the same percentage as the correct answer, whereas in the absence of misleading cues the wrong choices are more uniformly spread. Immunity against traps is an enormously useful capacity, but should it be tested along with arithmetic?

** Th. A. Romberg and J. W. Wilson (eds.), *The Development of Tests*, N.L.S.M.A. Reports No. 7, 1969.

also includes substitution problems where, in a general formula or statement, parameters have to be replaced with special values. These are achievements between which there may be gulfs of mental activity and cognitive level. There is a tendency to subsume analytic geometry under *Analysis* and synthetic geometry under *Synthesis*. Discovering the law behind a number sequence is *Analysis*, and constructing a number sequence according to a given law is *Synthesis*, though the second will in general be easier than the first. An algebraic problem with equality signs only will not score higher than *Comprehension*, while a smilar one with inequality signs involved has a good chance of being classified as *Analysis*, obviously because at school level inequalities are less often taught than equalities and therefore should be higher valued. A word problem without computation that requires translating from everyday language into formulae gets the low predicate of *Translation* (which belongs to *Comprehension*), whereas in a numerical context it becomes *Application*.

Sometimes the *Taxonomy* structure seems to reel before your eyes: a pure skill by rote problem like

> $3x - 5y = 2 \qquad 6x - my = 0$
> For what value of m will the graphs of the above equations intersect at the origin?

gets the high classification 4.20 in Grades 11–12, obviously because it involves some misleading cue; whereas a similar, more extensive one for Grade 10 is as cheap as 2.20. A problem for Grade 9 such as

> If $2a + 2b + 5c = 9$ and if $c = 1$, then $a + b + c =$
> a) 2 b) 3 c) $4\frac{1}{2}$ d) 5 e) 8,

which requires only substitution, gets a formidable 4.10, whereas in the same grade

> If x and y are different numbers and $xz = yz$, then $z =$
> a) $\dfrac{1}{x-y}$ b) $x - y$ c) 0 d) 1 e) $\dfrac{x}{y}$

which is as trivial and as dependent on skill by rote but includes a trap, is not higher valued.

In Grade 10 the theorem of the bisectors in the triangle is valued 5.30, though if it has previously been dealt with in the classroom, it should count as *Knowledge*; if similar theorems have been dealt with (for instance about the perpendicular bisectors), it is at most *Application*; and only if the pupils have not studied anything like this previously would a high classification like 5.30 be justified. The greatest absurdity is certainly (Grades 11-12):

> Without actually making the calculations, write out in detail a step-by-step procedure for determining
> a) whether 12087 is a prime number;
> b) the largest prime less than 5000.

This is a problem that does not require anything but *Knowledge* of the notion of prime number but is classified as *Synthesis*, because writing essays as opposed to answering choice tests is considered as *Synthesis*.

It goes from bad to worse if one opens the Bible of the test believers*, a monument of about a thousand pages of excellently formulated commonplaces, sparingly streaked with thin layers of level raising references to educational research of at least doubtful relevance. The chapter on mathematics is a contribution by J. W. Wilson we met earlier on as an editor. It contains examples from the chapter quoted above of Romberg and Kilpatrick, along with others which come straight from the horror and lumber cabinets of old mathematics instruction. The stuff is jumbled up, with all indications of grade omitted. Page by page, along with problems which would not be too bad for Grade 5, there are problems for Grade 12 or college, and nobody cares about the fact that what for the one is *Analysis* or *Synthesis*, might be mere *Knowledge* for the other. Nobody would deny that skills and routines must also be tested, but this collection that claims to be an authoritative interpretation of Bloom's system is full of that kind of routine which is nothing but tricks – knacks that are learned by heart to solve singular problems without illustrating any general theory – puzzles that test inventivity *in terra incognita* and are entirely insignificant if the tested one knows the trick to solve them.

An example (112): Compare the areas of two drawn isosceles triangles, one of which has a base of 8 units and the two other sides 5 units; and the second has a base of 6 units and the two other sides 5 units – a problem that for no visible reason whatsoever is placed into *Application*; it is at least

* B. S. Bloom, J. Th. Hastings, G. F. Madaus, *Handbook on Formative and Summative Evaluation of Student Learning*, New York 1971, McGraw-Hill.

Synthesis if the candidate is not prepared for it; whereas it can also be solved with the mere *Knowledge* that in problems right angled triangles with integral data are most likely to be of the kind 3, 4, 5.

A gross example is 149: Prove that for every positive integer n,

$$\frac{n^5}{5} + \frac{n^3}{3} + \frac{7n}{15}$$

is an integer – a problem classified as *Analysis* on which skilled mathematicians can break a tooth though it can readily be solved by pupils of the lower highschool grades as soon as they know the trick.

Even grosser is Example 137:

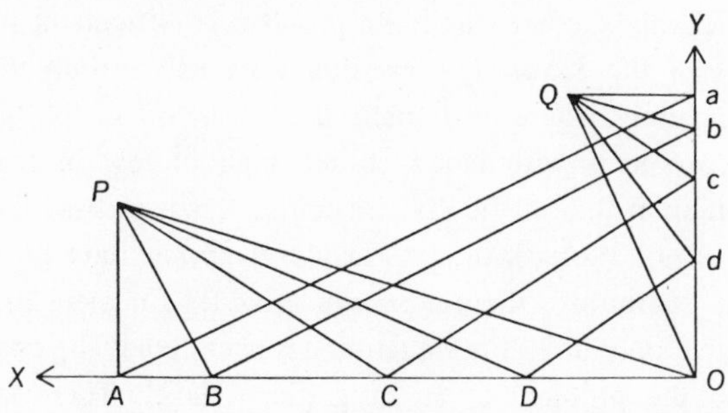

Example 137. In the figure above what is the shortest path from P to Q which touches both line XO and line OY? (a) $PAaQ$ (b) $PBbQ$ (c) $PCcQ$ (d) $PDdQ$ (e) POQ.

This is classified as *Analysis*. A pupil who can solve it without knowing the trick is not far from being a genius; if the trick is known, it is *Knowledge*.

The literature is full of this kind of example*. Romberg and Kilpatrick, in the cited contribution, admit that the classification of a test item depends on the previous knowledge of the tested one, only to forget this objection against the *Taxonomy* as fast as they advanced it. In Wilson's contribution I cited a few pages ago, this objection is not even mentioned; one behaves as though all classifications were absolute, and in a way this is the orthodox Bloom – indeed the educational system in which the *Taxonomy* was developed was so well-defined that this kind of objection could have been advanced only by malevolent fault-finders. It now depends on superficial criteria where something is placed in the *Taxonomy*, for instance under

*The record of taxonomic insanity I know of is P. W. Airasian's unpublished dissertation. Cf. Bibliography [94].

Synthesis if the answer to a question requires an essay. I cannot judge the mathematical understanding of the authors who pretend to fill the *Taxonomy* with mathematics, but I know for sure that they do not have the slightest insight into levels of mathematical understanding.

What can a teacher who prepares or evaluates a test do with the *Taxonomy*? As he knows the mathematical background of his pupils, he can localise his problems in the scale of difficulty in a more reliable way than a professional test producer, provided he ignores misleading guide lines and does not have his decision influenced by superficial criteria. He will soon notice that the terms of the *Taxonomy* are not operational, and on the basis of his experience he can more reliably predict whether a problem is difficult or not than if he takes account of the *Taxonomy*; eventually he will entirely trust his own experience, and only where he is obliged to show off in full bloom will he decorate the problems with labels chosen high or low in the *Taxonomy* according to their factual difficulty. Of course this is putting the cart before the horse: it is not the task of the *Taxonomy* to facilitate the valuation of problems; but conversely, the *Taxonomy* provides for mere trimmings that become effective only after the valuation has been fixed: the positional value is attached to the problem as an insignificant label. There is hardly any other way to do it, and indeed in all applications of the *Taxonomy* I saw – also outside mathematics – it was the way they did it.

Is there any other use for the *Taxonomy*? I pass over the proposals in the introduction of the *Taxonomy* where without any explanation or argumentation it is put that it would be nice to apply the *Taxonomy* to this or that. I read those pages carefully with the result that there are no more than two applications of the *Taxonomy* left that are worth serious consideration: first, by determining the places in the *Taxonomy*, the teacher can prevent choices of exercise and test problems from being too one-sided by one layer of the *Taxonomy* (for instance all *Knowledge* and no *Comprehension*); second, by using the *Taxonomy*, teachers can more easily communicate with themselves and others about what is mere knowledge and what is comprehension, and how high they should be valued in any particular case. Distinguishing knowledge and comprehension would indeed be a precious thing if it were to succeed, but it is more important in a form in which it is not at all considered by the *Taxonomy*: the teacher is properly not interested in knowing that the pupil has understood (long division, quadratic equations and so on); he should instead be concerned that the pupil has *now* managed to understand it – 'now', that is, in a certain phase of his learning process, which up to that moment has gone more or less smoothly. For instance: a child that figures out $8 + 7$ by counting 7 further from 8 on the abacus, acts on an as it were senso-motoric level. The discovery that $8 + 7$ is simplified by $8 + (2 + 5) = (8 + 2) + 5$ witnesses a high *comprehension level*. Once this is grasped, it becomes mere *knowledge of method*; as soon as the child has memorised $8 + 7 = 15$, it is *knowledge of facts*. At the same moment figuring out $38 + 47$ may still require *comprehension*; later on *knowledge of method* can suffice; for the skilled calculator it is mere *knowledge of facts*. Obviously the original *comprehension* need not be lost in the course of time; by well designed questions it can be tested whether it still exists, if it had ever been acquired, but these are questions of another kind from those by which it is checked whether a learner has understood it *now*.

These are plain facts, which certainly the taxonomists have been told a thousand times, but what did they answer? I know the kind of reaction. One admits the facts with no hesitation, only to continue on the same footing after a short, but hardly profound, reflection, rather than mending one's ways. It is the common and natural reaction if fundamental dogmas are jeopardised.

In the introduction to the *Taxonomy* Bloom *cum suis* asserts that in school practice expressions like 'comprehension' are 'nebulous' since everybody understands them in a different way, as shown by examples; the *Taxonomy*, he says, covers them with a bright light. I do not wish to decide whether Bloom is right in other domains; as far as mathematics is concerned, he is completely mistaken, as is convincingly proved by the host of unsuccessful attempts at taxonomising in mathematics. What the *Taxonomy* tries, is a cruel simplification, a Procrustean bed, the flashlight that blots out all nuances. The teacher who states that one pupil understands long division whereas another merely faultlessly applies the trick, does not indulge in nebulous dreams; he has good reasons to state it and he knows how to test it. Bloom *cum suis* is troubled by the phenomenon of mastering long division once classified as mere *Knowledge*, and in another case as *Comprehension*. He considers this as nebulous, which it is not. These are well-defined and clearly distinguishable usages. Whether something is *Knowledge* or *Comprehension* does not depend on its mathematical content but on its place in a learning process, or at least on its instructional context.

In the first sentence of the introduction, Bloom *et al.* refer to biological taxonomies. This comparison is lame on both feet. First, the biological taxonomies have a well-defined aim, namely to *determine* a plant or an animal by means of ever more refined ramifications; the *Taxonomy*, however, presents a comparatively rough classification according to levels of educational objectives and no practical method of subsumption under these classes. Second, the biological taxonomies deliver exactly what they promise, namely a classification of plants and animals whereas the *Taxonomy* promises a classification of educational objectives and produces a classification of subject matter according to alleged levels.

It is a fact that everywhere people tell you that notwithstanding theoretical deficiencies that can by no means be denied, the *Taxonomy* functions quite satisfactorily in practice. Teachers assure you they can work comfortably with the *Taxonomy* and that they have applied it successfully in curriculum development and the preparation of lessons – that is, general educationists who have been propagating the *Taxonomy* in the educational field tell you that teachers say so. I would not wish to deny such successes. Certainly there are practicians among pedagogues and didacticians who for the first time in their career were motivated by the *Taxonomy* to reflect about their own activity in teaching and that of others, and experienced this sensation as a decisive progress. This phenomenon is well-known and certainly not restricted to the *Taxonomy*; even the most absurd teaching appliances and methods can incite teachers who are confronted with them to reflect about didactical problems and by this even mark the awakening of didactical consciousness. In this way a system like the *Taxonomy* causes what is called in medicine a placebo effect.

This alone can certainly not explain the tremendous 'success' of the *Taxonomy*. The success of abstract educational theories, the worthlessness of which is patent, is a problem of educational sociology which will be touched upon later.

3. ATOMISATION

I do not remember by which strange accident I got the book that is now on my desk, a systematic catalogue of mathematical concepts of American school mathematics, no less than 2500: if the gaps I noticed are symptomatic, it should have been many more. An even more impressive catalogue of German extraction counts more than 1000 objectives of mathematical instruction for Grades 5–10, though if they had better learned their lessons, they would have subdivided systematically their sometimes quite complex objectives and produced five times that number. As a matter of fact I would adjudicate the prize to an American curriculum of objectives, sub-objectives, and derived objectives, where it is even specified how many objectives and sub-objectives are sufficient for mastery.

This atomism is the most fashionable wisdom of instruction theory – offspring of a shallow behaviourism. Behaviourism, too, has long ago left the stage where it studied *behaviour*. 'Behaviour' has been enriched with a plural 'behaviours', which means knacks and tricks, because this is the only thing you can come to grips with; petty behaviours which can exactly be described and measured, rather than the global attitude that is obviously 'nebulous'. At present behaviourism is globally identical with the most extreme atomism. All must be divided in diminutive pieces, partitioned, atomised; subject matter must be ground to powder and administered by spoonfuls. It is a demand of the test industry; operational objectives are needed to produce tests. Instruction has to accept the yoke of this philosophy.

Administering 2500 concepts, each day one, is equivalent to 200 a year, 2400 in Grades 1–12. This is a nice balance. Or isn't it so simple? The sentences of the test problems usually involve two or three concepts combined, which means that all concepts should also be trained by pairs and triplets. No, this would be an unimaginable number of combinations. Fortunately not all of them are effective; 'disjoint set' may occur combined with 'parallel lines' but not with 'square root'. Not all combinations need to be tested (and consequently to be trained).

I copy a specimen of the products of the atomistic philosophy. I trust no professional mathematics is required to appreciate this product at its face value.*

* Th. A. Romberg, Jean Steitz, Dorothy A. Frayer, Working Paper 5. Th. A. Romberg, Jean Steitz, Working Paper 56. *Report from the Project on a Structure of Concept Attainment Abilities*, Wisconsin Research and Development Center for Cognitive Learning, The University of Wisconsin.

AREA: SETS

DISJOINT SETS

1. Which of the following has members?

   A. the club for all people over 150 years old
   B. an empty field
   C. a football team

2. Your baseball team has:

   A. members
   B. denominators
   C. fractions

6. Which of the following is true for *all* disjoint sets?

   A. They are equal sets.
   B. The sets contain five members.
   C. They have no common members.

7. Which of the following is true of some but *NOT* all disjoint sets?

   A. They have no members in common.
   B. They are made up of at least two sets.
   C. They have the same number of members.

10. Disjoint is a kind of:

    A. set
    B. subtraction
    C. place holder
    D. operation
    E. factor

12. What is true about disjoint sets and parallel lines*

    A. Parallel lines have points in common, so they make up disjoint sets.
    B. Parallel lines can be made by two disjoint sets of points.
    C. Both disjoint sets and parallel lines can intersect.

* I do not know what pupils are expected to answer.

EQUIVALENT SETS

6. What is true for *all* equivalent sets?

A. They are sets about animals.
B. They have 3 members in each set.
C. They have the same number of members.

12. What is true about equivalent sets and subtraction?

A. When two numbers are subtracted, the answer is called an equivalent set.
B. If the members from two equivalent sets are subtracted, the answer is 0.
C. If the number of members from two equivalent sets are subtracted [sic], the answer is 0.

PARALLEL LINES

12. What is true about parallel lines and an [sic] empty set?

A. The empty set is made when one parallel line is longer than the other.
B. The group of points where two parallel lines meet make up an [sic] empty set.
C. The empty set tells about parallel lines that are curved.

PLANE

3. Which of the following is an example of a plane?

A. the corner of the room
B. where the floor meets the wall
C. a basketball
D. the blackboard

7. Which of the following is true for some but *NOT* all planes?

A. They are round.
B. They are flat.
C. They are made up of points.
D. They are made up of lines.

PLACE HOLDER

2. Fill in the blank. The 3 in 98,345 is in the hundredths place. One hundred is then called the __________ of the number 3.

A. distance
B. set
C. decimal
D. place value

5. $2 \times 3 < \square$ This has:

A. a statement
B. division
C. a place holder

6. Which of the following is *always* true for a place holder?

A. It holds a place for a number
B. It is an *X*.
C. It is a $\square$

8. A symbol which holds a place for a number is called:

A. a point
B. a division
C. a fraction
D. a place holder

Who is laughing? Well, a few years ago I still was, and many a mathematician would not be able to understand why nowadays it makes me angry. The mind behind this master work is neither a practical joker nor a crank but a prominent educationist, one of the leaders in American education technique, and this product is not due to a whim or a derailment but it is the conscious result of a philosophy of mathematical instruction which is served by a highly developed technique, and for this reason it is extremely dangerous. The author of this work has an image of mathematics in his mind which every mathematician will detest from the depth of his heart – and an image of education, which I am sorry to say will please many educationists all over the world. The protests of outstanding American mathematicians who are concerned about instruction were not listened to; curriculum research and development and production of textbook literature in mathematics for the American school is virtually monopolised by travellers on the irresistible band-waggon that squashed instruction reform.

Indeed, atomisation of subject matter is not merely a behaviouristic concern. It is the line of least resistance in technologicising instruction. Pedagogues and general didacticians judge mathematics to be their most appropriate victim. Indeed in mathematics you can isolate and enumerate all concepts in order to have them trained systematically one by one, in pairs, in triples and so on, as far as you want to go. It is a caricature of mathematics which is quite common. Therefore no subject is as exposed to ruin by atomism as is mathematics. It is too obvious that by atomistic instruction you cannot teach creativity in speaking and writing; the former atomistic instruction of foreign languages is superseded by language laboratories; natural science education is protected against atomisation as it were by nature itself. But mathematics seems to invite atomisation, and so mathematics is hard to defend. Isolating, enumerating, exactly describing concepts and relations, growing them like cultures *in vitro*, and inoculating them by teaching – it is water to the mill of all people indoctrinated by atomism.

An outstanding counter example to this radical atomism is the British integrating interpretation of educational innovation as is beautifully embodied by the well-known Nuffield project, which was directed by excellent mathematicians who at the same time were excellent didacticians – I do not know whether any general educationist participated in it. Other counter examples are the Hungarian innovation of T. Varga's *Munkelapok*, Emma Castelnuovo's work for the Scuola media, and in the last few years efforts such as made by our Dutch IOWO. It would, however, be an unwarranted bias to judge American innovation of mathematical instruction by the products of atomistic indoctrination, but these aberrations are its most efficiently advertised aspect and the one that determines the image of American education abroad – the 'American model'. A different picture of American education emerges if one visits good schools, casts glances into periodicals and books for teachers on instruction and education, participates at meetings and workshops of teachers. The creativity of the practicians of American education, pedagogues and didacticians convincingly belies the sterile atomism of its theoreticians. But all over the world practicians feel uneasy if a theoretician is around who might take them to task. Is it really so serious? No, if the general educationist casts a disapproving look, the clever ones among the practicians hasten to recite the behaviouristic creed although at present the Piagetian faith as subterfuge is becoming a legal denomination.

What is it in general instructional technique that procures this power? As far as mathematics is concerned I already answered the question: it is a wrong picture of mathematics that invites atomisation. As mathematicians we are bound to oppose it. We must stress that isolated concepts and formal structures are bloodless, and that both in mathematics and its instruction only a rich context is meaningful. Unfortunately this context is too often lacking in what is today offered as modern mathematics; too often attempts are made to teach pupils mini-languages that will long ago have been forgotten by the time educationally significant contents present themselves to be expressed in these languages. The blame laid at the door of those mathematicians who showed instructional technologists the road to denaturalising mathematics, or at least those mathematicians who failed to warn against this process, is not undeserved. Anyhow, it is a philosophy that any atomistic philosopher can identify with his own and it is a most comfortable philosophy. The instructional technologists did not need to be shown twice. What these mathematicians unsuspectingly presented to them, they imitated at a much lower level, while eliminating all mathematics from mathematics instruction.

4. THE ATTAINMENT OF CONCEPTS

The conception of 'concept' on the formal level espoused in many publications today of psychology and pedagogical psychology is one that has prevailed in philosophy for millenia. In fact it is Aristotle's conception of *genus proximum* and *differentia specifica* – the next higher genus in a hierarchy and the distinguishing characteristics. It has never been operational in science or prescientific cognition except – to a certain degree – in systematic biology, from which it was actually derived*. From the end of the 19th century onwards methodologists became aware of the inadequacy of this conception. Today it has become obsolete in methodology.

According to this conception of 'concept', knowledge is an explanatory dictionary – a kind of *Webster* – filled with such nonsense-definitions as

brother: a male human being considered in his relation to another person having the same parents;
ratio: the quotient of one quantity divided by another;

* It is true that in a certain measure it has influenced teaching, for instance the teaching of foreign languages according to a classification of words and phrases.

random number: a number whose likelihood of occurrence is equal for all numbers of the set of numbers to which it belongs (Remark: defined in singular);
unit: that after which anything is called one (Euclid).

The wrong idea behind this conception of concept is that concepts arise from *classification by means of attributes* and admit of *explicit definitions* within a – uniquely determined – hierarchy. However, as far as concepts arise by classification, it is most often not classification by means of attributes, but *by means of relations and structures*. As to the way concepts are defined, it has become clear from the beginning of the 20th century onwards that concepts do not form hierarchies and that the bulk of definitions in science and prescientific knowledge are *implicit*, that is, concepts are defined *operationally* within a system of experience and *contextually* within a written description of this experience. It can be shown by many examples from the sciences that neither an explicit definition nor a name are needed for the attainment of a concept.

I have never comprehensively studied the literature on the attainment of concepts. In a pedagogical content I became acquainted with one of its outstanding manifestations and it is just this one that aroused my criticism. It is one example and I do not know to which degree it is a paradigm*.

According to this theory concepts are attained on *four* levels: *concrete* (recognising a poodle presented from the same angle), *identity* (recognising the same poodle if presented from a different angle), *classificatory* (dealing with poodles as a genus 'poodle'), *formal* (defining the genus poodle). The mental objects constituted on the first three levels have never traditionally been called concepts, only ideas or representations. The activity on the fourth level would be irrelevant for anyone other than authors of *Webster*-like dictionaries. The examples of concepts (red ball, poodle, equilateral triangle, island, tree) preferred by the author of this theory show that he did not consider higher level concepts such as

cardinal number 5	length
cardinal number	area
ordinal number	volume

* H. J. Klausmeier *et al.*, *First Cross-Sectional Study of Attainment of the Concepts Equilateral Triangle and Cutting Tool*, Technical Report No. 288, The University of Wisconsin 1974; and Working Paper 119, ibid. See also H. J. Klausmeier *et al.*, *Conceptual Learning and Development*, New York 1974.

addition (in arithmetic)	weight
congruence (in geometry)	motion
equality (in mathematics)	change
yesterday	health
time	society
place	

all of them concepts which are only operationally constituted and contextually described, and which are all acquired at a concrete level, though not on what the author means by 'concrete level'. None of the author's four levels apply to these concepts, and none of them are relevant to any of these concepts.

Of course everybody is entitled to use a word such as 'concept' as he likes. But if he uses the word 'concept' as the author did, he is not entitled to state that "concepts comprise much of the knowledge basis of cognitive structure", and to quote "an article of faith that concepts are fundamental agents of intellectual work".

The author quoted undertook to test his hypothesis that the attainment of concepts occurs according to his four levels, and also some other hypotheses. As an example, he chose the concept Equilateral Triangle. It is quite normal in educational research to find that test producers do not understand the preconceived theories of the theoretician, or that there is no way to apply them in the concrete case to be studied. I think it was the second alternative that happened here. It is hard to imagine how any useful knowledge can be extracted from such an unproblematic concept as 'Equilateral Triangle' in a cross-sectional developmental study of the ages 5 to 16, even with many correlations and regressions added. The present test instrument proves it was indeed impossible. The test instrument has little if anything to do with the author's four levels, nothing to do with attaining the concept of equilateral triangle, in whatever sense, and nothing to do with the attainment of whatever concepts you want, or with learning mathematics.

It is well known that children as early as age 2 can identify such geometric figures as equilateral triangles in any position in which they are presented, that not much later they can identify the shape, and that they call such objects by names though perhaps not the conventional ones. In such situations the only thing the test producer can do is to focus on the features he is well acquainted with though they are inessential to the present research: that is, to formulate the items in an unusually involved fashion or in language that only occurs in tests, formulating vaguely when precise formulations could make the work too easy, withholding essential information, adding a bulk of material unrelated to the inquiry. What is then tested is the ability of children to understand more or less involved linguistic structures (which in the present case are only required to contain the term 'equilateral triangle'), to guess in any particular case what the test producer could have meant, or which information he could have been withholding, and in general, the ability to answer tests. These indeed are abilities that improve with maturation. So if those difficulties are built into the tests corresponding to the four levels, it can easily be proved that concept attainment develops accordingly.

Test Battery IA presents on every item one equilateral triangle in horizontal position and of varying colour and size, and beyond it a collection of 4 to 10 triangles and rectangles in various positions and of various colours, sizes, and shapes. For items 1–8 the (oral) assignment is

Mark the drawing that looks exactly the same

(as the model) and from item 9 to 16 it is invariably

Mark the drawing that looks the same.

The subject is expected to interpret "exactly the same" as "having the same colour*, being congruent, and having parallel bases"; "the same" is to be interpreted as "having the same colour and being congruent". Of course the subjects are not told this interpretation, because then everybody could do it and the test would not discriminate any more. The subjects are not even warned to pay attention to the change of formulation though a teacher who has read these tests more than once to children is very likely to unconsciously emphasize the transition, which then makes answering easier.

In Battery IB items 1–3 test whether the subject knows the term 'shape' and – passively – the term 'equilateral triangle' for a certain shape.

Item 4 shows triangles among which there are three equilateral ones (always with a horizontal basis). The question runs:

Are all of the three-sided figures above equilateral triangles?

a. Yes, all of them are equilateral triangles.
b. No, some of them are not equilateral triangles.
c. No, none of them are equilateral triangles.
d. I don't know.

* I cannot fathom why "colour" has been included here.

After the first three tests have made sure whether the subject knows a certain shape and the corresponding term, new complications must be invented. This happened according to certain linguistic patterns. Imagine a test of the following kind:

A picture of six horses among which there are three white ones is shown.

Are all of the equine quadrupeds above white horses?

a. Yes, all of them are white horses.
b. No, some of them are not white horses.
c. No, none of them are white horses.
d. I don't know.

Item 4 tests as much about equilateral triangles as it does about white horses or flying saucers. It tests linguistic abilities and formal reasoning.

Item 5 shows the same six triangles among which there are three equilateral ones. The question now reads:

Are all of the equilateral triangles above triangles?

a. No, only some of them are triangles.
b. No, none of them are triangles.
c. Yes, all of them are triangles.
d. I don't know.

Formulated in equine vocabulary it would be again:

A picture of six horses among which there are three white ones.

Are all the white horses above horses?

a. No, only some of them are horses.
b. No, none of them are horses.
c. Yes, all of them are horses.
d. I don't know.

Item 6 shows three equilateral and three right (that is always 'upright') triangles. The question is:

If you took all of the equilateral and the right triangles above and put them in a group there would be . . . there were three-sided figures*

* Here the test producer forgot to add 'above'.

a. fewer than
b. more of them than
c. the same amount of them as
d. I don't know.

The subject is not told what right triangles are. They are the only other kind of triangle that occurs in the picture, all of them upright, of the same shape and homothetic, though of different size. So the subject is expected to conclude that this is what the test producer means by "right triangle". The equine analogue is:

A picture of three white horses and three thoroughbreds is shown.

If you took all of the white horses and the thoroughbreds above together and put them in a group there would be . . . there were equine quadrupeds.

a. fewer of them than
b. more of them than
c. the same amount of them as
d. I don't know.

So it continues up to item 11 with questions like

Are all of these triangles polygons?
Are all of these polygons triangles?

and so on.

Items 12a, b, c are another kind, which is also a popular feature in the test production:

Below are four drawings. Put an X on the one that is different from the other three.

Of course the subject is not told in what respect different. In 12a one sees four figures with 3, 1, 4, 0 right angles respectively; three of the figures are open, and one is closed – there are more criteria possible. Of course most of them are traps. There is a unique figure that can be completed to get an equilateral triangle, and that is what is meant since the general subject of the battery is the equilateral triangle. In 12b three of the figures have two or more equal sides, and one has not; three of them are well-connected whereas one of them, the fourth, consists of two parts attached to each other in one point only. Again these are traps; there is a unique figure that contains an equilateral triangle, and that is what is meant. 12c looks obvious: three solids and a square. Or does he mean one round shape among no-rounds? These are traps. There is one that contains an equilateral triangle.*

Nothing in IB is even vaguely related to the four levels of concept attainment. Yet so it continues. IC and ID contain tests on some elementary geometry of the triangle, most of them artificially tailored to fit the subject 'equilateral triangle', but little if anything that is related to the four levels. The hypothesis that development proceeds according to them, cannot possibly be proven with this material. With the method used here one could as well prove that the concepts

Flying birds
Flying planes
Flying saucers

are attained in this order provided this hypothesis is tested by the questions:

If 3 birds are flying from North and 2 birds from South, how many are they together?
If 67 planes are flying from North and 24 from South, how many are they together?
If 793 saucers are flying from North and 118 from South, how many are they together?

Non-mathematicians, in particular education theorists, are inclined to consider mathematics as a catalogue of concepts. This is an entirely wrong view even if their conception of 'concept' is richer and more adequate to mathematics than the present one. Learning mathematics is viewed by them as the attainment of concepts, which is a wrong view, and if this view is allowed to influence teaching, it can ruin mathematics teaching. Mathematics is the most favored victim of such efforts. Much harm has already been done. Among the author's documents there are two 'illustrative' lessons on the equilateral triangle to prove my statement.

* Afterwards I saw that I flunked all three tests. The cues I interpreted as traps, were meant as the real cues.

5. OBJECTIVES OF INSTRUCTION

5.1. *How to Find Them*

After the *Taxonomy*, the atomism and the attainment of concepts I continue with specimens of what behaves as educational science. The *Taxonomy* was a crude classification of instructional objectives; atomism looks into the finest ramifications. In between the coarse and the fine structure there is a whole spectrum of opportunities from which I will also take examples.

Of all the themes in the theory of instruction that of instructional objectives is the most variegated. It is not to be wondered at that the question of the objectives of instruction has been put into the limelight. Education is a social phenomenon that must be justified in its social context. An architect who builds a structure fulfills exactly described objectives. Whoever indulges in pure research pursues aims which as a rule are only attained to a modest extent; but this then is *pure* research. As far as fulfilment of objectives is concerned, education flourishes in between these extremities; its efficiency is not negligible but also far from 100%. Education knows objectives but they are difficult to enumerate. If I board a train, the objective may be St. Moritz, or skiing or recreation or health – all can be correct together, at ever higher levels and with more vague contours. Objectives of instruction? The examination? Certain knowledge and abilities? Progress in life? Again objectives on different levels, in the general conviction *non scholae sed vitae discimus*.

Objectives of lessons in driving and programming can be sharply formulated, but this experience is of no help when looking at the objectives of mathematics instruction. One can try vague formulations which allow any content, and sharp ones that cut off the point.

These are well-worn arguments, which help us no further. On the other hand the quest for objectives of instruction is legitimate. The instructional objectives are to justify the tests. Innovators are rightly asked 'why?' and 'to what purpose?' But if instructional objectives are so important, why do people do so little about them? I mean about the true objectives that really matter, which means neither the sharp ones that cut off the point nor the vague ones that do not cut at all.

The other day I read a paper, by an educationist, in which all objections against 'instructional objectives' were carefully analysed and convincingly refuted. It gave me supreme intellectual and aesthetic enjoyment to read the paper. There was only one objection he had overlooked, a small one – simply overlooked. Or rather one question he had not caught – certainly this question had been asked him a hundred times in the past but selective deafness had allowed him not to hear it: How can we find instructional objectives and formulate them?

Of course a formal answer would be quite easy. A jungle of literature has grown up about it – papers, books, handbooks, where how it is done is explained in every detail. Sure, there are various models of how to do it, but they hardly diverge in principle. One takes programmes, textbooks, problem collections, exam problems from the subject matter area, cuts them into strips, and extracts the strips – if they come from the detailed tables of contents of textbooks one can use the strips directly. This is arranged according to areas and subarranged according to subareas. Then to each strip a starting formula is attached such as 'knowing that . . .' or 'knowing why . . .' or 'being able to . . .', or 'understanding, that . . .' or 'understanding why . . .'. Indeed, it becomes objectives to speak behavioural lingo. The style can still be improved by replacing 'being able to apply the formula $(a+b)(a-b)=a^2-b^2$' by 'showing by one's behaviour that one can apply the formula $(a+b)(a-b)=a^2-b^2$.' This is Behaviourese quite as it should be, and it is the safe way, because nobody cares about what this particular behaviour consists of. Properly speaking, the educationist is not obliged to do this work himself; he can hire labourers to do it; they will find the detailed prescriptions of what should be done if they consult the chapter on 'instructional objectives' of their educationist bible.

The next stage is the opinion poll. One draws up a list of respondents, pedagogues, industrialists, politicians, journalists, plumbers, parents and so on and submits the provisional list of objectives to the respondents who are asked to say 'yes' or 'no' to every particular item. In their atomistic isolation the questions cannot possibly be answered, and they cannot even be interpreted (at least as far as mathematics is concerned). A 'yes' or 'no' to one question influences the others, as one interpretation does with the remainder. It is as though one would show a group of people a novel or the introduction to a railways timetable for them to approve or reject sentence by sentence. The questionnaires are filled out at random by 10% of the respondents; on the last page there is some space left for general remarks, and people who cannot contain their flow of ideas are entitled to add an extra page; if even this is not enough, the educationist comes with the tape recorder to interview them. It is a great pleasure to have hundreds of people thinking for you free of charge, though it is a pity that those people do think in a disorderly, unscientific way – I mean, globally rather than atomistically. So you have to cut it all again into strips, which is a hard thing, but some day it comes to an end. Meanwhile the list of instructional objectives has become five times as long; they overlap and cross each other. It can no longer be systematized, the only way out is to arrange the objectives alphabetically or to number them – of course not without placing every item into the *Taxonomy* according to one's own imagination.

The educational Bible does not tell one what to do with the result. In mathematics and natural sciences, as far as I know research in these fields, one would say: throw it away. In educational research it is not much different though they know a penultimate phase before throwing away, that is, publishing. If a year later he reads the printer's proofs, one finds the educationist muttering, as meanwhile he has stretched out another area of instruction upon the dissection table, and he has almost forgotten about the old one.

Or has it dawned on him that something might be wrong with the method? Did nobody tell him, neither on the questionnaires, nor in the interviews? It sounds incredible.

5.2. *In a Green Tree*

What was wrong? One cannot analyse the objectives without being competent in the subject matter to be taught. No problem for the skilled educationist, whether it is instructional objectives or some other theme of educational research: he has got the money to hire competent folk, labourers by the day or hour, with the task of processing the material for him. The level of these serfs should not be too impressive; if their critical gifts were too well educated, their master could not play them as pawns. Or can he really? Does he have the leisure to supervise, and the competence to judge what they perform? Does he eventually become aware of the base alloy of what they coin?

But wouldn't it be an idea to have competent people find out on their own the objectives of the instruction in the area of their competence? Of course, not *ex tempore*. Applicants should first eat their way through the literature on instructional objectives. Take it for granted that they do not get through. Their appetite will soon be gone, to say the least.

It might be a good idea, but it does not work. Yet there is still one way left if objectives of instruction should be developed according to the principles of educational technology: the teaching matter of which the objectives are to be isolated should be the theory of education itself. The educationist should find out the instructional objectives of the instruction of his own branch of study. All research he publishes is to a certain extent doctrine – that is teaching – there are textbooks on educational theory, and educational theory is taught at universities and colleges. Is it too high a demand to ask that once in his life the educationist should drink himself of the potion he mixes for others? *Exempla trahunt*, the proverb says; examples convince.

Has no-one ever hit upon this idea? Or does the educationist fear slippery ground? Well, there have been courageous people among them who dared it. Perhaps it was a rare exception, perhaps the only one that exists, but at any rate it was an attempt of educationists to show with their own teaching matter how to formulate educational objectives. And it was not just an incidental attempt but an authoritative work* – the collective production of a group of prominent Dutch educationists, a course of didactics in three well-designed volumes, the first of which starts with general objectives and introduces every chapter by a list of the objectives of that particular chapter. A few years ago I analysed the first volume; I will extract a few paragraphs from that part of the analysis which deals with the instructional objectives, while abstaining from dealing with more detail of this – unanimously welcomed – work.

Chapter 2 starts as follows:

If you have studied this chapter you should have attained the following objectives:

1. Being able to describe which three aspects can be distinguished in didactic action;
2. Being able to tell which two meanings of theory are in use;
3. Being able to enumerate and handle the didactic key questions;

* L. van Gelder *et al.*, *Didactische Analyse* I, Groningen 1971. – Meanwhile I came across more textbooks on educational theory which exhibit their instructional objectives. They show the same features as I found in the present case. One of them teaches how to formulate instructional objectives: it is clear that this must be a particularly dangerous case, with a big chance of vicious circles.

4. Being able to draw the model of Didactic Analysis;
5. Being able to tell what introduction, instruction and assimilation of a lesson most often consist of;
6. Being able to distinguish the phases introduction, instruction, and assimilation in observed lessons. [My translation.]

In order to make sure whether I had already mastered the 'Didactic Analysis' before reading it, I tried to answer the questions. The first is of course perfectly simple. The three aspects of didactic action are the acting one, the act, and the one acted on. – Two meanings of 'theory' – the authors certainly meant it within quotation marks. But why two? I could easily turn them out by the dozen. And if I chose the wrong ones? – The key questions – I do not know, but it reminds me of the *Chrie* of my father's school days, the compulsory essay model of the seven queries 'quís, quid, ubí, quibus áuxiliís, cur, quómodo, quándo' (who, what, where, by what means, why, how, when). – Being able to draw the model of Didactic Analysis – is Didactic Analysis to be a drawing lesson? – The 'most often' in question 5 suggests the counter question: where do you find such statistical material?

I have flunked the test. I should first study the chapter. I did so, and behold, on the next page I found the answer to what was demanded as objective number one. My own solution was wrong though it was not my fault. The authors meant phases rather than aspects of didactic action; and the phases are, they say, preparation, execution, and evaluation of a lesson. Indeed, the didactic action is neatly partitioned into separate lessons.

After having attained the first objective of Chapter 2, I continued reading. An arithmetic lesson followed, the table of seven, which surpassed all terror I have ever dreamt of, but I could not discover the slightest relation with the explicit objectives of Chapter 2. Gallantly I continued reading, to no avail. Hi! A whole paragraph about 'prescientific and scientific theory'. (Does this division belong to prescientific or scientific theory?) A red underlining, and I reached objective number 2.

I continue. Behold, the key questions. Seven, indeed. Not too bad. I take off my hat to the man who contrived and so excellently formulated them. Moreover it follows so logically you could not add any eighth question. I can now enumerate them, but I should also be able to handle them. How? Should I use that arithmetic lesson to do it? But the seven key questions have as much to do with the table of seven as the seven dwarfs behind the seven mountains. I am now running forwards and backwards through the chapter, but there is nothing about handling the key questions.

A glance at the table of contents casts me from one surprise to another. The seven key questions are dealt with in Chapters 4–10, in each of them one, and there I can learn to handle them. How can they demand it as early as in Chapter 2? It is clear it is a mistaken formulation. Obviously here it suffices to enumerate them. It is how my eldest son learned 'years' in history: 'To-morrow our teacher will relate what happened that year.'

Objective 4 brings new trouble. There is nothing about a drawing lesson but even the expression 'model of didactical analysis' does not occur. I see, however, that the seven key questions are united in a gorgeous diagram. This cannot but be the model of didactic analysis. Arrows in many colours cross it like rockets: obviously drawing the model of didactical analysis means that I draw all of them. May I do it with other colours? – Objective 5: A lesson consists of three phases, introduction, instruction, and assimilation, and it is explained what is meant by this. 'In the introduction most often the discovery of a difficulty is central' – this is what the words 'most often' refer to (and not to instruction and assimilation), but when the statement was turned into a question, it was automatically included in Objective 5. They also explain what 'instruction' and 'assimilation' mean, and by the time I have underlined it I have reached Objective 5. Obviously I am neither obliged nor entitled to explain whether I agree with this kind of lesson organisation. Neither does it matter whether other people might understand decent instruction in a different way. Objective 5 of Chapter 2 simply means that I can echo the authors' opinion.

I do not wish to expose you to more of this. My word of honour, it continues thus from first to last page. Purely verbal enumerations which shall be underlined and memorised – these are the instructional objectives. Being able to tell the three most important aspects of *this*, the two categories of *that*, the two most important criteria of *this*, the two methods of getting *that* to happen, knowing three of *this*, at least six criteria of *that*, being able to enumerate five steps of *this*, three requirements for *that*, three factors of *this*, five forms of *that*, three conditions for *this*, at least four functions of the blackboard, two aims of grading, two characteristics of tests. Classifications only: and if by accident more is demanded, it is a slip of the pen.

The formulation of the instructional objectives is logically defective. The authors require the student to know *the* relation between this and that, to be able to indicate *the* three most important aspects of this, at least five steps of that, and so on. But they cannot possibly mean *the* relation between this or that, which does not exist; they mean the relation that is mentioned in this book. They cannot possibly mean that the student knows *the* three most important aspects of something according to the student's criteria of importance, but according to their own authority: without claiming even a shade of personal conviction the student is expected to declare as the three most important aspects of something that which he can and shall only verbally enumerate. They do not mean that the student should choose five steps, but that he should repeat the very five the authors indicated, without raising the slightest question as to whether it could be more steps. And that is also the way in which I have sometimes seen subject matter like this being examined. Question: 'What is a learner?' Answer: 'Somebody involved in a learning process.' Next question.

All the instructional objectives of this book require is that a few little pieces of its subject matter can be recited by heart. Altogether this amounts to about 10 pages of the 170 kingsize pages of the book, and the remainder is garnish. All objectives are formulated in terms of the book itself and none extends a hair's breadth beyond. *Non scholae sed vitae discimus*.

What has happened here? In former times textbooks contained repetition questions at the end of every chapter. For instance in geography: 'Give the names of at least three towns in Groningen where there are strawboard factories'. These questions now inevitably move to the beginning of the chapter disguised as instructional objectives: Being able to give the names of at least three towns in Groningen where there are strawboard factories. A primary school teacher who likes to mimic this, can fill the 'model of didactic analysis' as follows:

> Initial conditions: arithmetic book, bottom of p. 62;
> Instructional objective: up to top of p. 68;
> Instructional situation: dealing with pp. 62–68.

If I would have interpreted my present book as instruction and adorned it with objectives of instruction in the style of the *Didactic Analysis*, I should have preceded the section 'In full Bloom' by items like the following:

1. Knowing by what the author was thunderstruck;
2. Being able to guess the origin of the *Taxonomy* and its valuations;
3. Knowing at least three levels lacking in the *Taxonomy*;
4. Knowing which phase has to precede measuring;
5. Knowing which vicious circle is closed.

In behavioural language it should rather be:

1. Showing by one's behaviour that one knows by what the author was thunderstruck.

If the reader objects that in all of these questions the explanation 'according to the author' is lacking, he is right. I did it intentionally; it is an imitation of both the style here used to describe educational objectives and the dogmatic diction of textbooks in social sciences, in particular those of teaching theory.

Disguising such an extract as instructional objectives is dishonest. In the examination the student is expected to know the remainder too. It would have been more honest if on the first page one had put a notice like:

Instructional objective: knowing the contents of this book, on the understanding that students who take it as a minor subject can restrict themselves to Chapters 1–7 and the first half of Chapter 8.

I admit that I owe something to this kind of book offering explicit objectives. I see more clearly which requirements objectives should meet. It characterises these books that the objectives are formulated in terms of the book itself and are even defined by literal extracts: not summaries but diminutive extracts – if one should believe these extracts, the remainder would be mere decoration. I think the instructional objectives of a textbook should be formulated independently of the context of the textbook; a person who is acquainted with the subject matter and instruction in question, though not with this particular textbook, should be able to read and to understand the text of the objectives.

Perhaps this rule is too stringent. I can imagine textbooks that offer a wealth of subject matter rather than verbalisms, extracts, and personal views, and in this case formulating the objectives in the terms of the book itself would be justified. But I do not believe there are many textbooks like this in teaching theory.

5.3. *In the Dry Tree*

If educationists are wholly unable to satisfy their own postulate of explicitness of objectives – if they do these things in a green tree, what shall be done in the dry? What, then, can you expect from a group of mathematics teachers? The following is a sample from a catalogue of about 1000 objectives of instruction*. If you cannot help laughing, take the extenuating circumstances into account, and feel pity for those mathematics teachers and didacticians who have a reputation to lose and who under the command of educationists and sociologists are drilled in mental knee-bending.

1.5. ORDERING OF OBJECTS – 'LESS THAN' RELATION IN N

(1) **Being able to order the elements of an appropriately given set by means of an order relation.**
Use of strict or strictly linear order relations

†(2) Being able to distinguish between the 'ordering' and 'sorting' of elements of a set.

(3) Knowing the chain as a special case of an order.
Chain means here a strictly linear order.

†(4) Being able to recognise and indicate orders in the world around.

††(5) Being able to indicate order criteria for an appropriately given set.

(6) **Being able to say whether for a given ordered number pair the relation 'less than' holds.**
Possibility of the use of relation tables and arrow diagrams.

(7) **Being able to use the '<' and '>' signs.**

(8) Recognising that ordering the natural numbers by the 'less than' relation leads to a chain that does not end.

(9) **Knowing that the set N is not finite.**

(10) **Knowing that natural numbers can be used to number the elements of a chain and that by numbering the elements a finite set can be ordered into a chain.**

(11) **Knowing that to every natural number a point of the half line can be assigned.**
Introduction of the half number line.

22.1 BINARY OPERATIONS

(1) **Knowing that a binary operation in a set M is an assignment by which to every element of $M \times M$ exactly one element of M is assigned.**

* Der Hessische Kultusminister, *Rahmenrichtlinien*, *Sekundarstufe* I (Klassen 5 bis 10).

(2) Knowing that the carrier set M together with the binary operation rule $\square$ is called the operation structure $(M, \square)$.

(3) Being able to indicate a structure that is an operation structure, and one that is not an operation structure.

(4) **Given a binary operation in M, being able to draw up the corresponding operation table.**

(5) Given an appropriate set M, being able to find several assignment rules such that it yields, or does not yield, a binary operation.

(6) Given an appropriate assignment rule, being able to find several sets M such that in M a binary operation arises or does not arise.

(7) Recognising that the property of binary operation is a property of the structure $(M, \square)$ rather than of the set M and the assignment rule $\square$ separately.

(8) **Given a structure $(M, \square)$ being able to decide whether it is a binary operation structure.** [My translation.]

This is again a splendid example of what instructional objectives are not – a table of contents of a course or of a group of a few courses where the definitions, propositions, and titles of paragraphs have been decorated with 'knowing' and 'being able' lead-ins. The authors say it more overtly:

The mathematical teaching subjects were selected by means of an analysis of the existing literature using the experience of the members of the group.

Nobody thought of analysing mathematics and mathematical education themselves. The result was nothing to do with instructional objectives: it is a new textbook, provisionally restricted to a table of contents. Any relation between the mathematics and reality is lacking, as is any social motivation of mathematics or any understanding of levels in instructional objectives. It is full of logical, mathematical, and didactical absurdities, and carries a built-in didactics with it. In the arithmetic of fractions, for instance, it is not this subject as such but the subject according to a controversial, and to my view wrong, didactics that is prescribed as an objective. Besides learning fractions the pupils are obliged to learn riding the authors' built-in hobby-horses. It seems that in Hesse teachers are terrorised today with this 'objectives' monster. Do not object that they get absolution if they pay lip service to the system. It *is* terror.

5.4. *The Distribution of Chestnuts*

I cannot but analyse another example from educational literature – it is particularly illuminating. Sometimes educationists condescend to spice abstract theory with a concrete example. In 40 columns of a paper by a leading educational psychologist I discovered half a column where he specified his generalities. The fragment reads as follows:*

> On the basis of the objective 'being able to calculate' the following subobjective was formulated:
>
> The pupil shall be able to solve simple meaningful problems related to the quantitative aspects of the world of his experiences.
>
> From this objective the following concrete subobjective was derived:
>
> The pupil shall be able to work with the concept of ratio (of numbers and quantities). He shall see ratios between numbers as equal multiples of different numbers.
>
> *Operational objective*: The numbers of chestnuts of John, Peter, Bill are as 4 is to 5 is to 6. Together they have 75 chestnuts. How many chestnuts does each of them have? [My translation.]

It is quite interesting to look more closely at this fragment. The general subobjective is vague enough not to meet opposition. The adjective 'simple' is particularly useful for simplifying formulations of objectives, but with 'meaningful' and 'world of experience' controversy is sown; the chestnuts example, however, shows that this is also a simple thing to the author: if all arithmetic books are admitted to the world of the child's experience, all their problems become meaningful, chestnut distributions included.

Being able to work with the *concept* of ratio is subject matter typical of old and venerable didactics, such as has long ceased to be required; it is indeed the level of the didactician rather than the pupil, who should be able to work with ratios rather than with the concept of ratio.

The subobjective in which this is postulated is not, as the author claims, derived from the preceding objective – how could it be possible? But such claims are mere stale phrases in educational theory.

Now the subobjective itself. It is formulated in two sentences, and between these sentences a connection is suggested by means of the word 'ratio', which however has a different meaning at both places; in the first sentence it is premathematically to be understood, in the second it is fully mathematical**. The first part is acceptable though vague; as to the second I am not sure; I am inclined to reject this kind of mathematisation.

* H. P. Stroomberg, 'Onderwijsdoelstellingen en doelstellingen-onderzoek', *Pedagogische Studiën* **50** (1973), 497–517.

** This is not clear from the translation. The double meaning of *verhouding* is properly rendered in the first place by 'proportion', and in the second by 'ratio'.

The test under 'operational objective' is obviously related to the second part of the subobjective. If this is intended, it is totally wrong. The test problem can be solved by naive insight with no mathematisation of the ratio concept, such as primitive people would do: giving John, Peter, and Bill each at a time 4, 5 and 6 chestnuts, respectively, until the stock is exhausted. There is no remainder, and it is quickly done. In order to test what was intended, one should take larger numbers or have a division with remainder.

This sole example in an entirely abstract paper on education is wrong in all details but I did not fish it out as an unfortunate exception in a sea of good things. Its deficiencies are paradigmatic for a whole literature. In particular it is paradigmatic for the doctrine that objectives of instruction can be found by cutting the existing textbook literature into strips. Formulating objectives should be preceded by profoundly scrutinising analysis of the subject matter. There is no cheaper way; an educationist who does not know enough mathematics is better advised to keep off objectives of mathematical learning.

For the analysis that – at least in mathematics – has to precede the formulation of objectives, and which would be fundamental to other parts of educational research and technology in mathematics too, I chose the name didactical phenomenology: but the name does not matter; nor is that activity an invention of mine; more or less consciously it has been practised by didacticians of mathematics for a long time. In various earlier books and papers I have given examples of the didactic phenomenology of mathematics, and I hope to deal with it comprehensively in another book.

I have quoted the example of ratio as an objective of instruction from the literature because in the next chapter I will contrast it with a sketch of what didactical-phenomenological analysis might achieve for the formulation of instructional objectives. It should, however, be stressed that this analysis is only a necessary but not a sufficient precondition for the eventual formulation of objectives of mathematical instruction. I do not know whether the ideas I will specify there can be transferred to other domains, but I think in some way an end should be put to the frightening superficiality in the search for instructional objectives.

5.5. *Searching One's Own Conscience*

I fight the *fashion of*, not the search for, educational objectives. I could not insist upon the fact that no-one ever succeeded in producing a reasonable list of operational objectives of mathematical learning, and claim it to be impossible. But this would be too rash a conclusion. Before the first man flew, many pioneers tried and broke their necks. It cannot be proved that it is impossible. What remains for us is trying and trying again, and throwing away the trash – anyway this is the habit in the exact sciences. Nevertheless I will communicate an unsuccessful attempt. I take it from the 'football pool' theme of IOWO's project 'Coincidences' a piece of probability instruction in the 5th grade.* (IOWO is the Dutch Institute for the Development of Mathematical Education.)

2.1. Recognizing and inventing choice situations of k events ($k = 2, 3, 4, \ldots$)
2.2. Simulating such choice situations.
2.3. Symbolizing them (e.g. with numbers $0, 1, \ldots, k-1$).
2.4. Recognizing and inventing sequential runs of choice situations of k events.
2.5. Simulating such runs with random devices and numbers.
2.6. Symbolising them (with number sequences and tree diagrams).
2.7. Probability formulations according to the pattern 'it happens in . . . out of . . . cases'.
2.8. Probability calculations based on counting events.
2.9. Simulating choice situations without equiprobability of choices.
2.10. Simulating runs under the same condition.
2.11. Designing, carrying out, processing and describing a theoretical-empirical investigation on probabilities within the frame of the foregoing. [My translation.]

There is a striking difference between these objectives of learning and the ones I criticized. Though the objectives are formulated *a posteriori* on the basis of a rich and elaborate theme, the subject matter has thoroughly been analysed in the sense of didactic phenomenology; there is nothing left of the original subject matter; as far as possible levels in the learning process have been indicated.

I considered it progress then, but meanwhile we have learned that this, too, is wrong. Objectives of learning should not be formulated behind a desk, but in the didactic dialogue of the educational situation, with pupils, teachers, advisors, parents and other people concerned.

I explain this in more detail. We elaborate a rich piece of teaching matter, a 'beacon', a theme, a project, a piece that looks valuable to us, closely related to reality, which motivates the children and is socially relevant. We try

* *Euclides* **47** (1972), 265–272.

it in the classroom, and armed with a conscious or subconscious didactic phenomenology we observe the reactions of pupils, teachers and so on, and from these reactions we derive what pupils can learn and teachers can teach with the material – what they lacked before and possessed afterwards, abilities they acquired in the instruction. What results is underlined and formulated as instructional objectives – unless it is cancelled as irrelevant. Wherever the list of objectives suggests additions, we will try to build them into the revision only to proceed in a similar way with the revised teaching matter.

A delicate plant, as it is, this strategy has grown out of practice. It happened with a theme for the bridge class of our lower vocational instruction (7th grade of total school career). To somebody who had scrutinised it, it looked quite nice but he could not discover any objective of mathematical instruction in it. After the try-out in the classroom scores of them could be derived from the reactions of the pupils – objectives nobody would ever have dreamt of or included in any list of objectives whatsoever.

It was a detective story, in which the detectives had to find out the whereabouts at 7 o'clock of an inmate of the Groningen prison who had escaped at 6 o'clock and fled in a stolen car driving at 150 km an hour. The pupils had great trouble bringing together the three numerical data of the text in order to attack that partial problem – learning to do such things would be a reasonable objective. Eventually they succeeded: but then they hunted for the runaway at a distance of exactly 150 km from Groningen, as travel problems in arithmetic books are habitually of the type 'a train travels from A to B in 3 hours with an average velocity of 75 km an hour'. Well, the latter idea is certainly found in every list of objectives of mathematical instruction, but one will look there to no avail for the knowledge that a car with a maximum speed of 150 km an hour averages less than this; though mathematically it is at least as important.

The try-out of the story produced a lot of such examples. I only mention the last of them: at the end some pupils criticized the logic of the story. This is a high level objective: criticizing the subject matter.

These are positive sounds. I could not say so with regard to didactical phenomenology, but I am sure that the field strategy of finding out learning objectives can also be valid for domains other than mathematics.

6. OPINION POLLS

When I discussed 'Objectives of Instruction – How to Find Them' I mentioned opinion polls as a popular means of validating catalogues of objectives – an undertaking as foolish as voting sentence by sentence about the acceptability of a novel or the introduction of a railroad time-table.

Opinion polls can be valuable instruments of state and market policy. Years of practice and experience have allowed experts to develop a methodical system that, as it seems, can stand reasonable tests. People learned from their own mistakes and those of others; they are well prepared to avoid them when feasible. Once a marketing specialist regaled me with the most amusing stories from his vast treasure of polling experiences – up to the trick of asking a housewife polled about a particular detergent to produce a package of the brand she claimed to use. In so-called educational research it will be difficult, if not impossible, to learn from mistakes, as long as signalising mistakes is not the fashion.

There are many kinds of questionnaires: some that clearly do not admit any reasonable answers; a few others that evoke the impression that at least their authors honestly believed respondents could reasonable answer them; and finally a large number of questionnaires that look reasonable (yet which are not necessarily relevant). How large is the probability that they are answered in a reasonable way, and how can you check the trustworthiness of the answers? Lack of inconsistency is one criterion. Another criterion would be to mix questions about facts with those about opinion – reliability on facts might be an indicator for reliability on opinion.

I have always been sceptical about opinion polls in the area of education but a more recent experience has knocked the bottom out of my last vestige of belief in polls. It was when I came across a piece of research – the thesis of an outstanding man in the education field – on the use of teachers' manuals relating to textbooks for the seventh grade – twelve manuals, four of which belonged to mathematics textbooks. A large sample of teachers had answered (maximally) 88 questions of a questionnaire, among which there were questions, of course, such as whether there existed a teacher manual for the textbook they used, whether they used this manual, and how often and in which way. The concept of teacher manual was precisely defined and the warning was added:

The concept of teacher manual does not comprise booklets containing tests and/or answers to problems.

This is a stringent condition even though it might not have been intended as such by the author.

It appeared that among the mathematicians only a quarter availed themselves of the teachers' manuals; but this sample then answered in detail all the questions of the questionnaire on the use of the manual. Only a quarter used the manuals, the author exclaimed. Actually, the miracle was not that there were so few, but that there were so many. Indeed, none of the four textbooks could boast of a teachers' manual in the sense defined by the author; and for two of them there did not exist a manual in any reasonable, weaker sense.

Let us call the four textbooks A, B, C, D. Although the only reference book relating to Textbook A was a pure list of answers to problems, one quarter of the respondents claimed more and satisfied the author's curiosity about every detail of their use of the teachers' manual. Textbook B appeared not to be about mathematics at all, but traditional arithmetic, and two thirds of its pseudo teachers' manual consisted of answers to problems. As for Textbook C, an obsolete edition had been provided with a true teachers' manual, which in no way fitted the entirely revised current edition, but nevertheless a quarter of the respondents succeeded in filling in the questionnaire; a pseudo teachers' manual did exist for Textbook D, 80% of which consisted of tests and answers to problems.

At least the investigator should have known, with respect to Textbook B, that it did not deal with mathematics and that its teachers' manual did not satisfy the definition, since he himself was one of the authors of that textbook, though he is modest enough not to mention this fact; he could have ascertained in a minute that none of the others satisfied the definition if he had cast a look at them. It is improbable that he ever did. *Minima non curat praetor*. As he himself explained, collecting and processing the whole material was the business of subordinate people. I would not be astonished if he had not even written more than the profound theoretical introduction and had never read or corrected the statistical evidence, and if the present lines were his first opportunity to learn that Textbook B and its teachers' manual, of which he was a co-author, played a part among the statistical data.

How is it possible that secondary school teachers, who are not illiterate people, show such poor qualities as respondents? A few may have disregarded the definition of 'teachers' manual', others may have thought it might not be meant so strictly. Did the majority answer the question of the *existence* of a teachers' manual relating to their textbook in the negative, or did they admit its existence and deny *using* it? And the minority – who answered all the questions about teachers' manuals – did they do so because owing to the non-existence of the manuals they related the questions to the textbooks rather than to the non-existing manuals? Nobody knows what actually happened. One thing we can take for granted is that that opinion poll was extremely untrustworthy. It is the first case I have looked into closely, but it was an easy case. What about other opinion polls in the area of education? My scepticism does not diminish.

7. DIAGNOSIS

General educational theory aspires to the legitimacy of exactness by the use of expressions borrowed from natural sciences. We already met 'taxonomy', taken from biology. Investigations in which pupils take part as subjects, are adorned with the adjective 'clinical'. The white overall of the medical man suits a researcher well; maybe its pocket hides a stethoscope. A quite popular term is diagnosis – *diagnostic* tests are being developed and applied. Of course, everybody who teaches, is bound to diagnose. The new thing about methods such as Mastery Learning where teaching and diagnosing follow each other in systematic turns, is blindfolded diagnosis. Not looking at what pupils are doing, not posing questions to discover what they have not understood, but having squares on prefabricated test-papers blackened by them, and counting who failed, say, more than 20% of the tests, that is what they call diagnosing; while prescribing means that the feeble ones are administered a thinner dilution of the teaching matter they did not master.

Properly speaking it is even more sophisticated. It is not only the diagnosing teacher who gets blindfolded. It is the so-called double-blind method. The eyes of the designer of the diagnostic tests are also bandaged by means of educational theory. It is compulsory that he understands nothing of the didactical intentions of the course or textbook for which he designs a battery of diagnostic tests; he is bound indeed to investigate whether certain 'objective' instructional aims are attained – such as solving quadratic equations – rather than whether the learning processes intended by the author of the course took place.

I won't dispute that computers may be useful in medical diagnosis. But they do not supersede the physician who can distinguish German measles from scarlet fever with his naked eye, who can feel an inguinal rupture with his fingers, and who only needs to listen to his patient in order to know whether he is touched in the lower parts of his belly or in his upper story. Moreover I guess that medical diagnostic computer programmes are not written by blindfolded doctors.

I just analysed a copious collection of diagnostic tests designed for a mathematics course – tests for each chapter, each subsection. So somehow one ought to be able to tell what every particular test is expected to diagnose. But if anything one can only establish that such a test is diagnosing a quite different thing from what the test designer meant it to. The difference between solving an equation and verifying a solution, between constructing (say the graph of a function) and checking a proposed construction, between proving and searching for errors in a proof, has not yet dawned on the test designer's horizon defined by Bloom's *Taxonomy*. No test in the chapter on quadratic equations examines solving such equations; on function graphs there is no test that diagnoses whether the pupil can draw them. In order to satisfy the test designer's passion for fourfold choice tests, the pupil is obliged to entangle logical schemes which are not in the slightest way related to the subject matter, for instance after the order relation in **Z** has been taught:

A. For all $a, b \in \mathbf{Z}$: $a < b$.
B. For all $a, b \in \mathbf{Z}$: $a > b$.

1. Both A and B are true,
2. A is true, and B is false,
3. A is false and B is true,
4. Both A and B are false.

Yes-or-no queries are only for conditional sale. Rather than two questions, whether p is true, and whether q is true, one asks:

1. both p and q true,
2. p true, and q false,
3. p false, and q true,
4. both p and q false.

Even if the legitimacy of the multiple choice principle is granted for summative tests as a means to assure somehow the evaluative equivalence of the single tests, it can neither be understood nor justified in the case of diagnostic tests, nor can any argument at all be adduced in favour of the so-called objective test procedure. The coupling trick reminds me of a story of long ago: A Scottish peasant has heard that in the town they can recognise from one's urine whether he is ill and what ails him. So he goes to the dispensary with a big bottle of urine and stays there to wait for the diagnosis. Afterwards he writes home: I, you, all of our children and the cow are healthy.

I have just leafed through what is best characterised as the rape of a mathematics course by Mastery Learning: to each chapter are allotted learning objectives and corresponding tests. The course itself was constructed with great didactical diligence. For instance the arithmetic of positive and negative numbers was introduced by considering the functions $x \to x + a$, $x \to x - a$, and these functions were represented and grasped in three different ways, by means of nomograms, by inductively generated function tables, and as translations by means of translation arrows. None of this is mentioned as an objective nor accounted for in the tests. They do not diagnose whether the learning process intended by the author took place, whether one of the proposed representations has been applied, correctly or incorrectly, nor whether numerical problems have been interpreted by the functional pattern. On the contrary, it is suggested to the teachers and pupils that they skip all this stuff and try their teaching and learning strength with solid arithmetical problems. This then is diagnostics; and so it should be, according to Mastery Learning. It is a behaviouristic axiom that learning processes cannot be tested, and so even the learning processes elaborated by the author in a thought experiment are expunged. This happens with the cooperation of teachers who would very likely teach excellently without Mastery Learning. Out of reverence for his mystic words they let themselves be blindfolded by the general educationist; they let themselves and their pupils be educated to thoughtlessness. But who is blamed if this system fails? Mastery Learning or the course which was raped by Mastery Learning? Well, let us then design right from the start a mathematics course just for Mastery Learning, where each learning process is reduced to the memorising of rules!

8. PRODUCTION OF THE PACKAGE

I continue with the parade of what dresses itself as educational science. Products such as are exhibited under the title of Atomisation need not be fathered by the educationists themselves; it is possible, and in the case under review even probable, that the man who signed it and undertook responsibility for it, never saw it. It is the normal procedure: the educational technologist lays down the general direction and hires competent folk from subject matter areas to carry out the plans. The level of this labour force cannot be high – I repeat this – or else their critical judgement would be too well developed, and one could not play the game with them. The educational technologist on the other hand lacks the leisure, and certainly, the experience and competence to judge the level of the production. Indeed his task is defined and described independently of the instructional contents. The fundamental idea is, explicitly or implicitly, that in instruction and its technology, form and content can be separated from each other. All kinds of instruction have something in common, they think, which can be differentiated according to ages; and this allows educational technologists to specialize in kindergarten, primary school, secondary school, college: specialization according to competence, however, would be a minor concern.

I would not like to oppose this thesis if only some nuances were added, but I oppose the consequences which are wrongly drawn from it. The common factor in different branches of instruction is too superficially understood. It is as though somebody were to claim that with a book the essential things are its size and whether it is paperback or hard cover, whereas the content is a minor concern. This is correct – I mean in the practice of the library attendant who in fact need not consider that the books serve purposes other than to be moved in and out of the stacks.

All comparisons are imperfect and so is the present one – complicated things are simplified. All branches of instruction have much in common. The application of the knowledge of individual or social psychology is not likely to differ greatly from one subject to another, and certainly not if it is good instruction. Educational philosophy is likely to bridge the trenches between the areas of competence, at least if it is valid. The technique of class and school organization is widely independent of subject matter. The use of media is transferable from one area to another. But there is no reason to consider the differences of subject matter as inessential or negligible in developing curricula, teaching matter, tests, innovation, preparation of lessons.

To this the educational technologists will answer: we do not wish to develop curricula or tests, we do not wish to innovate, to design teaching matter and lessons, yet it *is* our task to prepare schemes, to be applied by competent people. We deliver the boxes for things to be packed in. It is our task to see that the boxes look attractive and can be comfortably piled up; and whoever uses the boxes must take care that the contents are tailored to fit. We even add indications as to the composition of the contents, which the packer must pay attention to, such as 30% *Knowledge*, 20% *Comprehension*, 20% *Application*, 15% *Analysis*, 10% *Synthesis*, and 5% *Evaluation*. For the tests, too, we deliver appropriate packing material.

Projects for research, curriculum development, innovation are conceived of in this philosophy as follows: A group of general educationists, the só-called nucleus, armed with the project bible design a grand plan with impressive flow diagrams in Indian ink on drawing paper, with boxes and arrows – dotted ones and connected ones – with in every corner an advisory group which together contains all the people who afterwards could criticise the undertaking or its results. If this work of art has served well enough to attract the subsidies needed, the next stage is a study year, and this is indeed indispensable as the literature is bulky and the educationist is *tabula rasa* by definition. Then follows a year of investigation of objectives with hired labourers such as I depicted earlier. Since the objectives are not worth a dime anyhow, a year to investigate initial conditions is included where mercenaries from the educational field and measuring specialists play their parts. Meanwhile the 'nucleus' has lost sight of the peripheral activities, which take place far away in the field. Curriculum construction which was planned to take half a year is left to competent people who need one more year even if they come ready. If they succeed, the educationists of the 'nucleus', as far as they are still interested in it, can take the package into the school, of course not to test it or to guide testing it, but to hire people who would do it for them. Evaluators, too, are hired; and after evaluation the material goes into revision, again by hired people. So it crawls along for years, withers away and eventually dies; and if a subsidy can be obtained it gets a sepulchral monument in three volumes, or else is buried in silence side by side with its precursors, or with the poor. But most often the 'nucleus' has exploded midway and torn itself and the project into pieces. Our educationists have meanwhile flocked together in other groups to start one or more new projects, those excepted who have acquired a chair to educate new generations of educationists.

Yet all they did was done in faithful obedience to the project bible. One detail, however, was not revealed in that bible: that you need millions, or scores of millions, and armies of skilled labourers to carry out such a project – the project bible was published in America where both the millions and the skilled people might be available. I am not sure whether even there the results can ever justify such expense. But one thing is certain, with a tenth or a hundredth of the required money available, no meaningful result is likely to be obtained. A project that requires the full engagement of a large and closeknit team cannot be carried on by working groups, meeting once a fortnight and labourers paid by days and hours. The packing of the project forged by the educationists is a Goliath uniform for a David, which as things go on is gradually reduced until eventually David gets trousers from Goliath's two gloved fingers.

In a recent paper an educationist asked the burning question why the general schemes of educational theory – I called them packages – are so lavishly produced and so rarely applied. He could not find an answer that satisfied him. Well, a specialised industry of packing material does not pay unless there are mass products to be packed. Curriculum and subject matter development, however, are rare events; there is not the slightest reason why you should not design for every such project a scheme that fits just this particular project, so there is no need for specialisation and specialists in designing such schemes. But even where the mass demand is available, proposing such general schemes (for instance for the preparation of lessons and the construction of tests) has no merit unless the proposer can make sure that, and show how, these schemes can be filled with meaningful contents. It is arrogance or fraudulent deception of the consumer to fabricate packing material and to demand that the buyer adapts the contents to the boxes. It should be the other way round, starting with the contents and looking for containers that fit them. This holds for curriculum and course development as well as for schemes of instruction procedures, preparation of lessons, construction of tests. It is simply not true that they can be determined independently of teaching matter and method.

Beyond the mistake about dimension the philosophy behind this kind of project is mistaken. It is again the atomism, which here expresses itself as specialisation. Of course specialisation is unavoidable, but it should never be undertaken in such a way that form and contents are separated. Curriculum and course development, innovation and research, ask for quick reactions;

therefore many tasks and abilities should be united in one person or a closely knit team, as I stressed earlier on. Organisation, design, guidance, evaluation must be in one pair of hands during the first approach, if reactions from those in the field are to be answered readily and quickly. The participation of people in the field – teachers, pupils and parents – is only effective if it reaches the final target unhindered. Pure educationists unacquainted with any subject matter area (or who have lost that acquaintance) are not welcome in such a team. Educationists should include in their own education acquiring some competence in at least one branch of teaching. In the long run society cannot afford projects the rationale of which is relief work for educational technologists.

Is this picture of a general educational technology too harshly painted? Yes, it is. Reality is not as simple. There are a lot of general educationists who are concerned with contents, who look into schools even if they are reluctantly received there by competent people and practicians. There are also educational technologists who design and publish dazzling plans with flow diagrams and arrows, and if hard pushed, try with or without help to fill such an empty box, let us say with the design of an arithmetic lesson that is so stupid that a teacher training student would flunk for it. There are among educational technologists artists who sense the design of abstract schemes as an aesthetic experience and who are struck with amazement if one dares suggest the schemes should be filled out. It is not the custom to put it down to theoreticians as a crime that their theories are not practicable: on the contrary it is considered a virtue. All great theoreticians have been ineffective in practice, haven't they? The separation of theory and practice is one of the symptoms of atomism.

There are some educational technologists who know how to cooperate in teams with subject experts, theoreticians and practicians. In the last few years I have become acquainted with, and learned to appreciate, so many that I readily accept they are the majority and that each would prove his capability, provided he was put in the right place. What by their specialisation on form they lack in understanding of contents can be made good in a team some of the members of which have subject matter and teaching competence. There rather than in an armchair as a schemer and in committees as a manager would the educational technologist do meaningful work.

9. THE ART OF DIVIDING

Educational theory, like neighboring disciplines, indulges in the fashion of general schemes the relevance of which is at least doubtful. Other sciences, too, have known this stage of development. Dividing according to pairs of opposites (for instance in the School of Pythagoras), or according to groups counted by holy numbers, inspired and dominated the first approaches of philosophy – four elements, four humours, four temperaments, five sense-organs, five zones, the eightfold path (Buddha), the seven cardinal virtues and vices and so on. Such partitions are first and last the wisdom of exalted theoreticians; demi and quarter gods may try hard, pressing what practice offers them into these compartments. In fact the partition schemes are not operational; it is dividing for dividing's sake.

Until recently, linguistics practised and cultivated dividing into parts of speech. They were as numerous as the biblical commands, from 1st article, 2nd noun, 3rd pronoun, up to 10th interjection. The division worked quite reasonably; words could be put nicely into these classes. The system was of practical use too. Until recently text books of language instruction – whether in the mother tongue or a foreign language – proceeded according to the same pattern: 1st lesson, the article; 2nd lesson, the noun (with declensions); 6th–8th lesson, the pronouns; and so on. Though utterly worthless, the division according to ten parts of speech was just the means of distributing the teaching matter decently, and of preventing such unruly excesses as throwing interjections like *ach* and *au*, *oui* and *non* at the poor childrens' heads as early as the first lesson. After the parts of speech the parts of sentences were taught, according to diverging theories, with no fixed holy numbers to justify them; and finally as a delicacy for gourmets – the various kinds of clauses. The partition passion put a stamp on the didactics of language instruction until recently. It is now gone, if I am not mistaken.

In teaching theory partitions have been cultivated with the same glee – cf. Comenius and the Herbartians – though these were operational patterns. In my schooldays I was taught along Herbartian lines. Continuity was the first requirement, though this was differently interpreted. If my German teacher had taught Wieland last time and intended to commemorate Eichendorff today, he would lead us along an artfully contrived path through the bushes of literature from Wieland to Eichendorff, and everybody listened in suspense, asking themselves 'What is his mind bent on?' – surprise interested us more than continuity. Our biology teacher did it with much less sophistication. If last time he had dealt with apes and he wanted now to turn to the ants, he would start the lesson with *one* sentence: 'The apes among the insects are the ants.'

In educational theory partition schemes are quite the fashion. They are prescribed by authorities; subordinates assure you one could work excellently with pattern *XYZ* ('a working hypothesis'); indeed it would be to admit their incompetence if they asserted anything else. If only these patterns were ever applied, but they are not. Or if they are, you are frightened to death. As a matter of fact, it is hardly possible to apply them both *meaningfully* and *operationally*, in particular if they are so general that everything can be fitted in. Why do they not learn from the history of natural sciences that filling general schemes meaningfully and operationally has more merit than constructing them. In teaching theory the estimation is still the other way, and learning that this is the wrong way still requires a long collective learning process.

On account of my experience of the natural sciences and their history I consider the deductive procedure – from the general to the particular – to be premature in educational theory. Natural science, too, started with general natural philosophy, which more impeded than promoted the development of the natural sciences. In the long run proceeding from the particular to the general proved much more successful, and once significant progress had been made along the inductive road, the chances of succeeding with the deductive procedure improved. Nevertheless even today general natural philosophy is still in its infancy.

The humanities and social sciences are much more difficult cases, which can only mean that the deductive method is still farther away. I see more promise in approaching general didactic problems via the didactics of special teaching areas than in pressing special didactics into the straitjacket of general didactics. It is *a priori* improbable that a common pattern exists for such different instruction activities as arithmetic and gymnastics.

According to a venerable didactic rule instruction should progress from the particular to the general, in the direction of increased abstraction and not the other way round. I do not wish to decide now whether this is correct, but, at any rate, general didacticians tell us to do it this way, and we shall do as they tell us to do (not as they do!) Because as soon as they teach teaching theory, they start with the most general theories, drawing dazzling abstract patterns; so they continue, and it may be a windfall if in the course of the teaching process they arrive at the point where they can try to fill out the abstract patterns with concrete subject matter.

In teaching theory one does not observe the rules one has prescribed for others; one feels oneself to be above the laws imposed on others. One ordains patterns of didactic action, but if one expounds them – which *is* a didactic action – one rarely cares about the rules. In developing his own curricula and teaching matter the educationist does not observe the schemes designed for others. If he did so and succeeded, he would have delivered the first convincing proof that they work, that the schemes are functional. It is strange that people rarely hit upon this idea, but I reported what happens if they do in the section on 'Objectives of Instruction – In a Green Tree'.

10. MODELS

It is sometimes admitted – and then with amazement – that most schemes are never applied. Often, however, it is stated that they are not applicable. 'They are models', it is said, 'and models never reflect reality faithfully; one ought to be content if one can work with them – working hypotheses I mean'.

It is not clear what 'working' is here. It does not mean that the model is applied in a concrete situation, but rather that it is the basis of continued speculation. With models one is not even allowed to exact demands of practicability, because if one does so, it is 'confounding model and reality', and this is like stealing silver spoons, as soon as something has been given the rank of a model. Once a meaningful term in natural sciences and in economy, 'model' is now devalued into a vague word in many humanities and social sciences, and "confounding model and reality" has become a slogan used to keep critics at a distance. Meanwhile this vogue has reinfected natural sciences. Recently I read a paper on hydrodynamics where every differential equation was termed a model. To express what it once meant, 'model' has become useless; whoever is in the habit of disciplining his own thought and speech is disgusted with 'model' and he almost hates to use the word even if he needs it. How 'model' developed from a technical term into a vogue word would warrant a thesis; incidentally I will recall what I remember of it.

'Model' has essentially two meanings, the model as *after* image, and *pre*-image, the *descriptive* and the *normative* model of a – concrete or abstract – subject, the model as *plaster cast* and as a *knitting pattern*. (The 'model' that poses for painters belongs with the vases he paints to the first kind; as far as the models of dress shows are concerned, I do not know whether their profession owes its name to the fact that they pose to fashion designers or that they expose models of garments.) The double meaning of 'model' certainly contributed much to the confusion around it.

In natural sciences the oldest use of the word 'model' is probably found with the planetarium models of the solar system, where the interplay of planetary and lunar movements caused by gravity is rendered in a coarse simplification by means of a mechanical device: being merely a model, justice is done to the kinematics though not to the dynamics of the processes. Well-known as the Rutherford–Bohr atom model is, it describes the atom with its manifestations as a little solar system, with strange restrictions of the possible orbits; the model character stems from the *ad hoc* conditions to which the orbits are subjected, and the *ad hoc* assumption of jumps from one orbit to another, which contradict the dynamical laws. A more recent example is the drop model of the nucleus, in which protons and neutrons are smeared out as a fluid – an idea which is typical of a coarse model.

A well-known feature in mathematics is the concrete model of an abstract geometrical shape, in gypsum or wire and cardboard, but beyond this one knows abstract, mathematical, models too. The first to use 'model' in the latter sense was, if I am not mistaken, Felix Klein. When he presented his model of non-Euclidean geometry, this geometry was to him as it were a Platonic datum which acquired a representation in the explicitly given projective geometry by reinterpretation of its objects; the model character here consists in the relative concretisation of the non-Euclidean geometry and its reinterpretation within projective geometry. Klein's example is the root from which the model concept for axiomatic systems has grown: what is implicitly given by the axioms is made explicit by means of a suitable mathematical object and in this way given a relatively more concrete shape. One can progress in concreteness from mathematical models to realistic models, for instance to what is called 'space' in physics as a model of a geometric axiom system.

In probability, the urn from which lots are drawn is, along with other random instruments, the model by means of which one attempts to mathematise everything in the world that seems to be conditioned by chance: pollination of a plant by another of the same species, marriages and deaths in a population, these are viewed – rightly or not – as though mating or dying are decided by casting lots. Whereas the models of physics and chemistry look as if they were pinned upon nature as paper patterns, the urn models often betray the fact that they were chosen in default of better ones; but almost as often, those who apply them judiciously are quite conscious of this deficiency. If the factors that influence the probabilities can be controlled and nothing of importance is overlooked, the urn model is not too bad, but often these conditions are not easily fulfilled. If there is no other choice one must apply the urn model in spite of its deficiencies whether one likes it or not, but then one will avoid too selfconfident conclusions.

It was 'model thinking' when Newton dealt with the flood wave of the tides as a pair of moons orbiting the Earth, and when Einstein imitated gravity by a rotating disk model to get insight into general relativity. Sticking too long to a model can be a grave mistake, as happened in the vain attempts to explain optical phenomena by elastic oscillation – eventually these elastic models were superseded by the electric field model.

Numerous examples of 'model thinking' can be cited from present-day technology: the circulation of air in a mine, and the circulation of blood in the vessels, are imitated and studied by designing models of electric circuits with resistances, capacities and self-inductions; in analogue computers the mathematical operations are translated by physical processes of which they are the mathematical expression; traffic flow is simulated by means of concrete random devices. Models of a similar standing are found in economy: for instance a rough picture of a national economy, where faceless consumers, wage-earners, savers, retired people, producers, intermediaries, importers, exporters – groups tarred with the same brush – are acting by transferring money and commodities; these models are then mathematically processed in order to predict the consequences of a decrease of the bank-rate, of an increase of income-taxes or any other measure of financial and economic politics.

This is a broad spectrum of examples of model thinking, but there is a common element in them: the – static or dynamic – system to be investigated is replaced with another that is simpler or more easily mastered, while conserving structural elements that are considered essential; concepts, conclusions, predictions will afterwards be played back from the model to the original system, while, if possible from the start onwards, deviations, deficiencies, errors of the model are accounted for.

Models are even preferred in those natural sciences where general theories are available which pretend to describe the physical aspects of nature completely. I mentioned earlier on that these sciences are not as deductive as they seem to be. The general laws expressed in mathematical formulae are almost never deductively applied; they function rather as frames for the construction of models which, strictly speaking, contradict the general laws. A widespread model is that of perturbation: consciously one sins as often as possible against Newton's law of equality of action and reaction; in order to be dealt with more comfortably, a – static or dynamic – system is cut into two pieces, a big and a little one, and one takes only the action of the big upon the little one into account and disregards – rightly or wrongly – the reaction of the little upon the big one. Or the model of feedback, where the reaction is accounted for in a schematic rather than a systematic way. The inaccessible Maxwell equations are circumvented by simplistic circuit models, field models, induction models; the equations of wave optics by geometric models, ray systems, wave fronts.

This 'model thinking' extends to areas where the general theories look much less coercive as frames or are even lacking. Applications of probability theory are often of this kind, and the larger the distance from physics grows the more frequent the models become *ad hoc* with no framing theory – models which then look like models of reality itself. 'Confounding model and reality' has its roots here.* It is an unfortunate way of speaking. It fits at most situations where the model is formed in the same reality as the original, for instance if a building is confounded with its model or a pump model of

* 'Confounding model and reality' must stand for many things. 'Zeno's paradoxes rest on confounding model and reality' is a ridiculous though frequent assertion. 'Point of time is a model concept whereas reality knows time intervals only': in fact both concepts are licit in the concept system of everyday life as well as in that of physics; a time interval is determined by its endpoints and consequently is as real or as much a model as they. I once witnessed an amusing quarrel about nothing, where one party claimed that continuity and infinity were model concepts whereas the reality was discrete and finite, whereupon his adversary turned the tables the other way round: in fact both of these concepts are licit on both levels.

blood circulation with the real blood circulation, which in fact are quite improbable confusions. What actually could happen, and has to be avoided, is changing from one model into the other with no precaution, from the model language into everyday language, or overstraining a model beyond the limits of its validity.

I have tried to explain the purpose and function of models in the sciences, from mathematics via natural sciences to economy. Looking for models in those domains where 'model' is a vogue term, one is gravely disappointed. What are there decorated with the label 'model' are partitions such as characterised earlier on, most often of a non-operational character. An investigation about some aspects of behaviour, the report on which is right under my eyes on my desk, had been carried out using the *PIN* model – *P* means positive, *N* negative, and *I* intermediate, and people were classified accordingly; the investigation shows that the *P* and *N* people possess all the properties everybody would expect them to have, whereas the problem of the *I* people remains unsolved until further notice. One model cannot meet all requirements, or can it?

There are, however, true models in teaching theory too, but they are never called models because they date from before the model fashion. For instance the Socratic method, which describes the teacher as a midwife, the taught one as a woman in labour, and the learning process as delivery. Or the model of the learning process that is called the Nuremberg funnel. Or the equally familiar mechanism 'in at one ear, out at the other'. Or the sausage model of the learning process: two ends and something in between, all interchangeable. Or the learning process of rats controlled by titbits and electric shocks as a model of the human learning process – a model with restricted applicability and high efficiency. I already mentioned the models of learning processes of Comenius and the school of Herbart. At present I don't think there is any serious search going on for models of learning processes or for other instructional models, perhaps as a consequence of the widespread misuse of the term 'model'.

The situation is also obscured by the double meaning of 'model' which I already mentioned. If I want to have an announcement of birth printed or to buy a letter-balance, the printer or dealer will show me a few 'models' from which I may take my choice. In the choosing of funerals or oranges, the term 'model' has not yet gained currency, but this is only a question of time. Using the term 'model' for a timetable is more than I can appreciate. I can, however, imagine models for the construction of timetables.

It is useful to contrast possible properties of the two model concepts:

descriptive	normative
valid	practical
quite determined	quite arbitrary
not numerous	plenty
in a way coercive	conventional

Examples which show these contrasts clearly are a model of the circulation of the blood and a model of traffic regulation.

How are the two kinds of models confounded and what are the consequences if it happens? Descriptive models are readily excused if they are restricted to a few selected aspects provided they do reasonable justice to these aspects – in the social sector this requirement seriously limits the domain of their validity, and there, overstraining a model may rightly be blamed as 'confounding model and reality'. Well, that excuse which may readily be accepted for the descriptive model is illicit when claimed for normative models where 'valid' is replaced with 'practical': I know and admit that my model is practically useless but demanding that it be useful is overstraining the model, and confounding model and reality. Conversely, the creator of a descriptive model does not claim its validity, but its practical value, which then means that others accept it as a frame, though with no practical consequences.

Descriptive models are produced arbitrarily and in large quantities, because this is allowable in the case of normative models. Conversely producers of normative models like to behave as though their models were well-determined and unique – in particular if they teach them. If a descriptive model is assailed, the defendant evades the arguments by saying it is conventional anyhow, whereas an unjustified compulsoriness is claimed for normative models – this is again a striking feature in the teaching of teaching theory.

There is no need to support these allegations by evidence; in many a discussion this confusion crops up, and textbooks of teaching theory abound with them: on the one hand one finds the dogmatic diction, and on the other hand, as soon as it is criticized, the excuse 'what do you want, these are only models'. Statements are not supported by arguments, because they are said to be conventional anyhow, but this does not inhibit continuing with the definite article and speaking about *the* model, *the* division, *the* meaning, and so on, in order to enforce the validity of the unfounded convention, if need be by means of an examination. Wherever references to literature suggest the existence of supporting evidence, it is in fact unclear what the citations mean: that somebody asserted or found or proved or tested or applied something. The slogan 'they are only models' nourishes in the learner's mind the idea of a science where all is permitted, whereas by the dogmatism the exercise of this freedom is restricted to the teacher and examiner. This frame of mind is not unusual in social sciences. I am not surprised by the rebellion of those who want to replace one dogma by another.

11. MATHEMATICAL MODELS

Often if models are used, one changes from mechanical, geometrical, electrical, biological or otherwise realistic models to mathematical models by replacing the real objects and processes with mathematical ones. I do not illustrate this, and I need not explain the significance of these models.* I will instead indicate downright grotesque misunderstandings which are met there as to what a model is.

Suppose somebody wants to dissect the art of painting mathematically and in the course of this undertaking he constructs a model of what people usually call a painting. Such a model would then look as follows:

A painting is an ordered triple $\ulcorner R, C, I \urcorner$ consisting of

> a rectangle R of the Euclidean plane;
> a set C the elements of which are called colours; and
> a relation I between R and C, where $I(x, y)$ also reads: in the point x there is the colour element y.

Or if somebody wants to analyse the techniques of meetings mathematically and invents a model of what is usually called meetings:

A meeting is an ordered set $\ulcorner M, P, c, s, C_1, C_2, b, i_1, i_2, S, i_3 \urcorner$ consisting of

* Sometimes, as regards their mathematical contents, the general theories of the natural sciences are also called models, which is not necessary but not objectionable either.

a bounded part M of Euclidean space;
a finite set P, that of the participants;
two elements c and s of P called chairman and secretary;
a finite set C_1, called the chairs;
a finite set C_2, called the cups of coffee;
an element b, called bell;
an injection i_1 of P into C_1;
a mapping i_2 of C_2 into P;
an ordered set S, the speeches;
a mapping i_3 of S into P with the property that c belongs to the image of i_3.

If i_3 is a surjection, it is usual to say that everybody has had the floor.

Contriving such models and presenting them used to be an amusement for people who organised an institute ball with a cabaret. In the last few years it has become a serious concern for model makers and an ornament to educational research. As a mathematician I am ashamed of it. Science, in whatever area, is never so cheap that it requires no more than mathematical jargon.

I have tried by these fictional examples to characterize what with increasing frequency are called mathematical models in educational technology. Can this development be stopped, or is it too late? Mathematically these so-called mathematical models are structures which are more subtle than rough partitionings, but they are still so trivial that nothing in them reminds one of mathematics – they are more trivial than $2 + 2 = 4$. Moreover they rest on the misunderstanding that it would be possible to change directly from reality, with no intermediate models, to a mathematical model. What results are verbal constructions with no operational value.

Mathematical models are also suggested by so-called 'flow diagrams'. An example to explain this idea is shown in Figure 1, 'Going Upstairs'.

What is served here is no esoteric wisdom: but neither is it so easy to develop such schemes; and they can have a use in instructing computers and robots. At any rate the scheme is operational: it is a model, that is, of a process and can function as such.

This cannot be said of what is dished up in educational technology and in neighbouring domains as flow diagrams. Frames beside and under each other are joined by arrows, and even if the text within the frames is meaningful, the meaning of the arrows remains undisclosed; for instance reading an arrow

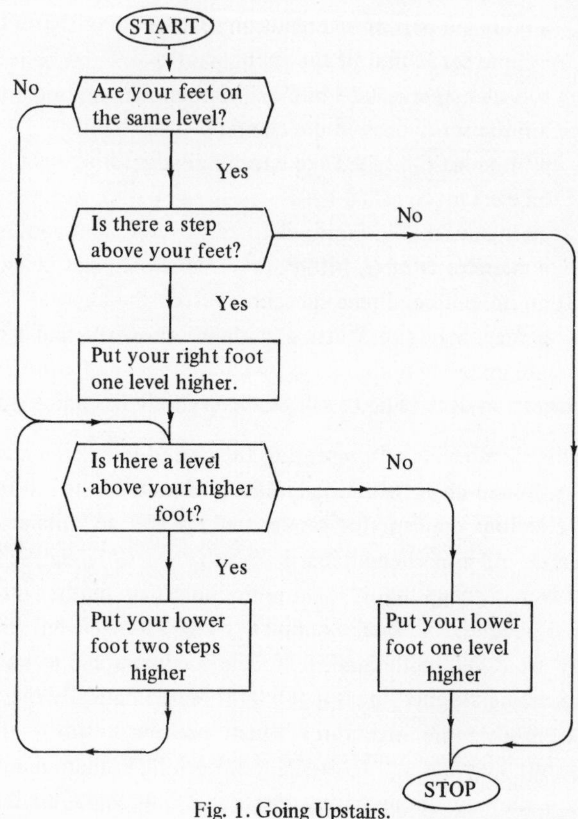

Fig. 1. Going Upstairs.

back and forth between two frames as a feedback may only mean that the term feedback is used, without any content. Nothing is left of the force of concreteness and visualisation of flow diagrams as pictures of processes. All remains as vague and abstract as ever, and the flow diagram is only a deceptive appearance.

12. EDUCATIONESE

A few – benevolent – reviewers of my earlier book found fault with its lack of citations and quotations. This restraint was a matter of principle for which

I had given reasons in the introduction. If, however, such criticism is preceded or followed by an exclamation "Can it really be so bad?" one feels inclined to do something to brush up one's credibility. Now reading again the last section I almost begin to doubt my own credibility. Is it really so bad?

I do not feel it a pleasure to pillory some individual who assiduously plays his part in the *cosi fan tutte*, as a bad musician. With a heavy heart I have decided to quote evidence; I would have liked to keep silent about the source but for fear of possible trouble I have not. One should not believe that the passage I will quote is a derailment. It comes from the chapter 'Research on Teaching Secondary School Mathematics' in a renowned and authoritative tome of more than two thousand columns, by means of which future and actual teachers are indoctrinated with the idea of the existence of something like a science of instruction.*

Teaching can be conceived as the ternary relation: x teaches y to z. Expressed in the notation of relation theory, this becomes $(x, y)Tz$, or more generally, $T(x, y, z)$. As popularly conceived, the domain of 'x' is the set of persons who act as teachers; the domain of 'y' is a set of knowledge, beliefs, or skills selected by a teacher; and the domain of 'z' is a set of individuals – humans and other animals capable of modifying their behavior as a result of experience – who are taught by a teacher. To continue the popular conception (which undoubtedly would not be expressed by means of the symbols being used), values of 'z' exist such that $x = z$, for on occasion we hear a person characterized as 'self-educated' or 'self-taught.'

With some modifications, this conception is a useful one for analyzing research on teaching secondary school mathematics. The proposed modifications follow. When one stops to think about teaching, he realizes that the teacher is not the significant factor. It is what the teacher does, in other words, his behavior, that becomes significant for research. Hence, the domain of 'x' in '$T(x, y, z)$' is more fruitfully regarded as sequences (sets) of verbal and nonverbal behavior the teacher manifests. Such a conception enables us to consider a person whose voice and image appear on a television screen and one whose voice emanates from a loud-speaker to be teachers if their objective is to produce learning in a group of people. Moreover, it allows us to consider a machine or a textbook to be a teacher if its function is the same as that of a human being who teaches. In all these cases, values of 'x' in '$T(x, y, z)$' are sequences of actions.

When we compare sequences of teacher behaviors, we find that they are not random but ordered so as to accomplish an objective of the teacher, usually to help a student learn some items of subject matter. Moreover, we find that the sequences can be classified into sets in terms of the common properties which characterize the set. The pattern, that is, the set of common properties that a set of behavior sequences manifests, will be called a *method*. This is in keeping with the conventional use of this term, for we speak of 'the

* N. L. Gage (ed.), *Handbook of Research on Teaching*, Chicago 1963: Chapter XIX, K. B. Henderson, pp. 1007–1008. Quoted by permission from AERA.

lecture method,' 'the supervised study method,' 'the discovery method,' and others, having in mind a sequence of acts which a teacher performs.

It seems reasonable to hypothesize that a method maximizes certain factors and minimizes others. For example, writing terms, mathematical sentences, and rules for changing the form of expressions on the chalkboard maximizes time; that is, it takes longer to write these on the chalkboard than it does merely to say them, but it minimizes the cognitive effort that the student must expend to remember the expressions. Discouraging questions from the students minimizes the time required to cover a topic, but it probably also minimizes the student's understanding and maximizes his frustration. To determine which factors are maximized and which are minimized by a certain method is the function of research on teaching methods.

We shall say, therefore, that methods – patterns of sequences of teacher behavior – will be the values of 'x' in '$T(x, y, z)$'. A distinct advantage of this point of view is that it allows textbooks and so-called teaching machines to be considered as 'teachers.' The people who design them can build in certain methods which then become values of the independent variable 'x'.

As in the case of the variable 'x', it is the behavior the student manifests rather than the student per se which is the significant factor for research, e.g., what he does in the face of temporary blocking, to what extent he can apply what he has learned to new problems, whether he sees a pattern in a set of problems, to what extent he exhibits behavior which inclines us to say that he is interested in the study of mathematics, whether he passes or fails in college, and so on. Hence, the domain of 'z' in the teaching relation $T(x, y, z)$ is profitably taken as the behaviors of those taught.

The concept of a student's knowledge about a subject fits into this model. Knowledge is an inferred entity rather than an observed one. Typically, we infer concerning a student's knowledge about values of 'y' from (his) values of 'z'; that is, we observe him do or say something and from this behavior we infer how much he knows about the subject.

One kind of research on teaching secondary school mathematics focuses on the binary relation ySz abstracted from the ternary relation $T(x, y, z)$. Research of this kind studies the relation between subject matter taught a student and his behavior subsequent to having been taught it and which are considered relevant to it. This kind of research may be thought of as curricular research. In its pure form, it attempts to identify members (y, z) of the relation which are invariant with respect to values of 'x'. That aspect of the work of the School Mathematics Study Group which culminates in selecting subject matter for various grades and mathematics courses may be considered research of this kind. This group has not sought to study any methods of teaching the subject matter they select. But by allowing the teachers who use their text materials to employ any methods they choose, the 'methods' variable is randomized. By the definition of the function of this Handbook, we shall not be concerned with this kind of research.

A second kind of research focuses on the binary relation xRz abstracted from $T(x, y, z)$. Research of this kind studies the relation between the methods a teacher (person, text, or machine) employs and those behaviors of a student which under various hypotheses are related to the methods. It tries to identify members (x, z) of the relation which are either invariant with respect to values of 'y', viz., items of subject matter, or depend on values of 'y', the nature of the dependence being the subject of research.

It is only honest to admit that this tome also contains meaningful and relevant information, and there is even a chapter at the beginning where the reader is warned about this kind of varnish. But, with regards to the quoted piece and similar matter in print, do not ask me what this has to do with mathematical education, or for that matter with secondary schools, or with education at all, or why it was originally printed on glossy paper, or why it should be learned. Please, I did not write it! I only quoted it in order to extend credibility to my earlier seemingly incredible statements. In the German edition of this book, which contains a translation of this piece, I promised to replace it in the English edition by the English translation of a German counter piece. The problem, however, is one of translation, and it seems insurmountable: there is no Educationese like German Educationese; though I agree it would mean an enormous enrichment of the English vocabulary if I succeeded in translating it.

13. RITUALS

A vogue word – not just in education but in the methodology and history of science – is 'paradigm'. Kuhn gave it its fashionable meaning; both as to the choice of the term and as to the content I disagree with Kuhn. It is too cheap a deal to view the trade of science as a society of builders and bricklayers: a few create revolutions, and the others industriously repeat paradigms. But even if this is admitted, I cannot identify paradigms with mere fashions, as Kuhn seems to do.

Even Kuhn's idea of 'paradigm' is too smooth for what is called the science of teaching. What was a paradigm once is soon calcified into a ritual, into something the origin and meaning of which is forgotten and which is applied dutifully and without thinking about it. This is one of the reasons why individuals should not be taken to task; all they do is observe rituals which they cannot infringe lest they are outlawed by their community. I have already mentioned the rituals of the objectives of instruction and of models, the rituals in so-called curriculum research. The holiest among the rituals of test development is known by the brand K.R.20; it is the twentieth in the collection of formulae of Kuder–Richardson, the formula by which the 'reliability' of a test is calculated. Neither Kuder–Richardson, nor anyone else either before or after, ever made it plausible, or even tried to make it plausible, why this magnitude should be called 'reliability'; or why it could be thought of as somehow measuring reliability – if applied to individuals or classes, or to comparing individuals or classes or suchlike – and how just one number could serve to measure such different 'reliabilities'. It is just a ritual to compute the 'reliability' of a test instrument and label the instrument with the numerical datum; for commercially available tests it is a kind of quality stamp. Reliabilities above 0.85 are considered as a recommendation, whereas those below 0.70 are met with distrust. Beyond this ritual I cannot discover any application of 'reliability' in the literature: that is, I do not know about conclusions drawn from this magnitude, neither do I know how it could ever be applied.

In general, much in the mathematical evaluation of the statistics of instruction and instructional experiments can only be understood as a ritual; but this I will illustrate a bit later. I will now discuss one ritual in more detail, that of Bloom's cognitive categories, which I dealt with earlier on.

I recapitulate that Bloom's *Taxonomy* aims to classify and hierarchically arrange the objectives of instruction. The objectives need not have been made neatly explicit in some catalogue of objectives; they can reside within a course, a textbook, a method, or without explicitation. Such a context defines the position values of what is graded by the *Taxonomy*.

Test problems which are not covered by any objective of instruction have no such position value; classifying them by means of the *Taxonomy* proves thoughtlessness. And yet it happens again and again, as a mere ritual.

A good example is the test production of the I.E.A. (International Association for the Evaluation of Educational Achievement), a company of prominent psychometrists, which occupies itself with having pupils' achievement compared internationally by testing. I view here the 'Science' study.* The test instruments, which are alarming as soon as you see them, and their taxonomic values, which are amusing, have been produced as follows:

A subject matter list was drawn up and filled out with tests, about four times the required number, while they obeyed the ritual command that the Bloom categories should occur in the test stock in a fixed proportion; the three uppermost categories, which are in any case a separate problem, were united into one category, *Higher Processes*, which procedure is also part of

* L. C. Comber and J. P. Keeves, *Science Education in Nineteen Countries*, International Studies in Evaluation I, New York–Stockholm 1973.

the ritual. The purpose of Bloom's categories in this context was the following: tests require a validation ritual; if, as in the present case (among numerous others) no yardsticks of validation of the *contents* of the instrument are available, one can use as an object of validation the distribution over Bloom's categories, which in fact as a formal criterion is more attractive to psychometrists than subject matter and educational content, and is more intelligible too. After the pretesting the 'experts' of the participating countries were asked to distribute the single tests anew over the Bloom categories. This is again a ritual which shows that all knowledge of and regard for the meaning of the *Taxonomy* has been lost. If at all, position values in the *Taxonomy* can be awarded to test items with respect to a well-defined instructional system, but not with respect to 19 different national instructional systems with widely diverging curricula (in particular among the 14-year-old pupils who formed one of the populations of the study). And with the I.E.A. definition of population it is even impossible in each single country. The I.E.A. populations of pupils are defined in the awkward way that one population substantially extends over 2–3 grades and often even over different types of schools; in each of these grades each test has an *a priori* different taxonomic position value. Nowhere in the report is it explained how the national experts were briefed about principles of taxonomic placement. But how can a national expert value a test taxonomically which does not belong to any objective of the instruction in his country for this or that population or for this or that grade? Where in the Bloom taxonomy is there a place for a chemistry test for pupils who had never had a chemistry lesson? (Indeed, populations were defined in such a way that this could happen.) I asked I.E.A., to no avail. Have they extended the six Bloom categories with a seventh, say *Illumination*, which was eventually included in *Higher Processes*? I do not know, and I cannot but presume that the classification was done in some honest way and accepted by Headquarters in good faith. But what happened then is so absurd that sometimes I feel as though a phantom played pranks on me.

Internationally the valuations of the national experts diverged widely. Nobody could have expected anything else. Just for this reason they could have been used in some sensible way, for instance, in order to eliminate tests with too large a dispersion of taxonomic value, or in order to pursue a test instrument with something like the same total taxonomic value over all countries. Nothing like this happened. What really happened – hold on to your chair – was that the valuations of the national experts were taken as – countrywise – a poll, and the tests were classified anew according to the result of the poll. (The four letter word 'poll' is my terminology: the report speaks about 'modal value' of the assessments rather than 'result of the poll'.) The result certainly looked like what one would get if one were to take the mean values of the corresponding components of all automobiles in the market in order to build an 'average' car. "The consensus of the experts is the criterion of validity" is the official characterisation of this procedure. Actually there was nothing that looked like a consensus; however, in such cases pronouncing the formula suffices. But what did they validate? The test instrument? No! The labelling of tests with Bloom categories? Not even that.

The result of the poll – surprising only for people who never assisted at one – was a high density on the intermediate categories and a low one on the extremities. Moreover some tests which had been selected for two populations had drifted into different categories. After this revaluation it became difficult to fill the subject matter table proportionally from the now ill-balanced test stock. Even by pushing and pulling they could not get the goat into the stable. But pull and push they did, and this probably severely damaged the test instrument. Nevertheless, agreement with the prescribed proportions could not be reached, not even approached; the divergence is enormous. The attempts at validation had entirely failed, but since they had taken place, the instrument was pronounced valid. If rituals are indispensable, would it not be time to replace the Bloom categories ritual by another where for instance committee and experts unite in a silent prayer?

The Bloom categories, which were invented to facilitate and objectify the construction of test instruments are rather detrimental, as is shown by this story. Under the pressure of the ritual of Bloom categories ill-balanced test instruments came into being. Uniform distribution over subareas of subject matter would probably have provided a bearable guarantee for international validity. This is now entirely absent, for after this failure no attempt at international validation was undertaken. And all this because of rituals which nobody dares to oppose.

14. EDUCATIONAL ACCOUNTANCY

Accountability in educational matters is too precious a thing to be debased into a slogan. Yet it is also too precious to be replaced by accountancy.

Accountability yes, but not by accountants but by educators who are able to weigh credits and debits more intelligently than can be done by numbers only.

Numbers as a tool in education have not come from outside, they have not been imported by imperious statisticians. I do not know for how many centuries marks have been given and pupils' achievements measured by test papers. But with the rise of statistics, numbers as a tool in education became an aim in itself, accountability became accountancy.

According to a well-worn joke there are three kinds of lies: lies, damned lies, and statistics. When the joke was invented, mathematical statistics had not yet come into being. Otherwise one would have added three kinds of surreptitious credibility: by word of honour, by oath, and by mathematical statistics. Or, three methods to assume a learned air: footnotes, bibliography, and correlation tables.

I am not biased against mathematical statistics. On the contrary, as long as I have known the subject, I have advocated applying it. Like many others I am scared by abuses which surreptitiously obtained their civil rights in many fields where mathematical statistics is applied. I want now to leave out of consideration the wrong recipes and the wrong use of correct ones; my complaints are more profoundly rooted.

I am not a lonely critic of the way mathematical statistics is applied in educational technique and beyond it in other social sciences. On the contrary the criticism pronounced by expert methodologists and statisticians – more expert than I – is unanimous and sharp. Critical descriptions I found in the literature vary from 'spurious respectability' to 'intellectual garbage'. They are, however, more often pragmatic criticisms than criticisms of principle: the applicability of the statistical method as such is not questioned. The contribution of an expert statistician to a collective work on educational research invariably begins with a characterisation – worth reading – of the methodological situation that invites the application of mathematical statistics. Inevitably he warns against applying mathematical methods to jumbled up statistical material; inevitably he demands that hypotheses should be stated, not *ad hoc* but within the framework of a theory, before experiments are conducted the results of which are to be evaluated in order to test the hypotheses. But after these prudent words and eloquent warnings the expert statistician abruptly proceeds to his trade in which to talk business is to talk of factor analysis, correlations and regressions, expounded in exactly the same way as he would do in a handbook on biotechnics, and no nonsense about applications. What his methodological postulates could mean in the particular case of the educational sciences is not explained in theory, let alone with examples. The pre-criticism remains ineffective; the statistician who expressed it washes his hands of the abuses, but as a detergent for the hands of others it does not work. It is not his fault if in the handbook to which he contributed, mathematical statistics is preponderantly, if not entirely, a varnish of scientific respectability.

The mathematical statistical methods used in educational technology come from biotechnics. They were invented, and are applied, for comparing varieties of cultivated plants, races of domesticated animals, nutrients, food and pesticides, and for evaluating methods of agriculture and breeding. The goals can be described unambiguously as well as numerically: a magnitude depending on many parameters, the output should be maximalized; the parameters – at least those from the biological sphere – are well-known and controlled in the experiments; their influence on the output, which is qualitatively well established, is to be quantitatively determined in order to control them most effectively; statistical tools serve to carry out this evaluation. Among the parameters I have in mind in the output of a cultivated plant are the variety, the nitrogen content and presence of different minerals in the soil, the temperature, humidity and light, and means of combatting pests. If the aim is to compare two or more varieties or two fertilizers, experiments are carried on under changing circumstances, that is while varying the other factors. These factors are not independent of each other, but the dependencies are at least qualitatively well-known. In a more general formulation the problem is that of refining quantitatively certain qualitatively well-known and well-understood relations on the strength of numerical observation data. As far as the mathematical character of these relations is concerned, mathematical assumptions are made on how the numerical parameters are involved. If there are no other indications, assumptions of linearity are made; indeed, within certain limits, numerical relations can be linearly approximated, though it is not known *a priori* how wide these limits are nor whether the assumption of linearity is at all useful. This then is the weak point of the analysis of variance and factor analysis. Nevertheless in biotechnics one can feel relatively safe; one feels less safe if biotechnic output is replaced with economic output. If the influence of the various parameters on the biotechnic output is determined, the next questions that arise are the cost of influencing each single parameter and their totality, and the economic value of a certain biotechnic output – queries, the answers to which include uncertainties depending on the market and its trends. Here the relevance of certain factors is easily overlooked or underestimated, and only by hindsight fully appreciated – a very telling example is the seemingly insignificant mercury load put upon the environment by nitrogen fertilizers which by mere accumulation becomes unbearable; and another is the eutrophic load put upon surface water by phosphate fertilizers.

But this is not to the point here. As a subordinate tool mathematical statistics is useful in biotechnics; it is mathematical statistics that makes it possible to provide qualitative connections having a quantitative precision. The qualitative connections are well-known and well-understood in fundamental physics, chemistry and biology. It is known that plants need nitrogen, and why, and in which way and combination it can be delivered to the plants; one knows why a plant does not grow with too little or too much water; one is familiar with the assimilation processes by which green plants convert and stockpile light energy; pesticides have been scientifically developed and their mechanism is well-understood. Some factors have still perhaps been disregarded or insufficiently appreciated – for instance the import of trace elements – but this again would be a shortcoming of fundamental science. On the other hand there is no doubt about the *kind* of factor on which the output depends and that factors like the religion or political conviction of the grower or benedictions and magic formulae, the moon and legendary rays are irrelevant. Finally whether one investigates or cultivates a certain plant, the objective aimed at is well-defined: one tries to improve the output quantitatively or qualitatively, to get trees that are resistant to certain pests, flowers which bloom with unusual wealth of colour or at unusual times, and fundamental knowledge is a guide to such aims.

The biotechnical methods have too readily been adopted by educational technology. It has scarcely been considered whether the assumptions made in biotechnics are at least approximately valid in education. I think none of them are; expounding sophisticated statistical techniques in educational handbooks looks to me like selling T.V. sets in regions where no T.V. programmes can be received.

The first difficulties arise if the biotechnical concept of output is to be transferred to an educational system. It would be an exaggeration to affirm the absolute impossibility of such a transfer; what I want to do is to indicate the difficulties, without stressing them too much – there are more essential arguments against too ready a transfer of statistical methods from biotechnics to educational technics. Biotechnical output (for instance milk yield per cow per day) is so defined that it can unambiguously be measured at least in its quantitative aspects, but even qualitative refinements hardly cause difficulties if they can be reduced to quantitative ones (for instance the quality of produced milk as defined by percentages of fat and protein); aesthetic factors which influence the quality (for instance in flower culture) can be measured through the economic output. It should be considered that measurement – qualitative as well as quantitative – often proceeds by samples; the reliability of the measurement of output or of other parameters by sampling is guaranteed by well-known statistical methods.

I do not question in principle the measurability of the output of education. It is a common place that examinations – an indispensable means both for the selection and control of instruction – are measurements. Seventy years ago when this might have been stated for the first time, it was a discovery to consider examinations from the point of view of measurement, and a challenge to make it come true, that is to subject examinations to the same requirements as are adopted for measurements. Indeed, if this is neglected, the examination as a kind of measurement remains an empty slogan.

What distinguishes the examination as alleged instructional measurement from biotechnical measurement? The biotechnical measurement is an operation effected upon the output (or a sample of the output) which does not influence the output itself, or if it does, it does so in a way that can be ascertained and accounted for. In instructional technology, however, the examination is in general part of the output, quite often even a part that is identified with the ouput; and this is rightly so if the output cannot be expressed in any way other than examination. Moreover as everybody knows, examinations influence the output of instruction by feedback even where its goals lie beyond the output measured by the examination.

There exist examinations where the examiner poses the candidate a number of questions, taken at random from a long list. If this master list reflects the teaching matter faithfully, we are indeed in the classical sample situation, but this will be a rare exception. It is more probable that the list is itself a sample from a still larger master list. If the sample has been taken in agreement with statistical principles, it does not matter: but if things were really so simple, one could work directly with this master list; this does not happen, which indicates that something is wrong.

The – real or fictive – list from which the examiner takes his questions is just not a sample of the teaching matter to be examined in a statistical sense. There are techniques in statistics to improve the representative character of samples (for instance stratification), by means of conscious and intentional infringements upon the principle of random choice (for instance in order to attain a population sample representing every age and profession in due proportion with the composition of the population itself). The examiner who draws up the master list cannot use such rough stratifying procedures but he is acquainted with methods of improving the representative character. Earlier on I dealt with – ever unsuccessful – attempts at systematizing this. There are two extremes of wrong strategy: representativity is pursued by patterns of partitioning where every class is attributed a certain weight, or by atomisation and the belief that all can be enumerated. I do not see what these methods can contribute to improving the usual intuitive procedures of drawing up a representative master list – apart from quite exceptional cases.

It is another question to ask whether a real or fictive master list can be representative at all. If it were so even up to equivalence, the only thing left would be to teach, or to learn, the master list, and if one yields to this interpretation of the instructional process – the inclination to do so can hardly be denied – the examination as a measuring procedure indeed becomes part of the output to be measured. In fact the master list is not an extract of the instructional contents; it is totally different and even as to mere size it can involve much more, so much that no learner would be able to master it – as an instance consider a mathematical theorem which in the master list is represented by a number of conclusions, or a mathematical method represented by a number of applications.

Anyhow there are enough arguments to doubt the representative character of the master list. This does not mean that it loses all of its value in measuring the output; its value is relativized. The examination becomes one indicator of the output, among others. Another, extremely valuable but little used indicator is a second examination, three months or a whole year after the first, in order to include perseverance of instructional achievement as a new factor into the output measure. For complicated matters like fair weather, health, welfare one knows several indices or indicators, and from olden times instruction knows process as well as product evaluation – I will come back to this later.

By the preceding I wanted to show that, when subjected to measurement, instructional output behaves in a quite different way from biotechnical output. This should be read as a first warning against too prompt a transfer of such statistical methods as are in principle applied on – allegedly – measured magnitudes. The main difficulties, however, are more deeply rooted. I explained a few pages ago what purpose the statistical method of *biotechnics* serves. One knows and controls the parameters on which the output depends and one wishes to express their influence on the output, which is qualitatively certain and understood, in a more precise way (that is, numerically); by observation and statistical processing one tries to get the data for this evaluation. Let us suppose that instructional output were as well-defined as the biotechnical one or at least that we knew beyond doubt – if need be by convention – which magnitudes can serve as indicators of instructional improvement, even then the question remains unanswered: Where are the parameters which should be influenced?

Let us consider biotechnics further. We can enumerate the parameters on which the output of a cultivated plant depends; physics, chemistry and biology teach us what plays a role and what does not, and in the experiment all these parameters are under control. The instructional output is produced by a teaching–learning process, starting with an initial situation; what parameters in the initial situation and in the process influence the output? There is no theory that tells us about it, with the result that people choose a few parameters at random and look for their variability: as far as the learners are concerned, it is age, sex, social extraction, training, previous knowledge, intelligence, achievements in other areas, structure of personality and so on; as to the process, time available, instructional density, arrangement of steps, number and kind of examples, repetitions, the logical depth of the theory, the use of all kinds of material, reward and punishment, the percentages of time allotted to class teaching, group work, individual work, and so on. These are parameters which come to mind but are not supported by theory as is the case in biotechnics (temperature, humidity, nutrients and so on): the really interesting ones among them are complicated and lack perspicuity; the numerically accessible ones are of no interest; and of none of them can one tell, except by mere guessing, whether and why they should influence the output. On the contrary, experiments are performed in order to find out what the parameters mean for the output; one wishes to decide whether, and under which conditions, this method of instruction is better than that; and silently, while the computer processes the data, one waits for something like traces of a theory emerging from the computer as a gift from the Gods. And this is the most favourable case. I have on my desk an investigation about the effect of guidance in the first semester of a technical university: the output of the guidance has been statistically analysed in 150 pages according to numerous factors such as age, sex, social extraction, personality structure of the guides and those guided, subject studied, studying habits, motivation, adaptation, intelligence, school grades and so on, with the overall result that the guidance does not affect the output. What the guidance consisted in is considered immaterial by the author, who is a psychologist; it is mentioned in just three lines, which tends to suggest that there was no guidance at all. Varying this factor was clearly too much for the investigator. Educationists who undertook such an investigation would have at least compared two or three methods of guidance – for instance traditional learning and learning by 'discovery', or class, group and individual instruction and similar distinctions. Even then it would hardly be specified what this means except that we are assured that the instruction has been given by experienced teachers – as though in zootechnical experiments one would mention the religious or political conviction of the stable man. This shows one's absolute inability to control at least those parameters one recognized as such and one would wish to influence, not to mention all the invisible and unknown ones which possibly influence the output more than the known and visible ones. What results appears to be an extremely doubtful collection of numerical material, but this does not matter. The sophisticated mathematical methods look as though they are created to refine bad material. It is a pity that methods like factor analysis, analysis of variance, correlations, and regressions can be useless even if applied to valid material if there is no theory behind them.

What do correlation coefficients mean? There is no fundamental inquiry into the problem what they mean and how they can meaningfully be applied. This does not imply they are valueless. In the framework of a *theory* they can yield indications for the dependency. of magnitudes, yet not in the framework of a policy requiring that correlation coefficients are computed of all parameters one can imagine, and as many as the computer can be paid for.

Well, a hundred correlation coefficients, more or less, is no disaster; they are not that expensive. The pinnacle of psychometric bliss however, is regressional analysis. There are no words to describe what is achieved in this area. I will shortly explain what analysis of regression can mean in educational technique; the example copies a pattern of the I.E.A. studies*. One gets a thousand pupils to be tested; the scores written in a row form a 1000-dimensional vector, the output vector as it were, which should be 'explained' by the instruction enjoyed and by other data. Such explaining variables were collected at random: training of the father, training of the mother, father's profession, size of family, number of books at home, private room of the pupil, age and sex of the pupil, size of school, school programme, quality of the school, kind of instruction, size of class, training of the teacher, salary of the teacher, number of periods of instruction, interests of the pupil, time spent on T.V., and so on. All these variables are of course quantified; as far as sex is concerned one can still discuss whether male should be 1 and female 2, or conversely, though it does not matter. The scales for most of the other variables are at least doubtful, if not nonsensical. Anyhow for a thousand pupils one arrives at a set of 1000-dimensional vectors corresponding to the enumerated variables.

And then it comes! The first vector, the output, must be linearly expressed by the 'explaining' vectors. Of course this cannot be done without remainder; there will be a residue that cannot be 'explained' further, and in practice this residue is quite considerable. No problem; the technique advances; next time more explaining variables will be taken into account to improve the result.

Yet what does this mean, big or small residues? The residue is a vector; what metric is used to measure it? Well, this question can satisfactorily be answered, but that is an aspect that does not matter too much now. Psychometric practice has pursued other paths; objections in principle that strike the one method as well as the other will be delayed for a while. What is actually undertaken is the so-called stepwise regression (sometimes a bit refined). The output vector is projected, according to simple Cartesian metrics upon the first explaining vector, which gives the first approximation. The remainder is

* Cf. p. 142.

projected on the second explaining vector, and so it continues until no significant explanation of the remainder is feasible. Up to this remainder the variability of the output is then represented as a linear combination of the explaining variables.

This method is not too bad if the explaining vectors are not too far from being orthogonal to each other – statistically this means that the mutual dependence of explaining variables is rather weak. The result of the stepwise regression depends on the order in which the variables entered the regression procedure; the more independent the variables are, the less influence the order will exert. But such approximately independent variables do not drop into one's lap. To obtain them, one must know, and intelligently analyse, the instructional system; one has to look out for variables that explain the output in a way more profound than just by statistics. It is an idle hope to believe that if there are enough variables offered, the computer will do the job. Take for instance such variables as size of school, size of class, school programme (that is academic, vocational, general by US standards), salary of teachers. There may be national instructional systems where these variables are strongly dependent on each other, for instance if the more academic schools are also the largest, those with the smallest classes and with the best paid teachers; the variable which enters the regression first gets the lion's share. In other instructional systems these variables may be less or conversely dependent; then, under otherwise equal circumstances, the regression will produce totally different results.

Regression dogmatists look for objective regression models. For instance a so-called causal model: first the pupil should be born, so the parental variables enter the regression first and swallow the lion's share; then there come the variables sex and age, actualized by birth or after many years. Then a school must be chosen for the pupil, so the school variables follow. After the pupil enters school, he gets instruction, which procures the next regression rights to the instruction variables, and finally instruction should stimulate interest, which allows the interest variables to collect the last crumbs under the regression table.

This is called the causal model which seems to definitively solve the problem of rank order in regression. But in fact it just opens the discussion. What is the use of regression analysis, of explaining the variability of the output by means of a number of explaining variables? Only to admire regressional equations – for each national instructional system an entirely different one? Or to be pleased by 'explained' variance and to be sorry about unexplained variance? No, the use should be to improve education by the knowledge acquired with the method. Rather than explaining, the people who apply this method also say 'predicting': predicting the output, if the values of the variables are chosen as such and such. But how can you choose the values of the variables as you wish? Father's and mother's training, father's profession, the number of books at home, the number of brothers and sisters, the sex of the pupil cannot be changed anymore, or can they? School programmes can be influenced to a certain degree, and school and class size too; teacher training and instructional methods are even more flexible, and the easiest to control are the interest variables. What help can the regression equations offer in this? The variables which swallow the lion's share can hardly be influenced; and those which can do not count in the regression. Should the order of regression not be inverted? This is the way regression is applied where it is meaningful, say to agricultural output: the regression starts with those variables that are the cheapest to influence, that is where influencing requires the least expense for a given output. Well, this would be a final rather than a causal model – pragmatism rather than dogmatism.

Would it be of some help? No. The regression model itself is wrong here and it does not matter in which way it is specified. The regression equations are entirely unfit for predicting, and they are so in principle. They have been computed *rebus sic stantibus*, for an exactly given instructional system. For other instructional systems they would come out differently, and they lose their validity as soon as the instructional system is changed. It is utterly naïve to believe that if school size and teachers' salaries are positive factors within an instructional system, increase of school size and salaries would increase the output, or that national instructional output would be enhanced if all children took academic programmes. The regression method has been taken over from biotechnics into education mechanically, with no regard to, or analysis of, the different conditions. Here it is meaningless, because the so-called variables are not freely variable; because changing one variable implies changing others; because changes that are not carefully weighed undermine not only the regression equation but the whole instructional system. For reasons of principle, *static* models such as regression do not match instructional systems that are to be influenced; these require *dynamic* models.

What can you do against the frightening thoughtlessness with which mathematics is applied in instructional technology? How can you prevent new generations for ever being educated to view mathematics as a slot machine that saves you the trouble of thinking – press the button K.R.20 and 'reliability' rolls out?

If a medical researcher compares a new treatment of a disease with the now usual one in order to prove or disprove its superiority, the design of the experiments is based upon considerations that come from scientific knowledge and experience; he treats patients who need the treatment in a way that is meaningful and promises the best results; he makes efforts to control parameters whose variability could weaken the demonstrative force of the experiment, and within the limits of his scientific knowledge he can tell how to do it in the most efficient way. Well, there is much at stake in that area, one is inclined to say. If mathematical statistics had been invented during the prescientific stage of medicine, would doctors have administered little known poisons to patients in order to test statistically the hypotheses that one was more efficient than another? But joking aside, is there indeed so little at stake if experiments of educational technology, the implications of which nobody can tell, are mathematically and statistically trimmed in order to make good for the lack of scientific theory by presenting a scientific looking façade? At least the growth of scientific responsibility in educational technology is at stake.

Perhaps some readers are offended by the application of yardsticks from biotechnics in educational technology. If this is a crime, it should not be put down to me. The horse of biotechnical statistics has lived for a long time in the Trojan stable of education. In good faith the gates were opened to him. It was an honest attempt to increase the credibility of educational experiments, which, however, terminated in superstition. Should we mathematicians be proud that others trust mathematics to be capable of ennobling spurious numerical material, believing its formulae and procedures can make up for scientific defects? I once said elsewhere that the main objective of mathematical education should be to shake the popular faith in mathematics. That part of educational technology which is based on mathematical statistics is one of the areas which need lavish education along these lines.

Testing hypotheses by statistical devices should take place within the framework of a theory; but it is itself no surrogate for a theory; and seldom, if ever, will it instigate the creation of a theory. I will illustrate this statement by a historical example.

Genealogists, cattle breeders and cultivators were from olden times acquainted with the phenomena of heredity; there existed phenomenological explanations in which seeming curiosities like the skipping of generations and the shifting to side-branches played a part. Something like a theory of heredity started statistically – with F. Galton's and K. Pearson's anthropometric and biometric investigations; mathematical instruments like correlation are due to these attempts; 'regression' originally meant the regression from son to father. It was statistics without a fundamental theory, though with a lot of background philosophy, in which terms like 'eugenics' had an important function. Genetics as a science, however, starts with something entirely different – with Mendel's laws, with concepts like genotype and phenotype, dominant and recessive. It continues with genes, mutations, crossing over, chromosomes, ribonucleic acid. This is the way genetics developed, to become a portly science, growing in depth and extent as a theory rather than by the force of statistics, though now and then statistics was allowed to supply contributions. Certainly good old Galton–Pearson statistical biometrics did not die; its youngest offspring do not disavow their noble extraction: there they still test hypotheses of background philosophy rather than of scientific theory – for instance if they allegedly prove by statistical evidence that intelligence is to be ascribed 80% to heredity and only 20% to environment.

Do I ask too much if I confront educational research with biotechnics? In the social sector everything is more difficult than in the natural sciences. But the greater difficulty should not be an argument to take things easier. With superficial applications of mathematical statistics one shirks the problems rather than trying to meet the need for genuine science. Fortunately what I have censured here are abuses of limited importance. As to quantity and quality it is no match for all that is achieved in education, and with a view to education, by practicians and engineers, and which is beyond my censure. The target of my criticism is what despite a lack of scientific character behaves like science.

15. EDUCATIONAL RESEARCH INC.

Several times* I mentioned the I.E.A. (International Association for the Evaluation of Educational Achievement), a group of prominent psychometrists who are engaged in international comparative investigations by means of achievement tests. In the projects** of I.E.A. hundreds of thousands of pupils, tens of thousands of teachers, thousands of principals, hundreds of experts were involved; the results are marked by millions of computer information units, and the expenses by millions of dollars. This is part of the I.E.A. advertising. If in one of the participating countries the achievements of pupils of a particular age in a particular subject, as measured by international yardsticks, appear to be below contempt, I.E.A. always finds the press, radio, and television ready to trumpet it forth. Sure as fate, if an expert, or even just somebody with a bit of common sense, takes a closer look at the affair, the discovery ensues that what is bad is not the incriminated instruction but the incriminating research on instruction.

Officially I.E.A. takes exception to these advertising practices. They do not organize international competitions, they say. In their last reports they even avoid the expression 'mean scores' above the tables of pupils' achievements in various countries; it is now "difficulty index". I.E.A. rather wishes to consider the national instructional systems as global experiments in order to analyse them comparatively, determine the influence of all kind of input parameters on pupils' and schools' achievements, and in this way provide educational politicians and administrators with material for decisions on educational reform.

A quite reasonable idea, if reasonably put into practice – the world as a gigantic educational laboratory! We already reviewed the gigantic numbers. The computer can digest all of them, from the hundreds of thousands of pupils to the millions of dollars.

From the start, I.E.A. assumed as an axiom that the same tools by which pupils' achievements and their dependence on parameters are measured *within* an educational system suffice to carry out comparative investigations

* See pp. 142, 152.

** They started with mathematics (1964). In the 'second phase' they investigated 'Sciences', 'Literature', 'Reading Comprehension', 'English' and 'French' (as foreign languages), and 'Civic Education'; reports were published on 'Mathematics' and the first three subjects of the 'second phase'. – Since this was written, more reports have been published.

between such systems. The question whether it is really so simple has not even been discussed seriously; if anyone dared to ask it, he was immediately outvoted. In this way, during ten years of activity, I.E.A. did not, and never tried to:

> develop internationally valid test instruments;
> define internationally comparable populations of pupils;
> define internationally comparable input parameters;
> develop methods to produce reliable statistical material;
> develop methods to meaningfully process statistical material;
> coordinate the collaboration of national centres.

These deficiencies are witnessed by the results: statistical data which as far as they can be checked are wrong and as far as they are interrelated are contradictory, witness thoughtlessness in collecting and processing the material. Meaningless mathematical rituals of processing witness lack of theoretical understanding. Groups of pupils, and even whole population samples were tested in subjects in which they had never had any instruction – and this is called *evaluation of achievement*. Populations and variables were defined as though an effort had been made to do it as awkwardly as possible and to be misunderstood as much as possible. National centres, teachers and students were given impossible questionnaires to fill in. In order to 'explain' a few percents of variance, variables were defined which are pure artefacts. The only internationally valid variable which proved capable of definition was the sex of the pupil. I.E.A. set out to compare reading comprehension internationally without even considering how such tests should have been translated if the test results were to be comparable. The collaborators at the periphery were given full play without any previous check on their abilities or supervision of their achievements. And the main thing: it was believed that the computer could ennoble worthless material if only it was bulky enough.

How could it go as far? I.E.A. are a group of people who know or take into consideration, concerning instruction, only that it can be tested. In the national field the power of evaluation is mitigated by instruction, innovation, development of, and research on, instruction; all these restrictions are lacking in the international field. There full play was given to evaluation for evaluation's sake, which was processed by means of mathematics for mathematics' sake.

At no commanding place did I.E.A. admit expertise: there were no experts in the relevant subjects, nor anyone who knew more about instruction than testing; and the national centres did not make good for this lack. There people were not even acquainted with the bureaucratic aspects of their own national instruction.

If I.E.A. as a company of evaluators, believed themselves to be entitled and competent to carry on international instructional research, how did they perform it? For subordinate tasks they attracted experts or at least people who were considered or defined to be experts. And this is what they called research: three or four times a year they met at conferences, filled each other with enthusiasm for future projects and took meaningless resolutions at the round table, which were to be put into practice at home by secretaries, statistical analysts and computers. What is the result? A meaningless chaos of numbers, which is not good for anything other than being published after having had the usual sauce poured over. Errors – who would notice them – the computer, the statistical analyst or the secretary? In order to notice them, one should know a little bit about instruction, shouldn't one? No, there are errors that strike every proofreader. In two of the reports efforts, at least, were made to gloss them over.

Big business in economy and science is a problem. Errors of subordinates are paid in the one case by financial losses, in the other by injured reputations. Each one of the I.E.A. fellows has a reputation to lose. Does it make no difference to them whether anyone commits blunders or obscures deficiencies on their behalf? In the natural sciences such big research business works quite well. The master's eye cannot see everything, but where it sees, it does so critically. In such business there are people who bear responsibilities and are able to do so, people who can survey the whole, who know whom they hire and with whom they cooperate, who read and understand what they undersign, and first of all there exist norms and the consciousness of norms. If, however, in spite of all, here and there disaster strikes, it can cost some grand man his reputation.

How could the I.E.A. people be as naïve as to believe you can do research with secretaries, statistical analysts and computers? Well, if something goes wrong, one can always excuse oneself by the size of the project, by the difficulties of a first attempt and by the complexity of education as a subject for research, and if one has done the best one could, these are indeed valid excuses. But who did his best?

Yet such an undertaking is not too risky. It is quite improbable that somebody with even the slightest degree of competence would look at the I.E.A. studies; if he hears about them he will dispose of them as an aberration, and whenever he opens such a report, he will stumble over the nonsense and close it as fast as he can. This is the way in which the I.E.A. carries the day to sound their own trumpet and have their reports reviewed by their equals. These reviewers have no idea that something could be wrong, no doubts about the validity of the statistical material and its processing – a frightening spectacle.

In an article of sixty printed pages* I analysed three of the I.E.A. reports. What I found was the most pretentious bungle I ever saw, wrong in all details and as a whole. Certainly with hindsight many will say that sixty pages were too great an honour, and that it were too cheap a pleasure to criticise such a shallow piece of work to the core. Cheap – yes, I never had so little trouble to fill sixty pages since these reports abound with mistakes. A pleasure – no. A bitter duty. But it was no Herculean task either. I took it easy, I did just what I could do with my forces. A bit of weeding where roots and branches should be extirpated. Will it be of some use? I do not have many illusions. But perhaps for a few people it will be of some use to know there are limits which are not to be transgressed without risk and there are no absolute exemptions from punishment.

16. A SOCIOPSYCHOLOGICAL VIEW

How could all this develop and never be resisted? How to explain the tremendous success of the *Taxonomy*? How the fashion of instructional objectives, the rage of atomization, the cult of packaging, the rituals? How could educationists who have nothing to offer but empty boxes and slogans get settled in the educational systems, first in the United States, but in an increasing density in Europe too? Empty vessels make the most noise according to a proverb. But why should this be so in educational science and not in other areas? Because education has not yet got a science?

Instructional research is a recent adventure. Two millennia or two centuries ago sciences which now boast authority did not fare any better. All sciences knew the era of hollow schemes.

* H. Freudenthal, *Educational Studies in Mathematics* 6, 127–186.

Right, but the science of education is a different case.

Firstly, the sciences of two millenia or two centuries ago that were not so much science, had not so much social importance either. The science of education, whether good or bad, is a socially relevant concern whether you like it or not.

Second, in educational research there is a tremendous lack of consciousness of quality and criticism. Eminent people are patient with charlatanism as though it were science and too much is covered with the cloak of charity.

How could all this develop? By hindsight one can understand why *general* didactics acquired authority. There was, and still is, hardly any subject didactics. Magistrates and politicians are not interested in the subjects of instruction, they like and grasp generalities better. About 1960 a historically unique wave carried mathematics into the view of magistrates and the public. Here and there this wave carried mathematics instruction into innovation; and though charlatans soon eagerly seized the opportunity, I would believe that, first of all subjects, mathematics will develop a science of education.

In the instructional field one feels a genuine need for instructional theory, in particular among future teachers and those who have the task of training these teachers – hunger and thirst that ask to be satisfied. Pedagogics alone is not sufficient, as little as historical and philosophical reflections on instruction are. Preparing a student for his future practice in school and classroom does not seem to be enough academic training; a science it must be, which is the only thing one can lecture *ex cathedra*, palpable stuff which can be divided into chapters and sections, which can be adorned by footnotes, and which radiates the shining light of science. In the course of the last quarter of a century this urgent need has been redressed. First in the United States so much educational science has been piled up that students can be crammed with it, four years or even longer, though the quality does not match the quantity.

There are thousands of professors of educational science. How many are still able, after all the indoctrination, to view critically what they teach students? A great many, I think. But how many among those who know better, would dare to cut the branch on which they are sitting, and thus deprive millions of teachers of their last and unique security? So the fly-wheel turns around and does not stop, and the machine produces ever new generations of researchers on instruction who pursue even more new and attractive packing boxes.

How to explain the triumphal march of something like the *Taxonomy*? It would be worth investigating thoroughly, but meanwhile hypotheses are allowed. Many a one is not satisfied by practicing just a technique; to them a *scientific* or *philosophic* justification of their action – or both combined – is a real need, the appeasement of which can sometimes lead to comic or tragic aberration. One who is not interested in philosophy, looks out for science, as a moral rather than a rational support, a straw as a life-line if nothing else is available. Dividing is a popular activity as a first approach to science – all science started this way. Dividing – the great wisdom which the *Taxonomy* had on stock.

Were there competing systems other than the *Taxonomy*? Were there reasons why the *Taxonomy* carried the day, or was it by mere accident? However it may be, there is nothing as successful as success. If a system is often enough cited, one cannot but cite it too, and as soon as a certain percentage – say 5% or 10% have accepted it, one could miss the bus, one could make a fool of oneself if one does not accept it or one asserts it is not acceptable. From 10% to 100% is a small step.

The need is undeniable, the need for help, for a straw if there is no better thing available. Teachers wish to know once and for all how to organize their lessons, teacher trainers are in urgent need of subject matter they can expound to their students by chapters, sections, and subsections, textbook authors urgently need patterns to design their production. That is the rationale of the packing material such as it is fabricated and sold. And the fear of missing the bandwaggon is the secret motivation of those who buy this material. This is the way fashions are created and sweep across the world – not only in educational technology. But why does this mentality have so many more awkward consequences in education than elsewhere? Well, I think, because of the lack of standards of quality.

Do the expedients help, are the gaps being filled, do the clients find the help they expect? The answer is: yes. Whether you like it or not, it is: yes. I called it the placebo effect. A teacher who never reflected upon his teaching is compelled to think as soon as he must arrange the contents of the next lesson according to the *Taxonony* or some other pattern; the teacher trainer feels safer if he can hang up his relevant but unschematized instruction on an – irrelevant – scheme; for the textbook author who formulates objectives of instruction it is perhaps the first time he asks himself: 'Is the pupil expected to *know* this or to be able to *perform* this?'

As far as this educational science is effective, it is placebo effective. Are we obliged to put up with the inevitable or should we say that it disgusts us? Are we demagogues, or is it our task to deal with our fellow men as reasonable and critical creatures? Up to quite recent times medicine hardly knew anything else but placebo effects, at least if its devices of the past are judged according to the present state of science. We cannot close our shop of the science of education all of a sudden nor keep it closed until we have to offer more sensible goods.

Quite right. But think about the consequences. Charlatanism, and no defence against it.

17. THE END OF THE MATTER

The title of this chapter contained the words "science of education", and in its first lines I asked whether this would not be a talk on the empty set. Indeed after the first chapter it was clear that I would exact high demands from what I would like to call science. After the chapter that is now drawing to a close it may also be clear what I aimed at when I formulated those demands: educating consciousness of quality and criticism.

Against the complaint of general educationists that there is no education to match their science I claim there is no science to match education. Not yet! I was able to assert this with so much stress and so circumstantially because I am optimistic. I am convinced that educational science is possible only because I know that what behaves so, is no science.

No, that is not the whole truth. There are, in my view, also positive indications as to the possibility of a science of education – no more than indications, vague outlines. If I had got more, I would write a 'Science of Mathematical Education' rather than a preface to it.

If anyone wants to learn from history – for instance from the development of the natural sciences – he will understand that a science does not start with general but with fundamental problems. General teaching theory is no science at all but an empty form the filling of which is a phantom. There is no instruction without content and no science of instruction without content. The science of instruction can only start with the science of a particular form of instruction. There one can forge the first tools, which are still lacking, and with these tools others.

I have good reasons for believing that the first area in which a science of instruction will develop is mathematics, though I cannot yet display these reasons in the present chapter. What I called indications and outlines is so closely connected with mathematics that I am inclined to guess it is proper to mathematics and not transferable. I delay this.

Among the indications, however, there is one that I think is more universal, and this is the reason why I mention it here, albeit shortly. So before this seemingly very negative chapter closes, some positive sounds will be heard, hesitating but hopeful sounds.

Didactics has something to do with learning, and the inevitable complement of the theory of teaching is the theory of learning. Would it be too bad an idea if didacticians – general didacticians and those in particular subjects – would start investigating learning? Is it really so mad an idea that anyone who utters it is given a cold shoulder?

Do not reply that investigating learning is a job for psychologists of learning. I do not propose didacticians to occupy themselves with the psychology of learning. It is simply learning they should study. Observing learning processes – spontaneous and guided ones. Do not object either that learning processes take place inside the learner and therefore are not observable. This is again such a nonsensical commonplace. We investigate what happens inside the Sun and inside atoms, don't we? A teacher who watches his pupils, has witnessed many learning processes and he knows that he has. Is there not a lot to be observed when people learn – others and the observer himself? Only it is so difficult to organise the wealth of observations, to describe, to evaluate them: but not until we consciously set out to observe learning processes can we create the means to organise, describe and evaluate them.

One has compared groups of children of different ages with each other, but this is no opportunity to learn about learning processes. One has investigated a fixed group at two or more instants and in this way observed the learning process of an average child or, if you prefer so, that of a hundred-headed monster. Let us try it once with the learning processes of individuals, in order to distinguish their most essential elements: the discontinuities. In the average learning process the discontinuities are extinguished; in this flattened out process all essentialities have disappeared, but only by coming to grips with its discontinuities will we get insight into the learning process.

Following a child in its development is certainly the best way to observe learning processes. There are investigations with titles like 'The Growth of the Child's Mind'. What is really shown and compared there are groups of children of different ages. It is true that one gets an impression of the exterior growth of a fir by putting firs of different ages in a row; but a fir interests us only as far as it is a fir; in the development of a human being it can be important to know that it is this being and no other. But even in another respect the growth concept of this literature is mistaken. Only a superficial observer will restrict growth of a plant to its height as a function of time; scientifically growth can be understood as a biological process. For a similar understanding of growth processes of the mind we still lack all preconditions; one of them would be observation and analysis of learning processes.

This at any rate is my – first – thesis: that *what matters in learning processes are the discontinuities*. I have proposed it several times before and illustrated it by examples; in the next chapter I will resume it.

Observing learning processes is no job for psychologists. In the laboratory there is little chance to observe anything but continuity, and the psychologist designs his experiments conscious of this restriction. Furthermore, the learning processes instruction is interested in take place in a class room or a group rather than in a laboratory.

Discontinuities can only be discovered in continuous observation, but even for teachers and educational researchers it will not be easy to observe these essentials in the learning process – the discontinuities. Observing must be learned, it is a selective activity, one has to understand what it is worth looking for. Fortunately observing can be taught by drawing others' attention to what one has discerned by oneself. Observing learning processes could be a task for those who wish to investigate instruction. But they should not spurn going into the classroom and they should have studied a subject matter in order to understand what is taught and learned there.

Such empiricism is the soil from which the science of instruction can grow. General didactics that aspires to more than technology and bureaucracy can only be developed if one starts in a particular subject, with the didactics of that subject. Listen to a good subject didactician. He can tell you infinitely more about instruction than the general didactician if only he does not bend his knees as soon as he learns the jargon of the general educational technologists and their masters.

Observing learning processes, yes. But this is not enough. Intelligent observation I called it. Not registering as a recorder. Before observing one should know what to observe, but one should not know it too precisely since then one only sees what one wants to see. How can we know what to pay attention to? On the strength of earlier observations, more precisely on the strength of what has been learned from analysing earlier observations. How then can we analyse our observations, where should we look for the tools needed? If there is nobody to hand them out to you, you have to create them yourself. But how to do it? After models. But who provides us with the models?

It looks like an inextricable tangle, a labyrinth of vicious circles. How to find one's way out? Or should it be blown up? Is it really so hopeless?

One does not begin with a *tabula rasa* indeed. Everybody has at some time observed learning processes, of his own, of his friends, of his parents, brothers, sisters, children, pupils. There are rich experiences in this area but they are difficult to communicate, to others but also to oneself. There is a lack of the tools of expression and organisation with which to speak about and process experiences. Well, for once one should start creating them. This I will do, this and no more. If all that results from these attempts proves to be wrong, the discussion that uncovers the errors will show the way to new approaches.

I do not claim that what I say here is world-shattering or even original. The idea of observing learning processes, the postulate of doing so consciously and systematically can by no means be new. But if one would reply that the idea has outgrown the stage of a mere postulate – and I expect these censures – I feel obliged to defend myself against this reply right now. Certainly there exists something, here and there, but how should I find it out? I am not digging for treasures. If there is really something around such as I am looking for, it is buried under the piles of what calls itself science of education. I know one book – indeed an excellent one – that bears the mathematical learning process in its title, and which contains exactly one chapter on this subject – indeed an excellent one – and in this chapter three paragraphs – excellent ones – where the mathematical learning process is touched on. Even this book cannot tell more about learning processes. The literature on learning processes, other than mathematical ones, is not my most direct concern. It might yield more lavishness. I do not know it but it amazed me when I heard from somebody who had made systematic searches that hardly anything is known about the childhood development of the syntax of sentential structure, and nothing about the processes of learning these structures.

I enter a *terra incognita*. I might go astray from the very start onwards, or progress only a few steps, but for once one should venture it.

Why do I wish to observe learning processes? Not just in order to know how they go on. There are even more trivial reasons – already in order to know what under certain circumstances may be worth learning. We do not know much more about it than the prejudices of school programmes and textbook authors. I will expound later on how to overcome these prejudices, in order to reshape the supply of subject matter as to meaningfulness and wealth.

Moreover I wish to observe learning processes to improve my understanding of mathematics. Do I mean my own learning processes and those of my equals? No, just those of children. Only one who does not know mathematics can suspect this is a joke or a romantic apotheosis of a child's mind.

Learning processes distinguish themselves from what psychologists call learning by the fact that they are always also teaching processes. Learning processes do not go on spontaneously, they are influenced; and this influence should certainly not be eliminated in the experiments since it is an essential feature of learning processes as they occur in the real world. Of course one should account for the influences. But this is difficult too, because much of this does not happen consciously – I add: fortunately.

Observing learning processes should in my view be the nucleus of the didactics in teacher training. But how can this be realized as admittedly we do not possess any theory of learning processes? Just for this reason it should, I would say. Since we have not got hold of even a little piece of theory, we are not able to train the future teachers *theoretically* in observing and analysing learning processes. We shall do it as the plumber who shows his apprentice, rather than telling him, how to repair a tap. Properly speaking it is an advantage that there is no theory of learning processes. By this circumstance the student is spared being taught a ready-made pedagogy instead of that to be made. Just as mathematics to be made is preferable to ready-made mathematics as a teaching subject, it would not be too bad an idea to replace the pedagogics taught *ex cathedra* with one that is lived through and created by pupils, teachers and trainers in a common learning process.

Of course it already happens in teacher training that trainers take the trained ones to the places where the learning processes go on, that they observe them together and discuss the observed facts and the facts of observing. It happens though, I am afraid, infrequently and not consciously enough. In a teacher training department I had closer contact with, it struck me that students were trained and stimulated to observe teaching rather than learning processes, to observe (and criticise) teachers rather than pupils. Future actors learn from observing skilled actors, don't they?

Observing learning processes is in my conception the source of knowledge about teaching as a subject matter to be taught and to be investigated – in the seminar where the foundations are laid when the future teachers are educated to observe and discuss their observations, in service where the results of this learning are put to use and developed, in further training where the thread of training is resumed and spun.

Observing learning processes is a play and counterplay of activities that influence each other intimately. Not only the others are observed, but one observes oneself in the learning process which one undergoes as a teacher, and under the impact of the reaction of the observation on the observed process one stimulates the pupils to become conscious of learning processes. Learning process, observation and analysis influence and reinforce each other. Observing supports learning, the becoming conscious of the observation in the analysis serves to improve the technique of observing. Later on when I can exemplify them by mathematical instances I must discuss anew the levels in the learning process. The levels as I have explained them are to each other as activity and meta-activity. Observing an activity may be a higher level than the activity itself, and analysis of observation again higher. The more intensive the interplay is the stronger the inclination to integration will grow; observing and analysing become implicit to the activity, the activity gets algorithmised and mechanised, it does not need any more the conscious check and control by observation and analysis, although if need be they can be brought back to consciousness again.

So all ends in routine. Teaching can go the same way. But the learner can counteract, he can influence the teaching process by his learning process, at least if he is allowed to.

Let us finish the chapter. The last pages were vague outlines of a theory. They rest on observations of mathematical learning processes; the tools of analysis came from mathematics itself.

CHAPTER IV

A SCIENCE OF MATHEMATICAL EDUCATION

ABSTRACT. There is no science of mathematical education. Not yet. Again, there are many marvellous activities – educational engineering in mathematics – sources from which a science of mathematical education may spring. But not yet, not in the present chapter, which is a mere collection of suggestions, supported and illustrated by experience.

Team work, in particular in curriculum development, may be such a source. In order to communicate, a team must create a working language. A language that covers some content can be not only a carrier, but even a source of science. Learning situations, and in particular open ones, learning processes, their levels, and their discontinuities are worth observing and analysing, in order to build them into theories. I try to show some features of *language as a vehicle of research* and of *motivation* as a motor in the learning process – motivation *by discontinuites in the learning process*, motivation *by goals*, motivation *by make-up*.

In a number of sections the author pursues the origin of general ideas, concepts, judgments and attitudes in the learning process, whether they are attained in a continuous process, by *comprehension*, that is by generalising from numerous examples, as is the common opinion, or by *apprehension*, that is, by grasping directly the general situation, which is my thesis. One way of apprehending creation of general mental objects is the *paradigm*: rather than a multitude – one example, which evokes the general idea. A series of examples of apprehending by paradigms is shown, and abortive quests for paradigms and discontinuities in learning processes are revealed. This, in particular, concerns the number concept. Another kind of apprehension is direct grasp of generality, illustrated by an apprehending approach to algebra, not unlike that of the school of Davydov, but on a higher level of learning.

I then turn to *levels of language*, illustrated by several learning sequences: the *ostensive* level, the level of *relative language*, the level of *conventional* variables, the *functional* level.

Another theme, extending over a number of sections, is *change of perspective*, again illustrated by many examples related to *grasping the context*, *logical conversion*, the switch from *global to local* perspective, and the converse, from *qualitative to quantitative* perspective, and the converse. *Grasping the context* is resumed in the section on *probability*, and many examples of *change of perspective* appear in the section on geometry entitled by the phrase "I see it so" by which young children justify their geometric statements.

The book closes with an example of what has been postulated on several occasions as a precondition of educational research in mathematics: a piece of *didactical phenomenology of mathematical concepts*.

1. INTRODUCTION

I anticipate the conclusion which will astonish nobody: a science of mathematical education does not – yet – exist. My preface is one to the void set. But it is not void of content. Like an index, I could enumerate words that I modelled in the course of the years – some of them might prove useful in the long run. I promised indications and outlines. This is not too high a pretence, and if anyone is disappointed at the end of the chapter, at least I have not deceived him. But I do not want to abuse this as an excuse for a chapter with no content. I will expound concepts and methods – most of them not at all new – which I think can be of some use in building a science of mathematical education.

2. THE ART OF MATHEMATICS TEACHING

If I come to the conclusion there does not – yet – exist a science of mathematical education, the reader already knows that I do not wish to deprecate what happens in that field – only it is no science in my terminology. Indeed there exists first of all mathematical education itself, and beyond and around it much of undisputedly high value goes on. If you brought together in one schedule all that happens in the world in congresses, conferences, workshops and working groups, sight and hearing would fail you. Much is published that deserves attention; material is produced; discussions are carried on; there is training and further training; and all hapens on a level of activity which is itself hardly, if at all, subjected to objective and analytical consideration. As general didacticians are not much interested in practical activities, they are rarely seen in these circles, so most of these meetings are spared the pseudo-scientific level-raising by the armchair fancies of general didactics. For reasons I explained earlier, mathematics is the one subject that has not completely escaped their grasp, unfortunately!

This altogether impressive activity – I restrict my statements now to mathematics – always goes on at the lowest level, on the level of an unconcerned activity, and if the influence of level-raising is at all expressed in the results, its source remains hidden and therefore ineffective. This characterisation includes even the most distinguished results of curriculum development. They are either most refined elaborations of a preconceived mathematical plan which seems to be uninfluenced by didactical reflexions or heavily fraught with didactics, but then of a – sometimes enchanting – naïveté. If there is more behind this naïveté, it is top secret and inaccessible.

The naïveté of staying at the lowest level is both reassuring and frightening; it is reconciling and becomes irritating as soon as one is convinced of the level structure of learning processes: how can the professional promoters of learning processes resist the impulse to climb to higher levels in their own learning? Or perhaps, how can they feign staying at the lowest level by reducing all to it? Or is this, as I explained earlier on, just a habit in mathematics where notwithstanding the wealth of levels the pressure to objectify extinguishes the traces of levels in the learning process?

Anyhow the result is – at least as it appears on the outside – paddling forth on the same level; and this pattern is imitated in most of the activities at the periphery, in the classroom, in the short and long term, in the accidental and fundamental preparations for activity in the classroom.

I would call it – forgive me – the plumber's mentality; if I contrast the plumber with the technologist or even with the physicist, it would not mean contempt of the craftsman. On the contrary, there is every reason to admire his instinctive purposiveness in action. Yet in the techniques of the natural sciences there exist along with plumbers also technologists and physicists, to which little corresponds in the areas we are entering now.

3. TEAM WORK AS A SOURCE OF RESEARCH

How can we change this? Up to about seven years ago I pursued my theoretical activities in mathematical education as an individual, though here and there, as it happened, I measured the strength of my arguments with those of others in oral or written discussions. Never satisfied with this situation, I lacked the opportunity or the force to change it. How fundamentally the team differs from the individual, I did not properly understand until the IOWO* came into being. Indeed I believe that a science of mathematical education can only develop in a team. I can rationally argue this belief that grew in the practice of the team against the seeming counterexamples of

* Instituut voor de Ontwikkeling van het Wiskunde Onderwijs = Institute for the Development of Mathematical Education

the history of natural sciences. Although today teamwork dominates there, did not individuals, up to quite recently, set the fashion in natural science? Why shouldn't the social sciences be allowed to start the same way? Well, I think it just took millenia to develop natural science because no teams existed; would we prefer or be allowed to wait for millenia until a science of education arises? Yet even in natural sciences there always existed some collaboration in schools, though the master-pupil relation was an obstacle to the forming of real teams. Of course there were lines of communication and tradition along which research was continued. To make this possible it was essential that along with the research a language was developed in which research could be communicated. This alone made transmission feasible without direct contact in schools or teams.

What distinguishes the social from the natural sciences today is the lack of plain linguistic tools. For this reason knowledge often remains the untransferable property of its discoverer and only for a short time accessible even to himself if he was not able to lay it down adequately.

Do not object that there is so much written and printed today where knowledge is laid down. In so far as the expression is lucid, it is numerical material of doubtful relevance; for instance if two methods of teaching are compared, no attempt is made to *describe* the two methods comparatively beyond what is expressed in mathematical formulae. And where an attempt is made to express more essential features, the eventual version uses a language that is already so far detached from the intended content that adequate expression becomes impossible and there is no expression of content any more.

In the social sciences the lack of exact linguistic tools is an impediment to continuity. This can be redressed by forming teams. In the team, lucid expression can more easily be dispensed with. In close contact one can communicate in a language of gestures like the plumber who teaches his apprentice. So it happens in working groups, at conferences and congresses. Orally one understands one another better, or at least one believes so, because all that is said can be explained once more.

Writing books at the desk – I never refrained from it – is the method of the individual worker, a method which functions decently in sciences that can muster a considerable stock of knowledge, to be edited anew and expanded. Here you can be sure that what is written will hit the mark since it is expressed adequately in a lucid language. Yet with only a diminutive stock of organised experience and knowledge available it is quite natural that gaps are filled from the stock of background philosophy, and if there are not even any tools of lucid expression available, it becomes philosophy in the bad sense.

This is an argument in favour of the team, the professional workshop; or at least it should be so. It depends on how the team is interpreted. It can also go wrong with teams, as examples show.

The team I have in view is one of engineers rather than of people who claim or believe they carry on pure research, and the activity of this team – I speak of my IOWO experiences – is curriculum development, a task that is as it were created for team work. How far can such a team nourish more fundamental developments?

At any rate a team can favour the development of a technical language, and if its task is as practical as that of IOWO, it might be a language that is rich with content. But this does not happen automatically and there have been teams that never reached this point. One can be stuck so firmly in acting that verbal accounting is neglected between like-minded members of the team – a communication failure that can be prevented and redressed. In the team of practicians there is a need for theoreticians, but then theoreticians so closely connected with practice that their words are not spoken into the winds.

The theory of instruction still lacks words, at least if only words rich in content are counted. In a team, a technical language can develop, perhaps preponderantly or exclusively for internal use. Moreover, in the team, less explicit terms can be well-defined in their use, operationally. What we at IOWO mean by expressions like 'project', 'theme' or 'beacon', outsiders can at most guess, but they cannot even do this if we speak of 'Visiting grandma' or 'seesaw'. It is good fortune if the team creates linguistic tools of more fundamental value.

Later on I shall deal with the role of language. Meanwhile I will explain further the influence of teamwork on the scientific development of didactics. The closeness of practice saves the team from the fate of a Pentecostal Community which has settled on a *Zauberberg* – even mathematical didactics was not spared such experiences. But while considering practice – plumbing – fundamentals should not be lost sight of. I mention this here in order to stress the 'yet' in my statement that there does not yet exist a science of mathematical education.

If curriculum development is planned in an era of innovation, we think it is mistaken, at least for practical reasons, to approach the school where the curriculum is to be tried out with teaching matter that has been developed long beforehand within a heavily programmed structure (for instance by means of a search for objectives of instruction and initial conditions). However well it might be prepared, it is too rigid a system. It is pretty certain that a considerable part of the teaching matter prepared will not function properly; and even if this were only a small part, it can be a source of confusion in the try-out school, and because of the logical enchainment of mathematical subject matter a menace to the functioning of otherwise serviceable fragments. Separating design and realisation is detrimental: it is not only *objectively* wrong since the feedback path becomes unnecessarily long; but also *subjectively* since intermediaries lack the information about learning processes that can promote their own learning processes.

In curriculum development the unity in the cycle of design, preparation and further training of the teacher, guidance in the classroom and evaluation, back to revision of the design, is a more promising strategy; it is the same man who designs the teaching matter, who prepares and guides the teacher's performance in the classroom, and who evaluates the performance and the design, in which activities he himself is accompanied and observed by a team. This serves to guarantee that the intentions behind the design are asserted, that malfunctioning teaching matter is immediately repaired and tried out anew in a temporarily shifted cycle in a parallel class.

Flexibility is a practical advantage of this organisation, at least if one is beware of misusing it. If the defects of the design can so readily be repaired one may become prone to experiment. The team which accompanies the designer should be on their guard against experiments for experiments' sake.

I did not explain this organisation because of its practical consequences. What I think is of great value and can bring us a step nearer to scientific research into teaching is the permanent contact with the learning processes, the opportunity, or rather the built-in constraint to observe learning processes – one's own, those of the teachers, of the pupils and of the collaborators. Can and should this be done only unconsciously? I think one should do all one can to make it as explicit as possible, and this includes drawing the attention of participants to their learning processes as long as they are not yet trained to discover them by their own means. (In fact I have observed that good teachers call their pupils' attention to some of their learning processes though they are not aware of doing so.) Observing learning and teaching activities presupposes training – we always notice it – and it is a particularly delicate affair if it regards one's own activities; this consciousness must not be bought at the price of frustrating one's spontaneity; one should not come to the situation of the man who, asked whether, when in bed, he keeps his long beard under or above the cover, cannot fall asleep any more. One should start by observing the learning processes of others. This, too, is difficult if the learning process takes place in a group one participates in – properly speaking this is the normal situation, whether one teaches another, plays with a child, has a walk with him, or answers his questions. Nevertheless a didactically trained person should in a learning situation manage to rise above this situation. He should have learned it in his own training, I would say. But to guarantee this one should first of all take care that the trainer is able to do it and that he is conscious of it.

4. THE THEORETICIAN IN THE TEAM

I cannot, however, say that up to now our team advanced more than a few steps in this direction. So far we have made only a few experiments in the systematic observation of learning processes. Mostly we just catch what the wind brings us. We make experiments to stimulate and initiate learning processes rather than to describe them, though we do not spurn observing those that take place. At present I could propose for every age a series of themes which would be highly appropriate for the method of observing learning processes, but I would not venture to try them nor propose them to others to have them tried. What we lack indeed is the ability – not the readiness – to be struck by what is not striking, to find our observations worth analysing, and in *need* of analysing. For a short time only did we work together as a team; there is still much to be learned – in particular, to train each other in capacities none of us can reasonably describe.

In this play the part of the theoretician in the team is not to bring along ready-made theories. It has been our experience that they do not take roots. Even theories, such as Gal'perin's and those of his school, are already so far detached from the experiments and experiences they ought to organize that the practician can no longer establish the connection with his own experience;

meaningless use of terms like 'interiorisation' and 'basis of orientation' then leads to what I have several times called banalising operationalisation. What the theoretician in the team should be able to do on the ground of his background knowledge is to react to the phenomena in the field, connecting them, placing them into larger frames without appealing to, let alone, settling on, pre-established theories. For instance, he should be able to recognize common elements in subject matter or presentation as a signal that promises success or failure even when no theory exists that in a certain situation allows the deduction of this result. An example to illustrate this: In the first grade composite additions and subtractions are put into a 'comic-strip': a bus with ... persons, boarded by ... more persons at the first stop, left by ... persons at the second stop, and so on, is pictured at every particular stop, and with the addends and subtrahends expressed by arrows with numbers. An unexpected difficulty arises: in order to be able to grasp this succession of pictures as a story, many children have this succession enacted ever anew from the start: if they know the occupation of the bus after the n-th stop, they repeat the calculation from the start onwards to obtain the occupation after the $(n + 1)$-th stop. It looks absurd but it ceases to be so if it is connected to similar, not absurd-looking, phenomena at different ages, for instance difficulties with stepwise procedures in arithmetic $(63 + 24 = (60 + 20) + (3 + 4))$, where the calculator 'forgets' what has resulted after the previous step as soon as he turns to the new step. From such connections one should learn that there are more fundamental abilities to be trained here than only composite additions and subtractions. I called it the tension between the local and the global view.

First of all, however, the theoretician should be the conscience of the team by watching its goals even if they have not been made explicit and were only formulated as a result of watchfulness and as a means of warning. In particular I mean formal goals which express a background philosophy. An example: subject matter designs, even projects, show that the better they are and the more often they have been revised, the sharper the signs of conscious structuration; where open learning situations were intended, all is eventually regulated in all details; in particular, rich content has finally yielded to overstressing formal features. The theoretician should notice and signal such deviations from the original intentions.

5. THE LEARNING SITUATION AS A SOURCE OF RESEARCH

In the bosom of the family, learning processes must often go on unnoticed; rarely will adults seize the opportunity to observe them. Adults, however, who dare to do so, lack the correcting supervision of the team; on the other hand they can see the learning processes in a developmental connection which can suggest unexpected corrections of interpretation, as I will illustrate by examples. Caution should be observed in applying such experiences to instruction because the learning situation at home is less of a teaching situation than that in the classroom; but fundamentally they can contribute much to understanding.

In the classroom, continuity of observation is lacking but as learning happens less spontaneously, the attention can more intentionally be directed towards observing learning processes. It depends on the instruction whether the learning processes take place in a way that they are observable. Instruction regulated in a traditional fashion will not yield much information respecting learning processes. The urgent endeavour of a child to take the floor may be an expression of the joy about a discovery; it is not unusual (and it can be justified in each case according to its merits) if the teacher disregards these urgent demands and yields the floor to more bashful children. To an even higher degree the subject matter itself can hamper the explicitation of learning processes by its content and structure. Most often, indeed, the subject matter is structured with a view to a continuous development of abilities. The big steps, for instance, the constitution of the concept of fraction, are imposed while being accompanied by palliating pseudo motivations, and then the continuous process of training starts.

From class conversation up to free exploration there are many shades of the open learning situation in which learning processes are visible and observable. The most beautiful example of an open learning situation I ever saw was a lesson in a 3rd grade of a school in Paris, which is taken care of by Mrs Douady of the IREM of Paris.

The children had pursued quite a lot of geometry in the square lattice before, and now they were given the assignment to cut from a sheet of coloured art paper at least 10 and at most 20 congruent rhombuses such that "little" was wasted. (In fact the assignment was formulated in a more concrete way; the rhombuses were parts of clowns' dress.) The teacher made sure whether the children had understood the words ‘at least’ and ‘at most’; one pupil asked a question, and when one group demanded squared paper (square centimeters), the others fetched it too. Then they worked in groups, and nobody intervened. They were active at all levels one would imagine. One pupil, who had no companion, calculated the area of the coloured sheet; it was 608 cm^2, which he divided by 20. He knew the formula for the area of a rhombus and put the product of the diagonals at 60 cm^2. He then tried diagonal pairs (2,30), (3,20), (4,15) and so on, but did not get enough on the sheet, since, moreover, he had the rhombuses radiating from one corner. All others took a rhombus as they thought fit; the majority constructed it on the squared paper, with lattice points as corners. Many cut it out, put it repeatedly upon the coloured sheet and drew around it; the clever pupils simply drew sequences of rhombuses side by side on the squared paper. The first group laid the rhombuses first along the lower edge of the coloured sheet and then along the left edge, which yielded an irregular and less economic covering. The others, who worked on the squared paper, found regular coverings; in a few, the vision of uninterrupted straight lines broke through. The weakest pupils had left blank spaces between the rhombuses. One group that had taken squares as rhombuses, suddenly started correcting them.

At the end each group sent a spokesman to the blackboard who explained what the group had undertaken. It was a manifestation of the great didactical virtue of the open learning situation. There was no doubt that the weaker pupils could follow the explanations of the more successful ones; while working they had plunged deeply enough into the problem to know what mattered and what was going on. Also the pupils who had found satisfactory solutions listened to other solutions and discussed them. Of course the problem was not exhausted with this lesson; I do not know whether and how it was continued.

Research is offered an abundance of points of attack by such an open learning situation. The broad spectrum of levels is a source of cognition of didactic phenomenological character and with respect to levels of learning processes. It is, of course, an art to create open learning situations or a sequence of them which are not boundless and which allow the recognition of the learning process clearly in the succession of learning situations. This must be learned, and it can.

The rigid, regulated learning situation, however, offers the advantage – or is it an advantage? – that it is pre-established what, if anything, will be learned. In the planned open learning situation, too, learning processes are predesigned in the thought experiment; the teaching practice can confirm or disavow the experiment – striking divergences can be observed. A detective story with which we approached a first grade of our lower vocational instruction (L.B.O., 7th grade) was judged to be very nice by one of our collaborators who had analysed it, though lacking any noteworthy objective of mathematical instruction; in the try-out it appeared that it was chockful of such objectives, which without trying out would never have been recognised as such.

This can be a practical output of observing learning processes. Under the given circumstances the designer of the subject matter presupposes pieces of knowledge and the abilities of the learner, which he more or less derives from the subject matter traditionally belonging to these circumstances. This tradition, however, has grown in instructional situations that differed much from those aimed at by the designer, which can mean that his design aims too high, too low, or far off the mark. The designer's activity is as much random as it is intentional; thought experiments are as indispensable as is the observation of the learning processes. It does not suffice to state whether a learning process took place or not; one wants to know what prevented, impeded or facilitated it to occur, or whether one should pay attention to it and promote it consciously; in the curriculum development by a team this is the place where the theoretician should intervene.

I would like to draw attention to a more fundamental fact. It is of profound importance that the designer of material can go astray in his judgement regarding the learning processes to be initiated by the material offered – I do not mean in the first instance what may be too easy or too difficult, but what is not at all supposed by the adult as worth or needing a learning process. It is perhaps the most fruitful result of an open learning situation that it makes these surprises possible. In the case of the detective story I just mentioned as material for the first grade of our lower vocational instruction, learning processes were needed for acquiring mathematical abilities which everybody would have presupposed with 12–13 year olds and which eventually were acquired without difficulty. Other experiments showed these pupils incapable of sharing work within a group but nevertheless capable of acquiring this capability. An 8 year old surprised me by the complete absence of the concept of weight along with the fast learning process and the Aha-Experience of the learner. A learning process of the same 8 year old led via a heavy conflict to the paradoxical cognition that a hundredth is more than a thousandth – a cognition which alarmed him to such a degree that he posed this problem in a fast succession to his parents and adult neighbours, and a fortnight later once more to myself.

Prejudices determine the opinions concerning opportunities and necessities of learning expressed by the traditional textbooks; with every step these prejudices are unmasked by learning processes in open learning situations. This shows the delusiveness of plans to draw up lists of objectives of instruction behind the desk. Even a careful didactical phenomenology is not sufficient as I will later illustrate by an example: I had analysed the ratio concept so circumstantially that I believed there was nothing left to be added, but the first essays with a group of pupils of the 5th grade showed me that one element indispensable in the learning process was simply lacking, the *qualitative* estimation of results of a problem on proportions, and later essays showed other fundamental gaps.

I somewhat vaguely mentioned open learning situations. I did not mean 'open ended', which to my opinion is too narrow. 'Problem solving' is an even sharper restriction of the open learning situation. Both are closely related: one proposes a problem that is not uniquely solvable – the start is the problem and the end is open. Illustrating examples, however, usually disavow the claim of showing open learning situations. I will adduce an example to show how cautiously a term like 'open learning situation' should be applied. For the third grade we had elaborated a theme Reallotment: On a square lattice (like a geoboard) a whimsical division into rectilinearly bounded estates – even disconnected ones – was given. This division should be improved by reparcelling, and to this end the various areas should be expressed in lattice units. This first objective is at any rate uniquely determined though in so many ways accessible that hardly any two pupils will do it identically. (There are three levels of performing this reduction which I will explain later in a suitable context.) If an open end is aimed at, one can eventually have the land available reallotted in a rational way, and then the objective is not any more uniformly determined, though the action leading to this result is uniform – only in a very superficial way is this an open learning situation. Now the practice in the classroom showed that even this design left too much freedom;

if it is more efficiently structured, there is every prospect that more pupils will sooner attain higher levels of dealing with it. Observing the learning processes has revealed steps and intermediate steps, levels and degrees, so a new design can show stricter programming in the sequence of the structured examples in a way that all necessary and accidental learning processes are strongly suggested to the learner. Then the open learning situation has disappeared. Or rather, the open learning situation has become a superficial varnish; careful analysis will show that step by step all is regulated.

It looks paradoxical: the wealth of experiences derived from an initially open learning situation allows the designer to construct an assembly line learning process, where all is preprogrammed – spoon-feeding with a mashed subject matter where nobody can break a tooth off, though modern technique rationalises and glosses over even spoon-feeding and mashing.

How can the subject matter designer escape the temptation of misusing the information from learning processes for 'perfecting' the material? First of all, he should experience this menace often enough to be conscious of it. Secondly, quite a number of techniques can be developed to use the information from learning processes in new learning processes without forcing the learner to run blindfolded through the subject matter in a well-programmed course. I cannot deal with them here, because they depend to a high degree on the form of instruction, in particular on the way in which the intervention of the teacher in the learning process is regulated. The most effective method is that of free exploration where the teacher intervenes with suggestions as soon as the exploration is menaced by a deadlock or runs aground. This, however, requires a great deal from the teacher, who should be allowed to confine his attention to groups of 10–12 pupils.

A working sheet system should show a sophisticated balance between programming and exploring; the assignments should alternate with each other in such a way that an unsuccessful exploration can be made good by a programmed learning sequence. Continuously during a programmed sequence the pupil should be given the opportunity to view the goal, albeit vaguely and globally; never should he be led by the bridle as a blind horse.

Another method of programming is indicated by the technical term of problem solving. It means cutting out from its natural context a problem which on the strength of thought experiments or experiences with learning processes seems to promise success, and to offer it as teaching matter. In the most favourable case it will afterwards adroitly be combined with others in a more or less natural learning sequence. If this is not the case it remains isolated within a conglomerate of as sharply isolated problems. It is quite natural that curriculum designers start their attempts with such isolated problems, as it were five-finger exercises, but this should not become a system as it has in some – indeed excellent – American experiments with natural sciences. It is a danger of this method that it can impede the learning of global understanding from the beginning onwards.

6. LANGUAGE AS A VEHICLE OF RESEARCH

At the beginning of the present chapter I mentioned a list of *words* I had modelled in the last few years into terms and which fairly well describe the contents of this chapter. To convey thoughts, one certainly needs terms, and if the thoughts are somehow new, one can be compelled to model words in order to create terms. Of course terms in themselves do not matter, but this fact is often forgotten. Terms should mean something, they should be rich with content. They acquire this content through what they express, and this should be more than mere words.

Being rich with content is, as far as language is concerned, one of the criteria for testing the scientific character. I believe I did not break this rule when in the course of the years I modelled a few words into terms of didactics of mathematics, but even the most conscientious obedience cannot protect against misunderstanding and misuse of terms one has offered the public – it is I who say 'misunderstanding' though of course I cannot forbid others to use words in a way diverging from mine. If *mathematisation* is sometimes used in the sense of *axiomatisation* (that is a very special and subtle mathematisation of already mathematical subject matter) or even in the sense of *formalisation* (mathematising a linguistic subject matter), it disturbs me, it makes me angry, because it takes the edge off my demanding mathematisation on *all* levels, and I cannot but warn over and over against this onesideness. However, mathematisation is an acknowledgedly clear concept which has been applied with success and mostly in a well-defined sense, and if on some *Zauberberg**

* *Schriftenreihe der I.D.M.* **1** (1974), 5–84.

cerebral contortions are undertaken to prove that mathematisation does not exist, it looks rather like a bad joke.

With many examples I outlined the concept of *local organisation* in order to claim legal rights and authority for a mathematical method which though cultivated by many mathematicians is readily rejected as inexact in pursuing wrong ideas on mathematical exactness. When I did so, I did not want to coin a slogan, which in some future – fortunately I think still far away – can be misused by any charlatan to justify mathematical nonsense; but if this happens, a glance at my examples will suffice to disabuse any honest person.

What I called *levels in the learning process* is, in my view, well circumscribed, though there is a want of many more examples – indeed many more than I could offer so far – in order to prevent misunderstanding.

The *didactical inversion* is hardly to be misunderstood and misused as a slogan, though I would like to deepen it by distinguishing better the 'direct' from the 'inverse' independently of the accidental mathematical action.

I feel the need to illustrate the *discontinuities in the learning process* by more examples, to structure the concept of *paradigms* more sharply by *comprehension and apprehension*. *Settling of conflicts*, *local and global perspective*, *change of perspective*, are words which only recently came into my mind when I observed learning processes. For a long time I have thought of a *didactical phenomenology* of fundamental mathematical concepts, but I did not dare to pronounce this term before I had succeeded in constructing an example of it, which eventually happened recently – I will present it as the last section of this last chapter.

My occupation with many other terms did not yet pass the critical point of understanding. The reader already knows that with regard to the *objectives of instruction*. Of the *general* ones I do not know as yet whether they can involve more than the expression of a background philosophy – of some use as such if they are cautiously watched. Of the *operational* ones I lack the proof of existence since they have not yet been represented by convincing examples. It will take time and trouble if ever it succeeds, to pull the objectives of instruction out of the swamp of slogans. It is a pity that show words as *taxonomy* and *model* more often than not radiate smattering rather than learning.

Earlier on I dealt with the team as a moulder of language. The team can go a long way with a language of gestures and mimicry; it can also develop a plumber and husbandry language, which works well in closeness to the reality the team is acting in; though detached from the practice – for instance if taken over by outsiders – it can degenerate into slogan or bombast. Two extremes may characterise the situation: Scientific progress can be impeded both by a premature and by a stagnant linguistic development. For instance the term 'sensitive phase', coined by Maria Montessori and much used by her followers, is no doubt legitimate though for the lack of an appropriate foundation it remains ineffective: as independent criteria are lacking, it can only afterwards, from success or failure, be concluded whether some pupil was, or was not, in the sensitive phase. The sensitive phase was, and still is, a premature linguistic moulding. As a contrast, around the term of motivation which badly needs refinement by adjectives, too little has happened linguistically; it is still too much under the spell of everyday language provided it has not succumbed to trivializing operationalisation and a cornucopia of empty research. With not even the slightest pretention to profundity I dare say a few words on the motor in the learning process.

7. MOTIVATION

7.1. *Through Discontinuities in the Learning Process*

In the first grade a few lessons on probability are given, without, of course, even mentioning the word. They play with a big die in front of the class and by chance and unintentionally the teacher asks questions like: Is it easier throwing an ace or a six? Is it easier for *me* throwing a six than for *you*? Unanimously and without any hesitation the pupils give the 'wrong' answer. They know from Ludo how difficult it is throwing a six; and they also know that adults are more adroit than children. After these introductory exercises, each pupil is given the cardboard networks of a cube to be cut out, to be stuck together and to be painted with the dice symbols. It takes a lot of time – the poor lefthanded with righthanded scissors, the glue sucked up by the cardboard, the dice collapsing when painted – I bitterly regret the waste of time. Some children knew that opposite sides must add up to seven; others did not. All start playing again, noting down the results, and comparing them, and casually the teacher asks once more: Is it easier throwing an ace or a six? Is it easier for me throwing a six than for you? Unanimously the pupils give the 'correct' answer – they even find the questions ridiculous. The gain proves transferable; in other instances in the same and the next lesson the magic of the dice is gone – how they behave if next Sunday they play Ludo I cannot tell.

Though I have observed other sharp discontinuities in learning processes this has been the sharpest, this complete reversion from a convinced 'yes' to a convinced 'no', and even then in a period where no proper instruction took place. The actual and troublesome construction of the dice is more convincing an argument than the tongues of men and of angels could be. It is one of the reasons why this story can be a marvellous starting point for multifarious didactic reflections.

I tell it because of another conclusion I would draw from it. The children did not seem aware of their conversion or at least their attention was not drawn to it. It may be asked whether the teacher should not have made explicit this discontinuity in the learning process. Is it right shaking the confidence of pupils who have acquired a certainty? Was the certainty not too easily acquired? Would it not have been better to have the acquisition more deeply rooted by obstructing it afterwards?

As far as I am concerned I would have drawn the childrens' attention to their learning process; I do it wherever I become aware of such discontinuities as I am convinced of the importance of making this conscious. I admit I could have met difficulties here. I should have faced a discussion why the one is wrong and the other right. Six-year-olds cannot argue it, can adults?

From my own learning processes I remember numerous experiences of intensely motivating discontinuities, and many times adults confirmed this by experiences from their lives. I observed that children I worked with remember for long periods the discontinuities in their learning processes, deeply rooted as they seem to be by their strongly positive emotional ties. In some instances the experience excited them so much that they could not contain themselves – I will mention a few examples here and later in other contexts.

Everybody knows that quite a few physical abilities are acquired all of a sudden. All of a sudden one has got it. All of a sudden the child stands on its feet – and gets so heavily excited by this achievement that it falls as suddenly. All of a sudden it pronounces its own name, or what adults interpret as such, and gets so excited that it stutters. All of a sudden one knows how to cycle, swim, skate. All of a sudden, and then training starts. Is it the same with mental abilities?

It is. I was once present when a child discovered what colour is (3; 4), and what is the use of relative clauses (3; 5); once I guess I was quite close to a child's discovering what counting means (5; 3); I was present when a child discovered cardinal number (4; 3), when it discovered what psychologists call conservation of volume (almost 5; 0). Each time the Aha-Experience and the unmistakeable excitedness. I have already spoken of the boy (8; 2) who discovered that 1/100 is more than 1/1000 and how excited he was. I would be able to continue this list for a while.

One afternoon I pass our Geological Institute with Bastiaan (3; 11) and tell him that two of his uncles had studied there. As he does not know the word, I explain to him that studying means learning. He asks what is the use of it. I lecture him about learning preceding being able. All of a sudden he ejaculates the words: "I can cycle". Like all children he got much too early one of those badly constructed pedal vehicles for the little ones, but eventually, just this morning he grasped the trick of transforming the treading movement into a rotation. He was excited, and now this excitedness is enhanced by the comparison of his own learning with that of his uncles. Not only does he learn, but he has discovered learning in its essential functions: learning in order to be able to.

7.2. *Through Goals*

If the joy of discovering motivates activity in general, albeit in a certain direction, goals are more specific. Earlier I discussed instruction programmed in all details and pupils led by strings. Sometimes this construction is hard to avoid, and it can be quite effective, in particular in the case of routine learning, though even then a goal visible beyond the programme is desirable.

It is not as easy showing somebody a goal before he attains it; but it is not so difficult, either, that it should systematically be shunned as is the case in school texts.

I say 'a goal' rather than 'the goal'. In the detective story for the first year of lower vocational instruction I mentioned earlier on, the goal that should seduce the children (as the artificial hare motivating the racing greyhounds) was catching the fugitive convict – a goal that somehow must be made credible. The subject matter designer had noted down some mathematical abilities the development of which would be stimulated by working through the story and afterwards he would check whether every gun fired as it should.

It would not have been too bad to tell the pupils afterwards what was intended with the detective story and to discuss with them what they had learned. Indeed, at least some of the pupils proved mature enough to see the design from a higher view point and to criticise it, that is to discover credibility gaps. The objectifying view on the subject matter is in fact, as we know, an activity which is useful by itself.

The pseudo-goal is expressly created in order to motivate, but if this goal had been attained, its effects need not have terminated. The actually intended goals stay in the context of the pseudo-goal and might be summoned from there if they are needed. 'This I learned at such and such an opportunity' can be, as everybody knows, a useful association and mnemonic aid.

The activities that are to be carried on by the pupil along a more or less strict programme with a view to the pseudo-goal, and that for the greater part are goals in themselves, have the tendency to lead away from the pseudo-goal. Our work with this kind of theme and project shows that many pupils need to be reminded step by step of the pseudo-goal – this holds not only for inattentive pupils lacking the ability to concentrate upon a subject, but also for assiduous ones that plunge deeply into every detail. The tension between a local and a global perspective becomes so strong that all connections break down. It is useful to have a continuous reminder of the pseudo-goal built into the material offered to the pupils.

If the pupil cannot be shown in advance the objectives to their full extent and with all lucidity, one will exert oneself to show him characteristic features with characteristic lucidity, as it were a foretaste that should motivate and an orientation point that should guide him. If for instance geometry is started with a pair of scissors and glue, one can trust that the manual activity has motivating effects for quite a while though rather as a manual activity than as geometry, and locally rather than globally. It seems, however, a better strategy to turn the pupil's mind to a more distant goal that is more objectively justified, for instance by showing him ready-made models of a few beautiful regular or semi-regular, bodies, say a rhombo-dodecahedron, which could be fully explored. The goal then would be to make such models and it is approached via less pretentious models – of cubes, pyramids, and so on, as preparatory exercises. Or one can propose the initially empirically accepted Pythagorean theorem as both starting point to a more deductive geometry course and as final goal of the exploration, an exploration which of course should begin with much more elementary facts. With a global goal in his mind that is continuously recalled, the pupil can more safely undergo a sharply programmed learning sequence than without such an orientation point. One can imagine a primary school course in handling computers (for instance as a means of teaching the positional system and its operations by means of old-fashioned crank machines); for such a course an effectively programmed system would be conceivable and justified. Programming pupils with eye flaps can then be perfected up to foolproofness; mechanically handling machines can motivate for a long while though only locally at every single spot. Even here global overview and insight would be a desirable and hardly dispensable objective, but it is doubtful whether this arises spontaneously in many pupils. I once proposed to have such a course preceded by a show (for instance a film) where the essentials are demonstrated in a captious and compact way which does not allow for immediate cooperative understanding. Afterwards in the systematic course, pictures in his working book remind the pupil of the place of each particular local activity within the global context.

7.3. *Through Make-Up*

I considered two kinds of motivation, the first using the discontinuities, the second the objectives of the learning processes (perhaps replaced with mock objectives). I see here starting points for a more scientific treatment. Opportunities for jumps in learning processes can already be searched for in thought experiments, but certainly it can be understood afterwards why in some processes discontinuities occur, and theoretically be discussed how they can be used. Even at the desk, methods can be contrived to show objectives and to observe which ones are the most effective. Moreover this kind of reflection and experience can adequately be communicated to others who may rethink and use it.

But most of the devices used or recommended for motivating spring from crude empiricism. They are justified by vague sentiments and cannot even be described adequately. This foreshadows a long way to a scientific approach, and just because of this methodical contrast I have tackled the theme of motivation. What I call 'get-up' or 'make-up' (of subject matter, teaching devices, learning processes) looks so arbitrary that one rarely gets a clue of the intentions behind the get-up – perhaps they are nonexistent, perhaps they cannot be formulated. (I speak of get-up not in order to dispose of the method but to indicate its arbitrary character.)

New arithmetic books (or what they call New Maths) distinguish themselves from the traditional ones in that in the old ones one could follow the author's intentions step by step whereas in the new ones only a global intention is visible, namely that of motivating. Guided by some psychologically adorned background philosophy, one aspires to closeness to life, which is interpreted within an alleged child's world of plastic playthings, gnomes, and dressed animals – no doubt with a certain justice because this is indeed the world in which life goes on according to the great majority of what is offered to little children.

Does a three-colour print on glossy paper motivate better than black and white on wood-pulp? (I mean the pupils, rather than those who visit education fairs.) Are funny pictures more motivating than serious ones? Are boys better motivated by pictures of footballs and girls by skipping ropes? What is more motivating, boldness, smartness or pomposity of language? It is hardly worthwhile asking these questions because even if there were somewhat reasonable arguments to answer them, no author of arithmetic books would bother about them; he would in any case produce what to his view promises didactic success or what can seduce others to believe it is didactically useful.

I do not at all turn against get-up or make-up. On the contrary, I readily believe they can serve motivation if they are functional. But as we observed they are not, or rather, not automatically. It is all the same to the children whether they count crosses or elephants, whether they must add apples and pears or boring Venn-diagrams. During arithmetical operations the character of the objects fades away, as do the illustrations during reading exercises. (Publishers of reading books are well aware of, and profit from, the fact that children do not notice if colour indications in the text and the illustration do not match each other, and they are not averse to even larger discrepancies.)

In order to function as a motivation, the get-up must be relevant in the counting and calculating procedure, but this goal is not reached without making an effort. The child has known for quite a while, at least unconsciously, that arithmetical operations function independently of the meaning of the objects. This indeed is the reason why it learns arithmetic and perhaps it is even aware of this fact. The pictures can only divert its attention, and as soon as its attention is diverted, it cannot calculate properly. The textbook author of course knows this. He wants the child to abstract from the object characters. Why does he act as though he wants to deflect the learning process into concreteness? What is the rationale of motivating the learning process by means of material that leads away from the intended learning process? Does the textbook author pursue any didactic objective at all?

Well, one objective could be to impede too quick an abstraction in order to vouchsafe the concrete character of the operations and their applicability. But if this is intended, the get-up must be meaningfully used. This means that rather than as an algorithmic datum each picture should be read as an illustrated story. If there are five dwarfs pictured, three standing and two going away, the child should read it for instance as 'five dwarfs, two running away, three staying' or 'five dwarfs running, two giving up, three running on'; but even 'three standing and two walking dwarfs are five together' cannot be forbidden. A number problem with a unique solution under the picture seduces pupils and teacher to premature algorithmisation, which unmasks the get-up as a delusion. Of course the interpretation of the picture as a picture story includes the assumption that children are allowed to invent their own pictures and stories – the child itself should furnish the arithmetic.

Many authors of arithmetic texts, however, seem to believe that a nice get-up motivates as such. No doubt normal activities can do so for quite a while; as to get-up that invites nothing but being looked at, a lasting motivating power seems quite improbable; three-colour print on art paper has only short-lived effects. One should demand that the designer reflect upon *how* the get-up could effect motivation and communicate the result of this reflection explicitly, or implicitly by incorporating it operationally into the design in order to have the get-up meaningfully used. If the designer meets this requirement, one can find approaches to a scientific evaluation of his approach. Comparing two get-ups statistically while their use is not controlled or while nothing can be precisely said about their use, is a pseudo-scientific exercise. The same holds with respect to furnishing the learning process with praise and reward – I cannot imagine how the conditions under which they are handed out can be made comparable. As a principle I rejected statistics offered as a surrogate for theory. I do not see any trace of a theory of the get-up as a device for motivation, and there are good reasons why such a theory would be a difficult, if not impossible, task. Though I would like to demand as I did that the designer reflect about how the get-up can yield motivating effects and that somehow he should communicate the result, I know very well that such a desire is not easily fulfilled. Acting instinctively on the ground of non-explicit experiences is one of the presuppositions of creativity which both designer and teacher cannot dispense with, if they want to motivate. Nevertheless one should attentively watch for possible approaches to genuine scientific analysis. Though not *a priori* one should try *a posteriori* as a designer to justify, and as a teacher and observer to understand, how a get-up can yield motivating effects (or at other places break down). It does not suffice that theoreticians and practicians, designers and teachers tell us that this or that is fun to the children (or is not). After a school television series for the 5th–6th grades (11–12 year-olds) on probability, an opinion poll among the participating teachers who had worked during six weeks with the programme showed to no question such a wide dispersion of answers as to that on the motivation of the pupils, which varied from extremely positive to extremely negative, from "exciting" to "boring", from "at last something different from arithmetic" to "it did nothing for my kids, who like doing arithmetic". It goes without saying that such statistics, even though mathematically analysed, cannot contribute anything essential to one's knowledge on motivation.

8. GENERALITY BY COMPREHENSION AND BY APPREHENSION

Many manual skills are acquired and perfected by continuous exercise and numerous repetitions. The belief that it is the same with general knowledge has hardly been opposed. By induction, philosophers say, general ideas, concepts and judgments are derived from numerous instances. The idea, the concept, of 'dog' is constituted out of the acquaintance with a large number of representatives of the species *canis*; we know that dogs bark because we have often heard them barking, and that non-supported bodies fall because we have often witnessed this phenomenon, according to this widespread philosophy. Indeed the criticism to which induction has been subjected since Hume says only that conclusions drawn by induction cannot be coercive, but if I may trust the literature, it has not been doubted so far that general ideas, concepts, judgments are acquired by induction where the number of instances is the main factor. This is the basis of all confirmation theories of knowledge as they are cultivated at present, whether they stress validation or falsification or behave probabilistically.

Methodology of science is pursued by methodologists not as an empirical but as an *a priori* science – as general didactics often is by didacticians. What actually happens in the various sciences does not much interest methodologists, who are more often logicians or philosophers than scientists. Their examples, like barking dogs and falling stones, are consequently most often taken from prescientific cognition, so they fail to notice that induction from numerous instances is not the only source of scientific cognition nor the most important. Compared with the prescientific attitude the scientific attitude is characterised by theory building, and what is confuted or confirmed there, are not single statements but theories, or judgments – and also hypotheses – embedded in theories. It is not true that to state the constancy of the velocity of light, a long sequence of experiments was needed; one experiment was sufficient and this one sufficed to provoke the need to explain the phenomenon, that is, to embed it into a theory. Sure, others repeated the experiment because they did not trust the report or because they wanted to convince themselves by their own experience, but each of them could be satisifed by one experiment. *One* Foucault pendulum sufficed to prove the rotation of the Earth; numerous repetitions were to convince a large public. *One* experiment decided whether light is a longitudinal or transversal oscillation; the wave character of X-rays was proved by *one* X-ray picture of *one* crystal, and if such pictures have been taken thousands of times, it was not to prove anew the wave character but to ascertain the wave *length* of a particular radiation or the *lattice constant* of a particular crystal.

Numerous repetitions of an experiment – yes, this exists, though for other reasons and purposes than that naïve methodology would make us believe. An experiment is repeated because it did not succeed and the experimenter is eager to know what went wrong, or in order to eliminate observation errors, or because the result aspired at is not a single magnitude, but a function or a probability distribution. Our scientific cognitions are theories or embedded into theories, and for this reason one single well-chosen experiment is in general enough to pose a problem or to decide between too alternative hypotheses; sequences of experiments are required to cope with errors of observation or measurement, or with probability distributions. It is not true either that credibility increases with the *number* of experiences. It is independency of new experiments that enhances credibility – this explains the large number of independent designs of experiments for the quantum character of light and

Planck's constant. Mere repeating does not create new evidence, which in fact is successfully aspired to by independent experiments.

This is the state of affairs in the *sciences*, in particular the so-called exact ones. Prescientific cognition could be different, but whether it is so, nobody has so far really investigated. Over and over they adduce the same well-worn examples of general ideas, concepts, judgements which should make us believe that they arise by induction from many events. It is, however, quite improbable that the learning of biological beings that are able to learn, is so badly programmed and inefficient that they really need numerous examples. There are good reasons to believe that their learning is pre-programmed in such a way that few examples suffice. A boy in the first year of his life who was still crawling had two rooms as living space, separated by a step. After the *first* time when creeping from the higher to the lower room he fell upon his head, he *always* turned around when he had to pass the step, and descended backwards. When seeking Easter eggs in the forest, which I had hidden around the trees three by three, Bastiaan (4; 0) looked systematically for three eggs a tree after the discovery of the first triple. One experience with an aggressive swan mother sufficed for longlasting fear of swans. In my house all floors are covered with a rough sisal mat. After the first touch of the mat with bare knees all of my grandchildren while crawling did so with raised knees; as soon as they reached carpets and linoleum they returned to crawling in the normal way. Once bitten, twice shy, the proverb says, but philosophers from Hume to Carnap (and many before and after) would talk us into believing that shyness develops slowly, by a continuous learning process. Only behind the desk where integral learning is dissolved into isolated learning processes, can people wonder how principles can be learned from one experience. The theoretical isolation of learning threads is a popular but artificial construction; learning is a wide stream.

Bastiaan (4; 2), who selectively collects what he finds on the street, picked up a piece of a wire fence, as it were a flat spiral of wire. Then he pulled out a thick rubber ring from his trousers-pocket and made it move on the wire while kept horizontal, as a 'walking path'; then he inclined the wire and finally kept it vertical so that the ring danced downwards along the wire. Then while we walked further, he took out a little ring of plastic from his pocket and made it fall along the wire, which was an even funnier spectacle. Next he took out of his pocket a flat aluminium beer-bottle top: "Now I must do something with this." I suggested to him that he should make a hole in it at home; this made a mighty impression upon him and caused a vivid technical discussion. Suddenly he said something like "a screw-nut has a hole where the screw fits in," dipped his hand, with an expert gesture, into his pocket, fetched a screw-nut from it (he had got two of them) and carried out the same experiment, an extremely funny spectacle. I said to him "You are a great inventor; what haven't you invented?," though I doubted whether he understood the word 'inventing', but after a while he himself said: "I thought out a thing." Proudly he demonstrated his invention at home.

I tell this story in detail because it includes a wealth of information. Never had the boy seen a similar event – otherwise he would have said so. As early as the first trial he performed the relevant generalisation: the thing must have a hole. My intervention only had the effect of introducing the *word* 'hole', though I shouldn't really have intervened. Not only did he generalise, he systematically searched for improvements. Moreover, he was sure he had discovered an important thing. Could he explain why the objects fall so funnily along the wire? Perhaps in a while. He acts very consciously and leaves little to chance.

Of course individuals differ widely. Once I observed the excitedness of a baby (3 months) that discovered his hand, and then learned seizing by incessant exercises, and another who almost from his first day onwards was unusually active with his eyes, who never indulged in useless trials of seizing but the first time when he tried to seize a thing, did so successfully. These are characterological differences which kept showing up in the development of both of them: the one measures his strength in useless attempts, the other undertakes nothing unless he knows he will succeed, but in both lives the moment of success is sharply marked, also emotionally.

I anticipate an objection: that the instances I gave – crawling babies, searching for eggs, the bitten child – do not concern cognition but expression of behaviour. One need not be a behaviourist to allow that cognition can also be shown non-verbally. In fact, doesn't the bitten child learn to say "oh"; and is it not only when it calls the biter explicitly "oh" that we are convinced it has *recognised* the biter as the "oh"? How consciously must a child weep in order to be credited with the *cognition* that pain behaviour moves pity? Should one distinguish at all between forms of behaviour that testify cognition and those that do not? The learning child does not do so, neither while reflecting nor acting. That trees are in bloom in spring, sheep bleat, horses run and cars drive, that red lights stop traffic, that the right hand is the fair one, all these are cognitions of the same order, for which the child asks for reasons with the same question "Why?" Not only the child. One has to go a long way in onto- and phylogenesis until this standpoint is vanquished, if this happens at all. The double meaning of the word 'law' as natural law and human statute – or is it a double meaning? – still clings to our mind.

I spoke of ideas, concepts, judgements, whether they are inductively acquired from many instances. From the start onwards I could have added 'behaviour'. I did not do so because it would not have enhanced the credibility of my thesis. For is there anything as obvious as the continuity of the process that shapes our behaviour, as the constant dripping that wears away the stone, as the legendary bird that whets its beak once a year at a rock, to show that when the rock is gone the first second of eternity has passed away. Yet men are no stones and they do not live an eternity. In few years of development is the behaviour of a man shaped – language, attitude, inclinations, and character, and where could he take the time and leisure for learning in little steps, for the numerous experiences which each single feature would need to get its shape?

However, there is some truth, a great deal of truth, in the parable of the constant dripping that wears away the stone, also with regard to acquiring one's pattern of behaviour. Such is not simply invented. 'I told you a hundred times', mothers say, and that is education. 99 times is not enough. In fact even 'I told you a hundred times', mothers say a hundred times; the 99th time has not yet convinced them that it is useless. Fathers like shorter ways, but the teacher imitates the mother. If 99 problems did not suffice to teach fractions, a hundredth must do the trick, or in a modern version, in differentiated instruction: the A-pupil learns by one example what is taught the B-pupil by ten and the C-pupil by a hundred. And the nagging question is whether it is not just the C-pupil who needs the unique problem. But in education and instruction the large number must do it. The little child is prompted to say the number sequence until it can rattle it off as a parrot. Poor child that refuses to repeat it, and poor mother that gets desperate – imagine the child will not learn counting! Or isn't it its strong character that prevents the child from parroting words it does not understand?

So, against my thesis, it is true that general attitudes, ideas, concepts, judgements are acquired by numerous instances and incessant repetition. It is true because this is the way people are taught. It is true, not as fundamental knowledge, but as a technique, which could happen to be wrong. It is as true as the pedagogics of sweet and whip, of stork and ogre. Only it is not as obsolete as these. On the contrary, the attainment of attitudes, ideas, concepts, and judgements along sequences of numerous examples is not only the principle of the current practice but also of many theories of learning and teaching, and on the whole this will not change as it is the path of least resistance. It takes much less trouble to sprinkle the learner with a shower of examples than to search for the one that matters. It is often enormously difficult to find the one, because this does not happen at random.

Everybody knows how lavishly nature spreads its abundance: one among thousands of fish-eggs becomes a fish, one of millions of sperms fertilises the ovum, one out of billions of planets grew life. The farmer already behaves more economically: each seed should bear fruit. But in order to attain this, he did not fetch at random what he sows, and he does not scatter it at random. Observation, experiences, and more recently even science, help him to act purposively. The lack of all this impedes the educator to act as purposively though he could even less afford spending as lavishly as nature.

I deal with these problems here in the chapter on the science of mathematical education because from mathematics I acquired the insight in what I said and I am going to explain it in more detail. I acquired it by observing learning processes, my own first, then those of others in thought experiments and actual experiments. No subject matter leads more easily to this insight than mathematics. But this does not mean that its scope is restricted to mathematics. Though research on instruction cannot but *start* in a particular subject, it certainly should *not stay* there.

I used the words *comprehension* and *apprehension* to distinguish two ways of acquiring generalities. I took the liberty of moulding these terms comprehension and apprehension more sharply than I found them, and I did so not without a bit of etymology in the background. *Com*prehension, the 'taking together', *ap*prehension, the 'taking on'. Generalities by *gathering* many details, versus *seizing* a structure, albeit by an example, by one example. I do not restrict myself in using these terms to the acquisition of general ideas, concepts, and judgements but I shall include, as is clear from the preceding exposition, patterns of behaviour, though my examples and arguments will be taken from mathematics. Again the main goal is to look around for possible approaches to a future science of mathematical education.

Teaching is the intentional promotion of learning processes, but the results of a learning process need not match the intentions. While being taught, one learns many things that are not on the programme and that are not recognised as essential learning results even by the teacher and are deemed to remain by-products of the learning process. This implies the risk that once in a while they will be skipped. Making conscious what is attained, and therefore can be attained, by some learning processes should always mean a gain in the educational techniques. I do not assert that it always is a gain. It might happen, and I will argue by examples that it does, that awareness prejudices rather than improves the techniques of teaching. I already mentioned counting. It is true that the number sequence is learned according to the principle of perseverance – perseverance of the adult. Yet one may doubt whether this contributes anything to acquiring the skill of object-related counting. Indeed counting out a set by means of the numerals while each member of the set is touched precisely once – palpably or mentally – is an ability that is acquired in one blow, independently of the qualitative and quantitative progress reached in reeling off the sequence of numerals; and I think it is not far-fetched to suppose that the mechanically exercised number sequence frustrates rather than promotes the ability of object related counting.

Another example: under the influence of set theory broad circles have become consciously acquainted with the fact that the equipotency of sets can, and should, be found out independently of counting out by means of the number sequence. This indeed is an unconscious ability that was acquired in the traditional teaching of arithmetic though it was never intentionally exercised – I have made sure that adults master it, often even consciously. The new insight, however, has become didactically operational in prescribing systematic exercises where the equipotency of two sets must be corroborated by explicit one-to-one relating. This is done with innumerable pairs of Venn diagrams which are related to each other by junctions, two pages of examples, one after the other, for each of the cardinalities 0 to 10, and the only diversity in this insipid activity are the coloured pictures on the art paper, which are spoiled irrevocably by the pencil lines.

This is a most typical example of a shower of exercises instead of one that hits the mark. The children who are to perform these exercises are already in the possession of the cardinals and the ability to count. They state the equivalence of two sets by sight if the sets are small, and by counting out if they are bigger. The ability that is aimed at, that is, comparing by one-by-one relating, cannot be exercised, it can only be blocked by a shower. One grasps how at one blow to teach this ability or to test its presence as soon as one thinks about how one applies it oneself as an adult. Indeed, as I have stressed a great many times*, children are entitled to be dealt with as reasonable people; the Venn diagrams remind me of the baby language in which some adults like to address children.

In fact there are a large number of examples that fulfill our requirements. I take a vase – or its picture – decorated around by a girth of alternating suns and moons – its rear, of course, being invisible. "Are there more suns than moons, or conversely?" is the question. Or the same in a more sophisticated version with wallpaper patterns. Or a long open chain with alternating two red and two blue pearls, or its picture, or with the complication that the ends may, or may not, be of the same colour. Or the question whether each layer of a – drawn – wall counts the same number of bricks, or how to play a game such that everybody gets the same number of turns. Not only can first graders answer these questions by yes and no, they can even argue their answers in a meaningful way – I mean by using one-to-one mappings but of course not this term, and by this they prove that they have seized the one-to-one mappings as a device for comparing sets in a more convincing way than they would do by pairs of Venn diagrams. Likewise adults are in possession of this capacity, and more frequently than with children, I have observed with them the Aha-Experience, the discovery of coming to consciousness of a deeply rooted unconscious experience.

The preceding should be evidence that the coming to consciousness and explicitation of subject matter which has traditionally been unconsciously transmitted need not be considered progress. Such subject matter might owe its inconspicuousness and importance to the fact that it is acquired by apprehension. If the teacher has become aware of it, then there is a real danger that its didactics is framed comprehensively, as I called it, with a shower of examples instead of the one that really does the job.

The concept of cardinal number as such belongs to an earlier stage which I

* *Mathematics as an Educational Task*, e.g. p. 118.

will deal with later on. In the present first grade arithmetic books it is practised abundantly with the numbers 0, 1, . . . , 10. All my observations affirm that this concept is attained earlier and then at one blow; I will explain later on how I think it happens. There is not the slightest indication that addition and subtraction of numbers are acquired comprehensively, as is obviously assumed by the textbook authors. The manner of comprehensive learning applies indeed to the attitudes that are finally expressed in the mastery of the tables of addition and multiplication. Engraving this subject matter on the memory looks more like the constant dripping that wears away the stone, but even here its efficiency should not be overestimated. I have the impression that a didactics which starts with the learning of addition and multiplication by apprehending, and separates the domains of the apprehensive and comprehensive acquisition of concepts and attitudes more clearly, could also facilitate learning routines.

The method of many examples and continuous exercise, which springs from the philosophy of inductive acquisition of patterns of attitudes, ideas, concepts and judgements is always applicable; only it is a question whether this method is not just the cause of many learning failures, whether it often does not block learning. No doubt many pupils can be programmed like living automata in order to acquire algorithmic skills which can be tremendously useful. From olden times this programming has been carried on by the stimulus-reflex-method, which has been discovered, rather than invented, by behaviourism, and which was practised long before behaviourism. It appears, however – and this too is an old experience – that in arithmetic and mathematics at most half of the pupils pass beyond the domain of the most primitive responses, and that among those who succeed in progressing beyond this limit the great majority remain far below the level of achievement – and below the capacity of achievement – of computers, which can be programmed with much simpler and more reliable methods than those that are current in programming men.

The disadvantage of the apprehensive method is that it requires such a tremendous amount of insight – insight into the subject matter, insight into learning – that this insight is difficult to develop as long as we lack schemes of thinking about them and observing them, that the results of this insight can hardly be disseminated as long as the communication devices to this end are virtually non-existent, that teachers and educators are not prepared to receive and apply such insight, and that curriculum developers and text book authors can take few risks and certainly not those of replacing comprehensive methods of old repute by untried apprehensive innovations. Well, I do not expect revolutionary changes either. Too much preliminary work must be done, too much must still be explored in the armchair and in the field. Rather than sprinkling with a shower of examples I asked for the one that matters, but I could not tell how to find it.

9. APPREHENSION AND PARADIGM

I called such examples paradigms – exemplary learning is another term that means that the paradigm is stressed in learning. The origin of the term 'paradigm' is well-known, it comes from learning the grammar of foreign languages. The 'a' declension of Latin, for instance, was memorised by means of the noun 'mensa', for the 'er' conjugation of French, generations of pupils recited the forms of the verb 'aimer': it was taught my generation with 'donner', but I do not know what is the fashion now. For irregularities there were again paradigms, for instance 'partir' for one group of verbs and 'croire' for another. A more recently invented device for learning foreign languages is paradigmatic sentences, simple and composite ones. If this use of the term paradigm reminds the reader of old-fashioned methods of teaching foreign languages, he is misled by a superficial association. The paradigm in a broader, less rigid sense is indeed an important, albeit mostly unconsciously used, device of linguistic instruction in general, that of the mother language included – at least I guess that there, too, approaches which are far more apprehensive are buried under a seeming abundance of comprehensive elements.

At present one sometimes says 'paradigms' if one means patterns of research, perhaps in order to alternate with the word 'model' that can mean the same; in an even grosser way it is used by Kuhn who says 'paradigm' if he means what at a given moment is all the fashion in natural sciences. I restrict the use of 'paradigm' to learning processes and there it does not sound to me to have any depreciative undertone. The paradigm 'mensa' of the 'a' declension is consciously to be learned by the pupil and consciously to be transposed to other 'a' words, but this is not my interpretation of the didactical paradigm. It is of a much higher degree of efficiency, it is required to function with no mnemonics applied and does not need consciousness in order to function; it looks more like the paradigms by which the child learns to master the grammar of its mother language. It is another thing that afterwards such a paradigm can be brought to the consciousness of the user, in order to contribute, if it is useful, to knowledge of a higher level such as is the explict grammar of the mother language.

With this exposition, a philosophical-historical-etymological introduction, I have indulged in a didactics which is the generally accepted one although it is just the one I have said I reject. If I intend that others emulate my deeds, I should begin paradigmatically myself. I now pass to the deeds and in order in my own teaching to observe the condemnation I have often pronounced against the didactical inversion, I begin with the event that for me, if my memory does not deceive me, was the paradigm of the paradigm. Certainly I had pressed for paradigmatic instruction for long, and I could sprinkle others and myself with examples of paradigms, but not until a talk with 8-year olds (8; 2 to 8; 6) did I discover the one paradigm that I really found convincing as an example of a paradigm. The area to which it belongs is not included in traditional arithmetic and mathematics teaching – this made my experiences possible – though it would fit at least into the second grade, but even kindergarten teachers who participated in our refresher courses tried it convincingly.

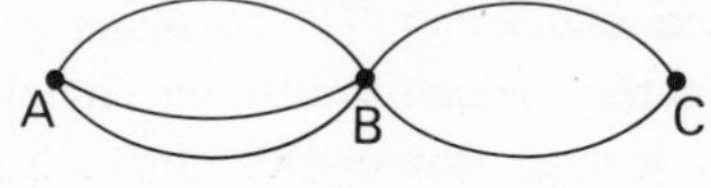

Fig. 1.

Meanwhile I expounded this paradigm many times: I drew a map with three towns A, B, C, where A and B are joined by three roads and B and C by two. The question is: In how many ways can I travel from A through B to C? (Figure 1.) It is characteristic of the fundamental weaknesses of our traditional arithmetic instruction that 8–9 year olds have difficulties with this problem, and that even adults, including people who have enjoyed a higher education in the arts or social sciences, often do not know how to tackle such problems.

What is the trouble with the problem? Only with sequences of carefully separated objects, with ten marbles in a row or ten cherries on a plate do children learn counting. But what should we do with the confusion of roads in our problem? The things to be counted are not properly present, they must still be created, these composite roads. Is this the trouble? I believe not. Indeed the child has known for a long time that inaccessible absent objects can be counted, or at least he has practised this activity. As I will explain later on, this ability or even the knowledge about this ability might be the essential discontinuity in learning processes that bring together the ordinal and cardinal number concept – as an example take the story I related about counting the legs of a company sitting around a table that hides the things to be counted.

Rather than the absence of the objects to be counted it is the confusion of their presentation that causes the trouble. Like the rats grown together by their tails, the objects to be counted are entangled with each other. Where and how should counting start? When the problem is proposed, it is good that the children fully experience the difficulty, that they work hard to get the solution. As a matter of fact it is most interesting to observe them. They do not proceed unsystematically; on the contrary I always observed a certain system: systematically they vary both partial roads at the same time, that is if the first choice was road 1 from A to B and road 1 from B to C, the second may be road 2 from A to B together with road 2 from B to C. It is a pity that this is a bad system but this is a thing children have still to learn.

The didactics of teaching this problem is to divert the children's attention from the drawn map, a tactic that seems to be easier with children of preschool age than with 2nd to 3rd graders. Children are indeed able to count objects imagined, and it is a didactic necessity and duty to make children aware of this ability in order that they use it when needed. I should say that I never saw this happen in teaching – such fundamental facts are generally unknown.

The visible picture is confusing, and drawn over with a pencil it becomes even more confusing. Only in a mental picture can the concrete picture be dissolved – a mental picture that can have been concretised by verbalisation and rhythmisation (this-this, this-that, and so on) or dramatisation (performing the problem in the classroom). Indeed, the representation need not be optical, senso-motoric ideas are perhaps more efficient, and they are certainly so with preschool age children (which, however, in our experiments were given a variant of the problem). It seems to make things easier if the problem

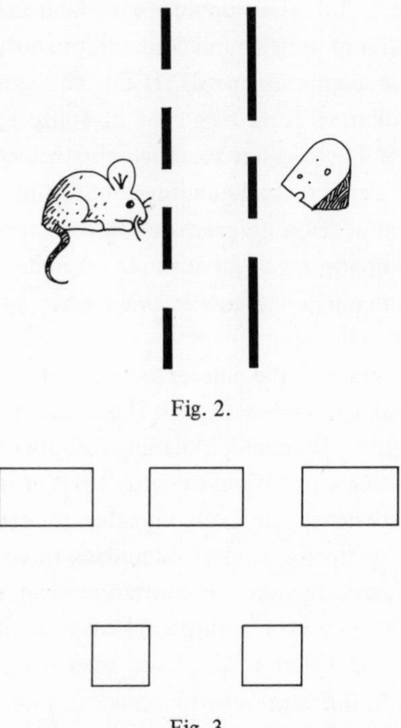

Fig. 2.

Fig. 3.

is proposed independently of its pictorial representation, but in the total context of education local facilitation is not necessarily a global advantage.

It took the 8-year olds to whom I proposed the problem individually about half an hour to find the solution. About a fortnight later I gave them a whole sequence of problems: Two parallel walls, one with three holes in it, the other with two holes; here the mouse, and there the cheese; in how many ways can the mouse run to the cheese? (Figure 2.) It was answered without any hesitation. Either they said immediately "six" or answered with a rhythmic cadence: "dadà-dadá, dadà-dadá, dadà-dadá – six". Three houses and two garages, from each house to each garage one path is leading; how many paths are there? (Figure 3.) Three shirts and two trousers, three blouses and two skirts, how many days can you dress differently? So one can continue for a while, waiting for the exclamation "it is all the same". (This can fail to come – one of my subjects afterwards pitied my dullness: she told her parents I had given her ten times the same problem without being aware of it.)

Rather than saying "it is the same", we speak about isomorphism though in a broader sense than that of pure mathematics; the isomorphism does not break down if the numbers 3 and 2 are replaced by others. The strength of this paradigm is rooted in the wide range of this isomorphism, and in that this isomorphism makes aimful acting possible. It is not at all required that the actor becomes aware of the isomorphism - on the contrary there will often be a lack of awareness which can mean a strength rather than a weakness. Even less does the isomorphism need to be accessible to verbal formulation; giving arguments for the isomorphism is a still higher level, which requires considerable mathematical insight or routine - think about how to visualise the isomorphism of situations in the two problems of the roads and of the mouse. If the children are hard pressed to tell how they knew it, they answer "I see it this way"*, and this is all right. Indeed it would be wrong to compel the child to rationally motivate a thing it sees clearly and distinctively; rational analysis is not required unless vision fails, and closing the eyes intentionally is a mathematical level that is not reached by many, whereas leading children away from intuitive cognition is, as mentioned earlier, a didactical task that can be undertaken on the basis of earlier detachments of thought from the support of visual intuition.

The reason why I call the above example a paradigm – and even my paradigm of paradigms – is the quickness and sureness of transfer of the solution to isomorphic problems (or rather problems I considered as isomorphic at that time) after the paradigm itself had required a great effort. Anyhow I claim that in this particular case I found the one example that can be substituted for the shower of examples – the shower will now come afterwards when the insight is to be complemented by routine.

How important a paradigm can be, is also convincingly illustrated by wrong applications. After a variety of problems of the above type, I asked the following (Figure 4): Here are four houses; there is one path between each pair of them; how many paths are there? "Twelve", the child says with no hesitation. "Draw them!" "No, it is six." "You thought four times three, didn't you?" "No, I thought twelve, but it is six", she hesitates, "because between two houses there is only one drawn." "So, you thought four times three." "No, I thought twelve."

* Dutch: "ik zie het zo" – I cannot tell what English speaking children would answer. Maybe "'cos"?

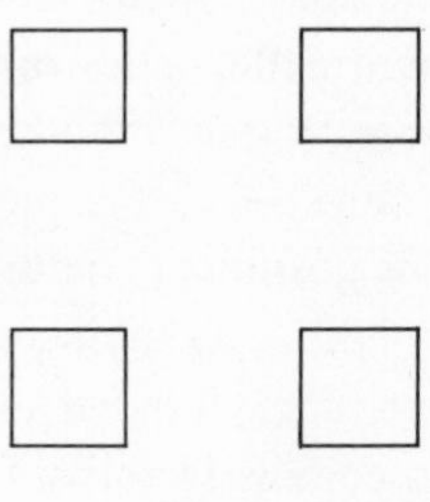

Fig. 4.

It is a high level mistake the child made when she said twelve. Her mind's eye could most easily have viewed the square with the diagonals between the houses, but this concrete picture was already superseded by a more abstract structure, probably a structure of $3 + 3 + 3 + 3$, which was not yet algorithmically interpreted as a multiplicative one. The mistake is a symptom of the attained mathematical level. A next level would be putting this kind of mistake into a scheme, again defined by a paradigm.

How many line segments can be drawn between four points? If four persons meet, how many handshakes do they exchange? In how many ways can two objects be chosen out of four? The problems are isomorphic, of increasing abstractness. The six lines between the four points can still be seen together, the six handshakes can be imagined one after the other, but the six pairs of two things invite confusion by their intricate overlappings. Nevertheless under the influence of the isomorphisms pupils are able to solve these problems, and only the 'why?' requires a mathematical level beyond the "I see it this way."

The paths problem proved highly paradigmatic in my experiments, though at present I would object against it, as a first approach, that it is too simple. I would now prefer another, richer, approach, for instance, the following: a sheet with 12 drawings of flags with three bars each, which must be coloured; for the highest black, white and brown are allowed, for the middle red and green, for the lowest yellow and blue – all flags must be different. The eight-years olds start unsystematically, or rather according to the system to change all together until finally when the supply becomes scarce the scales fall from their eyes and they discover the right system. I did not give this problem to the children who solved the sequence starting with the paths problem so I do not know whether its paradigmatic character extends as far as the flag problem. Conversely I do know that children who started with the flags did not have any trouble with the paths.

The overall ability aimed at by these problems is systematic counting or rather the habit, the need, and the skill to proceed systematically when counting. This can be trained by quite different examples: the stars in the flag of the United States, the candles in a Christmas tree – which are structured in their totality to make counting easier – coins counted in towers of equal height, heaps in the shape of rectangular parallelepipeds and of pyramids, which are structured in layers, and many more – structures to be discovered in the data of the problem.

In the paths problem, the structure is not directly given, as the elements overlap; but once the structure has been discovered it impresses itself like a concrete datum. It is a striking observation that children who started with the paths are prone to reduce all similar problems to the paths model – I will come back to this point. Starting with the flags, rather than a model, a strategy develops: "First I take all flags with black at the top, then the second bar can be red or green, and both can be combined with yellow and blue . . ." Here all oozes away in a verbal scheme of enumerating. But with appropriate examples one can then stimulate model forming, and the result is the tree model. From there one can lead the learner to the paths problem and demonstrate isomorphism by uniting nodes on the same level (Figure 5). Children who started with the paths, have more trouble with the inverse operation. Finally the paths model carried the day because of its greater compactness, in particular if more than two factors are involved, though one might judge the paths model not intuitive enough because it seems to hide the product structure. The fact that it carries the day proves that the child has learned to discover more abstract structures in the concrete material. The paths model becomes so strong a habit that it imposes itself even in cases where it would hardly have been expected: Six roads between A and B (Figure 6): go from A to B and back but not on the same road; how many possibilities? Or more complicated: the journey *ABAB* with no road twice. The reader will have no trouble in guessing which combinatorial principles are covered by this application of the paths model.

I continue with the sequence of experiments that started with the paths problem – I interrupted the story by the flags variant and its consequences.

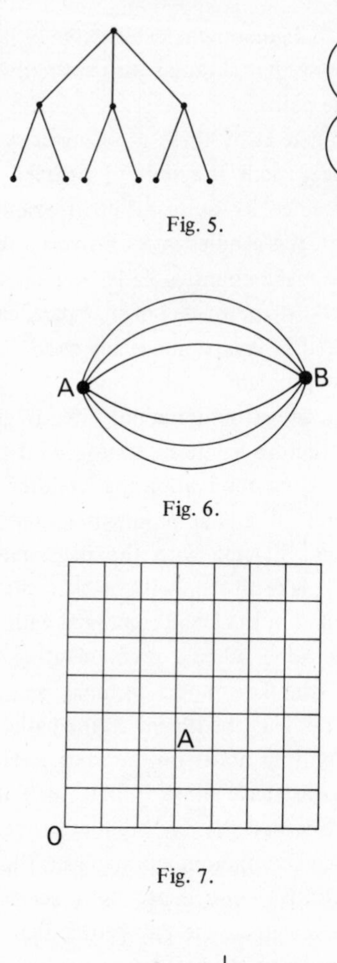

Fig. 5.

Fig. 6.

Fig. 7.

Fig. 8.

The next step was the ways in the square lattice, or as we called it, the city map with 8 streets (horizontal) and 8 avenues (vertical). How many ways with no detours – but what are detours properly? – from one corner to that diagonally opposite? Or, as this is too confusing, let us begin with the ways

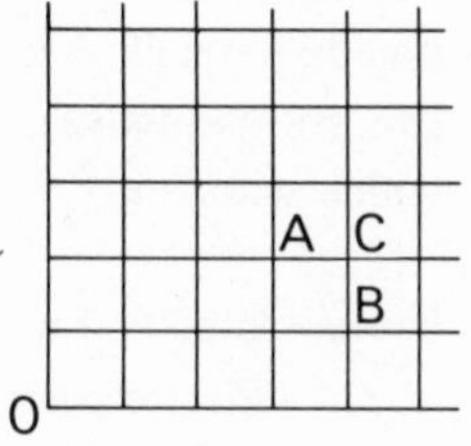

Fig. 9.

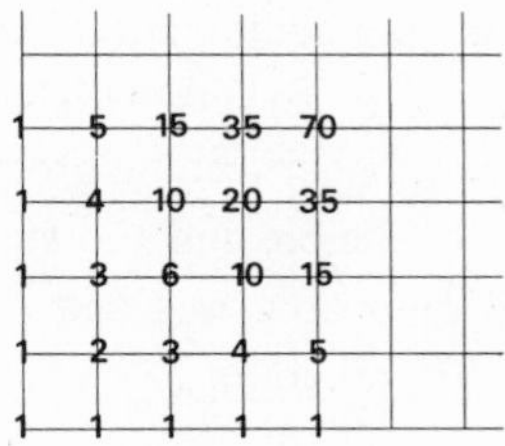

Fig. 10.

Fig. 11.

from O to A. Again it starts with badly systematised trials. How do you lay down what you have had? The child *draws* ways like that on Figure 8. Don't you know an easier method? Impulses are needed to have it proceeding symbolically and *writing* down the ways, of course abridged with H for horizontal and V for vertical, for instance

H V H H V, . . .

How can you put an order into this list? Again an impulse is needed. Do you know how a dictionary is arranged? By this remark a paradigm is activated that so far was only passively experienced, the paradigm of the lexicographic order, a paradigm of far reaching importance within and outside mathematics.

From here the way can lead further, to more profound mathematical knowledge. The next important step would be to recognise that the number of ways from O to A and B together equals that of O to C (Figure 9). This knowledge makes the recursive (or inductive) construction of a number pattern (Figure 10) possible, which with the 1 corner turned upwards yields the well-known Pascal triangle.

I interrupt this exposition because later on I will come back to the triangle of Pascal in another context, as the didactic paradigm for a remarkable level forming. At the present point the triangle of Pascal emerges as a paradigm for a recursive definition, or if one wants to go to greater depth, of a recursive or inductive proof. There are of course mathematically simpler, more fundamental examples of recursion: the adding and multiplying of whole numbers can be defined recursively, as can powers with whole exponents; formulae such as that for the triangular numbers can be proved recursively (Figure 11), though these examples are too simple and too static to be paradigmatically efficient. Pascal's triangle is more dynamic and richer, in particular if it is related to the combinatorics of probability.

10. IN VAIN QUEST FOR THE PARADIGM

I discontinue the sequence of paradigms. I could evoke the impression of turning them out by the dozen, which would be a quite wrong impression. On the contrary it is difficult – tremendously difficult in general – to find a good paradigm, a paradigm that is indeed worth trying hard for. Instead I will show – again in an exemplary way – an unexpected difficulty one can come across.

Some time ago I tried experimenting didactically with the so-called drawer (or Dirichlet) principle. I set out with a well-known question: "Are there two people in the world with the same number of hairs on their heads?" (It is useful to exclude bald people from the start.) As a matter of fact this question is, as it were, the shiboleth of the drawer principle, or seems to be so. Though I knew the question was too hard to be answered, I began with it. It is my habit to descend from difficult to easy in order to ascend at the end. After the question had indeed proved too difficult, I switched to the sequence of questions:

> Are there in your class two children with their birthdays in the same month? (Yes, John and Mary).

> Is it the same in every class?
> How large must a class be so that you can be sure two of its pupils have their birthdays in the same month: 10, 11, 12, 13, . . .?
> Are there in your school two children (teachers) with their birthdays on the same day?
> Is this the same in every school?
> How big must a school be to be certain to have two children (teachers) with their birthdays on the same day?
> (Variations with 'village' instead of 'school'.)

All these questions functioned even with 8-year olds. The answers were given with such persuasiveness that I did not ask for arguments, which in fact I would not have obtained either. A mathematician would argue as follows:

The set X of the children is mapped by the birthday into the set Y of the months; if there were no two with the same birth month, the mapping would be one-to-one and consequently the number of children would be less than, or equal to, the number of months. If, therefore, there are more children in the class than there are months, two must have the same birth month.

The children I gave the problems had received traditional arithmetic instruction without explicit one-to-one mappings. How might they have argued unconsciously? For instance: "one child in January, one in February, one in March, and so on – there are at most as many children as months"? I do not believe so, and the reader will understand after my exposition why I would not accept this solution.

My next question was the first time:

> Centipedes* have at most 100 feet; are there two centipedes with the same number of feet?

The answer was "Ha, ha! All centipedes have 34 feet". I do not know whether it is true; the girl had read or learned it somewhere. I tried to argue as would become a mathematician: "Let us agree that by a centipede we mean something with at most 100 feet". She had great fun with my subterfuge, but rather than accepting my proposal she thoroughly enjoyed the fact that she had taken me in. I chose another example.

* The corresponding Dutch term means 'millipedes'.

> A used match-box contains 100 matches at most; are there two of them with the same number of matches?

It is my experience that this problem does not function with 8 year-olds; 10 year-olds, with whom I do mathematics regularly, manage it hesitatingly – then the transfer to the problem of the hairs is smooth. Why is this question so different, what distinguishes it from the preceding ones?

Obviously here too the children could have argued: one box with 0 matches, one with 1 match, one with 2 matches, and so on, therefore 101 at most. They did not do so. Why not? Because it is a natural procedure to enumerate the months according to the calendar, but not the match-boxes according to the number of the matches in them?

Let us analyse it mathematically. X is now the set of match-boxes; Y, one would say, is the set $\{0, 1, \ldots, 100\}$ and then f would be the mapping that assigns to each box the number of its matches. In the first examples Y was the set of months, or days of the year – sets of the real world. Calling upon a subset of $\mathbb{N}$ as a mathematical tool is a strange idea; moreover the mapping f defies imagination. Y should rather have been a set given by the problem – one which was functional within the problem. Are there other options? Well, the set of numbers of matches in a match-box, but this is not a concrete enough set either. The numbers $0, 1, \ldots, 100$ must not appear as such but as numbers of matches in match-boxes. To solve the problem the child's unconscious must form this set, and it is just this problematic set which makes this problem give much more trouble than the former ones.

In order to solve such problems there is no need for the child to know what sets are but it must be able to form mental objects which are operated on as sets; and it is not at all certain that this is facilitated by an explicit set concept – I will return to this point; but something like the idea we call 'set' should be operationally available.

Adults who are able to work explicitly with sets consider the first and last problems as isomorphic and so did I until the children set me right. "Isn't it in both cases the drawer principle, in that one set is mapped in another, numerically smaller one?" 'Drawer principle' is a nice expression: the drawers are the months and the children are being pushed into them. Well, even this would not be too bad, but how if the drawers are the numbers of matches where the boxes must be pushed in? Superficially we state an isomorphism where there is none; surreptitiously one obtains isomorphisms by means of expressions like 'drawer principle' which in fact are of no use until one has grasped this isomorphism. Well, if it is known which set must play the part of Y and which mapping that of f – if the appropriate set has been constituted as Y and the appropriate mapping as f – the problems are isomorphic: it is always the same old tune.

Unfortunately set theory in today's schools is no training field for pupils to become acquainted with sets. The style vacillates between a formal definition of what is a set on the one hand, and wrong concretisations on the other – often both together. The pupil is seduced into believing that sets can be produced by drawings on paper, by Venn diagrams. Of course you can produce sets in this way, though not just those sets for which it pays to introduce sets. Assigning to a man not the set, but the number, of hairs on his head – well, it can be illustrated by a drawing (I mean afterwards, when it has been understood). It is much more important, and indeed the essential feature in the set concept, to form sets that cannot be shown on paper.

A typical example, which shows how strongly attached textbook authors are to a wrongly understood concreteness, is the frequently occurring universal set (or universe), which is cheerfully drawn on paper, and according to which complements, for instance, are formed. If it remained in this naïve concreteness, it would be bearable. But, along with the Venn diagram, one gets a definition of the universe as a fixed set that comprises all sets under discussion. Fortunately the set of all sets is not discussed, but anyhow after half a page the sets $\mathbb{N}, \mathbb{Z}, \mathbb{Q}, \mathbb{R}$ enter the field; and a few pages further even product sets and power sets – albeit of finite sets only – and finally also partitions and other mappings. Fortunately the pupil meanwhile forgot the universe, which cannot cause any harm because the only notion for which the universe was introduced, the complement set, is never applied in the sequel (which does not mean that other notions will somehow be applied).

Handling sets paradigmatically is not facilitated by explicit set thory. This is obvious, but beyond this it seems to be a fact that the didactician is seriously hampered in finding paradigms by the knowledge of explicit set theory. When a little while ago I explained about the successful experiments with the drawer principle – the birthdays in the same month and so on – I could not explain why one example functions paradigmatically and the other does so only in a restricted way. I could not even tell which non-analysed complex of ideas – "I see it this way" – is effective there and what restricts its power. I would not know either where to start the analysis, and I am afraid all I would do to find it out would be dominated by my own prejudices. The birthday problem lacks paradigmatic force in the sense that it does not allow the child to pass beyond the "I see it this way", and the observer to understand what happens there. One should dig deeper to make this possible. The problems around the drawer principle are not paradigmatic but the difficulties are symptomatic. Symptomatic for the phenomenon that sets and mappings, as results of an *accomplished* mathematisation, prejudice those of the mathematisation *to be accomplished*. Later on, where I touch upon the development of the cardinal number concept, I will again ask the question which part, if any, the set concept plays there. We lack not so much paradigms to the drawer principle but – more fundamentally – to the concepts of sets and mappings. How can we attain the situation where something is operationally grasped as a set or a mapping; and how should the operationally grasped idea be made conscious, verbally expressed? And even more fundamentally, how can we attain the situation where – in quest of paradigms – we are not struck with blindness by our explicit knowledge of set theory?

11. IN VAIN QUEST FOR DISCONTINUITIES IN THE LEARNING PROCESS

Elsewhere I have already said the necessary things on discontinuities in the learning process, their significance for understanding the learning process, and the urgent need for observation of learning processes to discover discontinuities. Here and there I adduced examples (or turned them out by the dozen, one would think again). The situation, however, looks much like that of the paradigms, and therefore I append the present section to the last. Moreover, as to the content, it is connected to the preceding section.

There are good reasons why discontinuties in learning processes are more easily observed the younger the learner is. The little ones manifest the discontinuities without restraint by Aha-Experiences. The older they are, the more blasé they have to behave, and finally all that is left are one's own Aha-Experiences: if only one knows how to observe oneself. I also reported about learning discontinuities which unfortunately were not exploited unto the Aha-Experience (the magic of the dice, p. 185).

Ever since I began observing learning processes, the most mysterious for me have been those concerning colour and (cardinal-ordinal) number. One fine morning there they are operationally; and nobody can tell when and where they have come from. As to the colour concept I once observed its sudden appearance (*once* among many trials). The child (3; 4) pointed to a ditch which it knew very well and upon which – it was late summer – a thick layer of duckweed had suddenly formed, and with great agitation asked: "What is the red?"* In fact he thought the surface could be walked upon. It was his first use of a colour word and that as a noun. The colour was discovered as an object. It is of course immaterial that duckweed is yellowish-green rather than red. It took quite a long time before he learned to master the colour words flawlessly: in fact two and a half years later this point had still not been reached. In the development of the colour concept an apprehensive event seems to be followed by a long comprehensive learning activity which is as little understood: why does it take such a long time, compared with the acquisition of other vocabulary, until that of colours is settled? Has it something to do with man's phylogenesis? Why are the languages of classical antiquity so poor as far as colour words are concerned? From my own childhood I remember my obstinacy in using colour names, which lasted even to the beginning of elementary school. Once, when a new suit was bought for me – it must have been around my fourth or fifth birthday – I got a little lilac flute from the shop-keeper. I was charmed by the flute as well as by the word 'lilac'. On the way home, however, while I played, it fell through the iron railings in the front garden of a villa and was never found again. From then onwards, and for quite a long time, I named that house the lilac villa, which, as it was not lilac, was to the adults a new symptom of my colour blindness.

In spite of all efforts, I have never observed a discontinuity in the normal developmental process of the number concept.** Or was I very near to it when a child got excited as it discovered it could count invisible objects?

What could be the clue in the constitution of number? There are numerals that in many languages are dealt with as adjectives: few, some, many. In languages with inflections the proper numerals above a certain limit do not

* In Dutch: "Wat is het rode?"

** See, however, the description of an extraordinary one, p. 281.

undergo declension. A feature common to all languages I am acquainted with is the absolute impossibility of using numerals predicatively: "the horse is brown" along with "brown horses", but not "the horse is three" nor "the horse is few, some, many".

However, 'three' is a property. Of what? Not of the horses but of the troop. 'Set', the mathematician says. Is this the decisive element in the genesis of the number concept that a set should be constituted? I am led to accept this idea by arguments I take from what I related in the preceding section. There, on a higher level, with the drawer principle, I succeeded in explaining the failure in the number concept by the default of the basically required set construction.

I shall put it as clearly as is needed to avoid misunderstanding. In no way would I affirm, as is the habit today, that set *concept* should be constituted before the child forms numbers. The constitution of the set concept, if it takes place at all, is of a higher level. What matters is forming certain mental objects of which the numbers are properties; I call these objects sets because this is what we do with mathematical objects of this kind. Several times I signalled the confusion, which is all the fashion now: rather than forming sets, which is important for the number concept, one attempts to instil the set concept in the children. And one step further, rather than numbers one wishes to teach the children the number concept. It is ever and again the skipping of levels in the learning process. In the genesis of the set and number concept the lowest level is constituting sets and numbers, and only at far higher levels is the constitution of the set concept and the number concept at home.

In a rational development of mathematics, cardinal numbers can be constituted as equivalence classes. This is an example of what is called concept formation by extension; and the constitution of weight by equivalence classes of equally heavy bodies and hardness by classes of scratching materials are other examples. The view on abstracting learning as a comprehensive process leads one to believe that the naïve learning process develops according to the pattern of equivalence classes or at least similar patterns. The Piaget experiments, which are called upon as evidence, prove to be just to the contrary.

For the mathematician the equivalence relation which constitutes numbers is that of one-to-one mapping. It is, however, improbable that it plays the same part when a child invents number. It is quite another thing that problems, in which one-to-one mappings are effective, can be used to check how far the genesis of the number concept has proceeded (we mentioned such tests on p. 199). The decisive element, or one of them, is constituting sets: a troop of horses is one and the same object however they run and stand, if only none run away, and no others join; it is the same object all the time, yesterday, today, tomorrow. I think I can explain linguistically why I could not discover set constitution in learning processes: there are in the language of 4-year-olds few, if any, terms for a set rooted in concreteness. At a higher age there are a lot of them: family, community, people, society, pack, troop, gang – a sequence that is easily continued up to the word 'set' itself – but what in the vocabulary of 4-year-olds can indicate to us the constitution of sets?

Sets will not be formed, unless there is some need that they should be. In the laboratory experiment the child is expected to view some hotch-potch as a set, but why should it? What could be the genuine need to form sets? A most obvious need could be the one that the child wants to delimit some possessions, say playthings of a certain kind, from those of others. Loss of old and gain of new elements are clearly recognisable events. If nothing of this kind happens, the set is unchanged.

A fashionable term is 'conservation'. It is indeed an important idea, much more important than that of one-to-one mapping. The one-to-one mapping is indeed a high level concept. In the beginning it can only be constituted if the sets considered are separated. All examples for introducing it presuppose that the sets which are to be one-to-one related are separated. It is in fact the only way to do it. Overlappings or even inclusiveness within the pair of sets cannot but seriously trouble the development of this concept. The applicability of the one-to-one mapping is enormously restricted by this fact; it cannot contribute much to the constitution of number.

By contrast with equivalence through one-to-one mapping, conservation as a constituting principle of mental objects is natural and simple. Only it is projected on the wrong spot by those who use it theoretically. It is not number but set that is constituted by the conservation principle, and the principle itself can be formulated as we did above: if none run away, and none join, it remains the same.

'Conservation', however, is no magic word. One should not believe it can explain much. Volume and mass rest on conservation principles quite different from that for sets. A marble that is pulverised – what is conserved there? What is reversible there? Psychologists presuppose the child's conceptual system to be largely and lastingly detached from reality and do not consider to what degree this detachment is not a process determined by important factual experiences, though I agree that in the laboratory setting of their experiments they cannot do anything else. I think it is worth reporting the only observation on conservation (other than those of set or number) I had the opportunity to make in a learning process:

One day I went for a walk with Bastiaan (almost 5; 0) along the Amsterdam Rhine Canal, where excavations had been made and are still to be continued in order to broaden the fairway. Suddenly he burst into a stream of words I could not make head or tail of. Eventually when he calmed down I gathered that he wondered where the water came from to fill the gap caused by the excavation. My answer was put into a broader context, including even the global circulation of water in nature. Though further experience is still lacking, I feel that Bastiaan's problem indicated some decisive point in his development with respect to conservation.* At any rate it shows a feature that is entirely lacking in artificial laboratory experiments.

I have not been able to observe the process of acquiring sets mentally. I only know that 4-year-olds can manipulate sets but I cannot tell how they acquired them. As I have not observed Aha-Experiences in this learning process, I am prone to believe it happened comprehensively. At this age children can also estimate the cardinal numbers of sets, and they can do so with an astonishingly accurate approximation without counting (as did Bastiaan (4; 3) with the number of little ducks around a mother duck, and the number of piggies by a hog). But this does not prove much as it does not in general happen spontaneously but after the question "How many?" Is this already the constitution of number? I do not believe so. The constitution of number requires sharper features.**

I suppose that a child constitutes numbers as properties of sets, but I cannot believe that this happens without any provocation. Whole tribes have never managed it. Why? There was nothing that could induce them to do so.

One would like to object that those tribes do not have numerals either.

* In his further development he never showed any lack of 'conservation'.

** See p. 281.

Quite right. In our society, children learn numerals early on, as they do colour names, and even counting. Only they are unprepared to do anything with this skill. Counting the same items again and again with the same result, also independently of the order, creates the ever strong associations, psychologists claim, which lead to number. I need not emphasize that I do not believe in continuous learning where essentials are involved; essential concepts are not acquired in the way tables of multiplication are memorised. I look for the discontinuities, the compelling events, the strong inducements.

What could provoke such jumps? I conjectured that delimiting one's own property from that of others is an inducement to form sets. If this is true, the need to check whether one's property has not changed could be an inducement to constitute number. As long as the elements of a set can individually be distinguished and identified – for instance the members of a family – as long as the set as a whole is easily surveyed, the need is not urgent. The misfortune of the little duck that lost its mother, which could not count and consequently was ignorant about the gap in the crowd, did not at that stage convince Bastiaan (4; 3) that rather than estimating one should count. The problem had not yet seized him. In the right situation, with the right material, the need can suddenly be felt, and it is good luck to be able to witness it. In order to make sure whether nothing is lacking, the child counts, I suppose – most of them learn it long before the constitution of number. I do not know how far Bastiaan (4; 3) can count; he does not take orders. Once when he threw three sticks into the water one after the other, he counted 1, 2, 3. One counts first steps of processes rather than sets.

Counting out a set does not mean anything. If counting is a means of proving that one's possessions have not changed, the constancy of the number that results from counting must be recognised as a criterion of the constancy of a set. How can the child arrive at this assumption?

A short while ago I uttered a hypothesis: was not counting invisible sets the decisive discontinuity? Indeed this could lead to the criterion of the constancy of sets: the child counts the visible set; the set disappears but can still be counted, in the memory, long after it has disappeared; it comes back, and behold, it can be counted out all the same.

There would be three steps leading to constituting number: first constituting sets, for instance as of possessions, a process that might go on comprehensively; second, the counting out of sets that under the pressure of adults develops comprehensively – rather than apprehensively, which would not be impossible – while the constancy of the result is not yet grasped as such; third, the possibly apprehensive seizure on counting as a means of checking one's estate, for instance at the opportunity of counting absent or partially or transitorily absent sets.

Is this the way number develops? Certainly there are many ways, as children differ greatly. The disturbing feature of this development is that children go a long way in counting before the numbers are constituted. This seems to be normal. The only deviation from this pattern I know is Bastiaan who refused to count before achieving cardinal number – the story about it, which happened after the present section was written, will be told later on.*

At any rate, up to that point, according to my hypothesis, the one-to-one mapping plays no part. Even if the child grasps that all people have the same number of fingers, that on all dice equivalent sets are pictured, that boxes of play bricks of the same brand contain the same number of bricks, it is a comparison of congruent, or similar, or equally functioning sets rather than a one-to-one assignment. If these devices of comparison fail, sets are counted, for the child readily learns that this is the most effective tool. For the older child one has to contrive tricks in order to have him or her compare sets by one-to-one mappings – earlier on I mentioned a few of them (p. 199), the decoration of the vase with alternating suns and moons, the chains of pearls of alternating colours. Almost always we compare sets by means of the set of natural numbers because mostly the two sets to be compared are not simultaneously present. If the table is to be laid for six persons, we must count out the plates; after this, it is true, the knives and forks will be laid by one-to-one assignment. This then is the way we should do it with the first graders, the majority of whom have already constituted number: let them count where adults count, and leave them to one-to-one assignment in situations where adults too practise it. Certainly they should learn it, because it affects systematic counting. Albeit strongly mathematised situations at higher age level that invite one-to-one mappings have been beautifully described by A. Kirsch**, for instance comparing the sets of all three digit numbers with

* p. 281.

** A. Kirsch, 'Eineindeutige Zuordnungen im 5. Schuljahr, Begründung des Zehlbegriffs oder Förderung der Kombinationsfähigkeit', *Die Schulwarte* 7–8 (1973) 29–36.

a 2 at the end,
a 3 at the end,
a 3 in the centre
a 3 at the beginning
first and last digit equal,

and formalising the one-to-one mapping, which belongs to an entirely different level.

With the synthesis of cardinal and ordinal number concepts the development is still far from accomplished. How much is still left to be observed: grasping the transitivity of equality – likewise of magnitudes – the order relations, the insight into the infinity of the counting process*, and the part played in all this by mappings.

12. AN APPREHENDING APPROACH TO ALGEBRA

Guided by arithmetic and algebra instruction I once more confront the traditional with the paradigmatic method in order to pass to a third method and a fourth, which is apprehensive though not paradigmatic.

The usual method of traditional arithmetic and algebra instruction is to introduce the operations and to corroborate the laws governing them by examples; as opposed to this the geometric and the algebraic method, if truly understood, aim straightforwardly at generality. As I have stressed, examples are not a bad thing, if only they are really exemplary, that is paradigmatic. The example of the roads from A over B to C has such a convincing power that its validity – even without being generally formulated – spreads as a skin of oil. If the development of language has not yet progressed far enough, a general formulation may be less conclusive than paradigmatic examples and can even hamper the generalisation of content. Examples, on the contrary, if they are paradigmatic, can be mathematics of good standing.

If a learner has transferred one paradigm often enough in order finally to arrive at the general formulation, one can be misled to the conclusion that the generalisation was the result of numerous applications. This, however, need not be the case at all; such a belief can witness insufficient insight into the levels of the learning process: a cognition is confused with its formulation.

* I reported about one observation in *Mathematics as an Educational Task*, p. 173.

As to the content, the generalisation can have taken place at the first instance, that is with the paradigm – this would be proved by the ease of dealing with new cases by means of the paradigm. The numerous examples then were required to elicit the *need* for a general formulation and to exercise its linguistic conditions. Of course there are cases where the generalisation, also as to the content, is and must be accomplished by painstakingly piling up material of the same kind, but this is hardly characteristic of the areas we are now entering.

A method, classical in algebra though now highly perfected, is the arithmetical one. It consists in teaching pupils to solve problems like

$$-3-5 = \ldots,$$

$$3-(2-7) = \ldots,$$

hoping that it will help them to grasp rules like

$$-a-b = -(a+b),$$

$$a-(b-c) = (a-b)+c$$

and to apply them. Not only does one hope, one even 'argues' the general formulae by such numerical 'examples'.

In fact these examples are not at all paradigmatic, they are 'antidigmatic', I would say. It looks like drawing a right angled triangle, writing 3, 4, 5 at the sides, and $3^2+4^2=5^2$ below, and explaining: "That is Pythagoras, $a^2+b^2=c^2$." The solution of $-3-5=\ldots$ is paradigmatic at most in the way that it 'easily' transforms to $-4-8=\ldots$ and so on, but the formula that matters is $-a-b=-(a+b)$ in general and not only for $a>0$, $b>0$. Even if the textbook does not claim or suggest that this suffices, and carefully distinguishes four cases, it is no help to attaining understanding since such fundamental things cannot be understood in distinguishing cases.

With the second kind of problem, $3-(2-7)$, it is even worse. Indeed, the result is simple $3-(-5)=8$, and all subtleties of the formula $a-(b-c)=(a-b)+c$ have disappeared in the worked out numbers. Here the numerical example does not help even partially.

To this arithmetical method of establishing algebra I opposed a genuinely algebraic one*. It rests on what I called the algebraic principle: For instance

* *Mathematics as an Educational Task*, p. 224.

$-x$ is defined by

$$x+(-x) = 0,$$

and from this, formulae like

$$-a-b = -(a+b)$$

are derived by – explicitly – using known arithmetical rules:

$$a+(-a) = 0, \qquad b+(-b) = 0$$

$$a+(-a)+b+(-b) = 0$$

$$(a+b)+((-a)+(-b)) = 0$$

in which proof, a and b could also be replaced with – paradigmatically exemplary – arbitrary numbers. At the cited place I have circumstantially discussed the possible objections against this method. I have shown that, in particular when introducing fractions, this method is preferable to the arithmetical method, which today has been perfected by unheard of sophistications, but is operational only in the sprinkling phase.

Shortly I repeat what I said at the same place about a geometrical method of establishing algebra. The operations are interpreted as mappings of the number line, for instance, the subtraction from -3 as the mapping

$$x \to -3-x,$$

which intuitively is the reflection interchanging 0 and -3. It is intuitively evident what under this mapping happens with 5 or any other number on the number line, without distinguishing cases. Now, the mapping

$$x \to 3-(2-x)$$

is the product of two reflections, thus a translation, namely that translation which carries $x=0$ into $x=3-2=1$, thus

$$3-(2-x) = (3-2)+x.$$

Again this one instance is paradigmatic, and no particular cases need to be distinguished.

I would, however, try to lay the foundations of the geometrical method more profoundly, not simply in the paradigmatic way. If this has to happen, it is an indispensable didactical condition that mathematical instruction has been geometrised early and fundamentally – it is a postulate I will argue in more detail later on.

In that case the child has early become familiar with geometrical mappings, and by regular rounds this knowledge has gained depth. The child is familiar with reflections in the plane and has recognised the translations as products of reflections at parallel lines. These planar mappings are now restricted to a fixed line, which will later on carry the real numbers, but at this moment is still a homogeneous geometrical object – a rigid oriented ruler with no scale. The mappings are dynamically experienced as translations and reversions – so far I have tried it with 9 year olds. The following is a thought experiment:

The totality of translations is experienced as a group, and likewise the totality of translations and reversions together – of course without using group theory terminology.

Then a fixed point of the line is assumed and denoted by '0'. A translation (reversion) is characterised by the image of 0: an intuitively obvious fact. The translation (reversion) that carries 0 into a is indicated by $a +$ $(a -)$. This includes identity $0 +$, and the reflection at the origin $0 -$. A sequence of 'computing laws' for these operations are derived, while using the fact which kind of mapping is the product of a pair of such mappings – a conceptually paradigmatic activity in which the computing laws acquire geometrical content. After the additive structure the multiplicative one is dealt with in the same way: the dilatations are the mappings leaving invariant the additive structure; a point different from 0 is denoted by '1'; a dilatation is characterised by its 1-image; if a is the 1-image, it is denoted by the multiplication $a\,\cdot$. In a similar way as for the addition, 'computing laws' for the multiplication are derived from the group structure.

On this geometrical line the numbers must be localised and the arithmetical operations recognised. At which moment should this be done? I would say: not until the geometrical apparatus functions, both conceptually and algorithmically, at least to a certain degree, after dealing with addition, but before multiplication. As a matter of fact, the commutativity of multiplication can hardly be justified without an appeal to numbers.

If the numbers are localised on the number line, it is first *natural* numbers only. Then the *negative* ones enter automatically. It is no new definition that the mirror image of 7 at the origin gets the name $0 - 7$ (abridged as -7) but a fact that can simply be stated on the strength of earlier definitions. It is remarkable that the troublesome double role of plus and minus signs as both state and operations signs is non-existent. There are operation signs only, and $-a$ is simply an abbreviation of $0-a$.

Rational numbers are of no concern at this stage. They need not emerge until the dilatations are dealt with, but they do emerge as soon as dilatations with whole multipliers are inverted. The whole procedure is similar to that which I described in my earlier book*; it is the gradual numerical penetration of the – pre-existent – number line rather than its creation.

This geometrical approach to algebra is decisively distinguished by the feature that the computing laws are obtained not surreptitiously by unparadigmatic examples, but by a general conceptual seizure, apprehensively though not by paradigms. Since it depends on many preconditions, there is no need to decide in general whether this approach must be elaborated in the form of mathematical proofs or whether all remains at the level of geometrical insight – later on this level will be described in more detail.

It is in no way settled, nor can it be done without making the thought experiment more precise (and without transforming it into a true experment) which age levels the various steps of this approach would fit. Geometrical preparations can start early but it depends on experience which is still entirely lacking, how far they can progress. Conceptual sophistication and formalisation should start early, but even if they would come so late that if compared with the present situation formal algebra were retarded, it would not be a loss. It is no secret any more that formal algebra, though instructed earlier, hardly functions before the 9th grade (age 15).

In order to show what the approach I sketched above involves logically, I am going to delineate its mathematical background. The following should be read with the eye of the mathematician.

13. THE MATHEMATICAL BACKGROUND OF THE GEOMETRICAL APPROACH TO ALGEBRA

Axioms A–E are accepted.

* *Mathematics as an Educational Task*, Chap. XIV.

Axiom A. The straight line bears an orientation and a group G of ('rigid') one-to-one mappings, which either conserve the orientation (translations) or invert it (reversions); the square of a reversion is the identity (the reversions are 'involutions').

Consequences of A:

1. The products of two translations is a translation.

2–3. The product of a translation and a reversion (in both ways) is a reversion.

4. The product of two reversions is a translation.

Axiom B. For any two points a, b of the line ($a = b$ is admitted) there is exactly one translation and exactly one reversion that carries a into b.

Remark: The reversion carrying a into b interchanges a and b.

Notation: A certain point of the line is denoted 0. The translation carrying 0 into a, is denoted by $a\,+$; the reversion interchanging 0 and a is denoted by $a\,-$.

Then it follows:

5. $a + 0 = a,$

6. $a - 0 = a,$

7. $a - a = 0.$

From B it follows:

8. If $a - b = 0$, then $a = b$.

From 1 it follows that the transition from x to $a + (b + x)$ is a translation, hence for appropriate c:

$$a + (b + x) = c + x.$$

What is this c? Put $x = 0$. Because of 5

$$a + (b + 0) = a + b,$$

and $$c + 0 = c,$$

thus $$a + (b + x) = (a + b) + x.$$

Similarly from 2,

$$a - (b + x) = c - x$$

for appropriate c. Put $x = 0$. Then

$$a - (b + x) = (a - b) - x.$$

And similarly further. Together:

9. $a + (b + x) = (a + b) + x$

10. $a - (b + x) = (a - b) - x$

11. $a + (b - x) = (a + b) - x$

12. $a - (b - x) = (a - b) + x.$

Commutativity is harder to prove: One applies 10, 11, 7, 5, 7 in this order:

$$\begin{aligned} (a + b) - (b + a) &= ((a + b) - b) - a && \text{by } 10, \\ &= (a + (b - b)) - a && \text{by } 11, \\ &= (a + 0) - a && \text{by } 7, \\ &= a - a && \text{by } 5, \\ &= 0 && \text{by } 7, \end{aligned}$$

and from this by 8:

$$a + b = b + a.$$

According to B there is one translation carrying a into b. How can it be denoted? It carries 0 into some c, thus

$$c + a = b,$$

which is solved by $c = b - a$, because by 12, 7, 6

$$(b - a) + a = b - (a - a) = b - 0 = b.$$

Thus:

13. For any a, b there is exactly one c with $c + a = b$, namely

$$c = b - a.$$

Up to now we have not met expressions like $-a, -a + b, -a - b$. If they are to be introduced following common usage, a notation is to be convened:

Notation: $-a$ means $0-a$.

Thus

14. $$-(-a) = a,$$

because of $0-(0-a)=(0-0)+a=0+a=a+0=a$,

15. $$a+(-b) = a-b,$$

because of $a+(0-b)=(a+0)-b=a-b$,

16. $$a-(-b) = a+b$$

because of $a-(0-b)=(a-0)+b=a+b$.

A sophistication: How can all reversions be found?

Let f be a reversion. f maps 0 in some a. There is a reversion interchanging 0 and a, namely $a\,-$. Consider the translation

$$(a\,-)\circ f.$$

It fixes 0, thus is the identity. Thus f is the inverse of $a\,-$, thus identical with $a\,-$. Consequently:

17. Any reversion has the form $a\,-$ (with appropriate a).

According to B there is one reversion interchanging a and b. How can it be denoted? One looks for c with $c-a=b$. This is solved by $c=b+a$ because of

$$(b+a)-a = b.$$

Likewise the equation $c-a=b$ for a is solved by $a=c-b$.

Thus

18. The equation $c-a=b$ has for given a, b the (unique) solution $c=a+b$, for given b, c the (unique) solution $a=c-b$.

From A it also follows:

19. If $b<c$, then $a+b<a+c$ and $a-b>a-c$.

Notation: Instead of $a>0$ ($a<0$) one says a is positive (negative).

Axiom C. On the line, a group H of one-to-one mappings is present, which leave 0 and the additive structure invariant (the dilatations from 0), and leave invariant or invert the orientation.

Axiom D. For any two points a, b (both $\neq 0$) there is exactly one dilatation from 0 that carries a into b.

Axiom E. H is commutative.

Notation. Some point different from 0 is denoted by 1. The dilatation from 0 carrying 1 into a ($\neq 0$) is denoted by $a\,\cdot$.

Thus

20. $a \cdot 0 = 0,$

21. $a \cdot 1 = a.$

The invariance of the additive structure is written as

22. $a \cdot (x+y) = a \cdot x + a \cdot y,$

23. $a \cdot (x-y) = a \cdot x - a \cdot y.$

The existence and uniqueness of the dilatation from 0 that carries x into y, is expressed by

24. For any x, y (both $\neq 0$) there is exactly one a, such that $a \cdot x = y$.

As was done with addition, one considers the product of two dilatations in order to corroborate that

$$a \cdot (b \cdot x) = (a \cdot b) \cdot x.$$

It is useful to admit 0 as a left factor and to define

$$0 \cdot x = 0.$$

Then from the commutativity of H it follows generally

26. $a \cdot b = b \cdot a.$

$a\,\cdot$ preserves the mutual order relation of the points 0, 1 if $a > 0$ and changes it if $a < 0$. Thus $a\,\cdot$ preserves the order on the line if $a > 0$ and inverts it if $a < 0$. Thus

27. From $x < y$ it follows
$ax < ay$ for $a > 0$,
$ax > ay$ for $a < 0$.

I stop here.

It should be noticed that all details can also geometrically be recognised except the commutativity of multiplication. That of addition can be put in a larger context, the vector addition in the plane. In order to justify that of multiplication, one must recur to arithmetical experiences, or to quite different geometrical experiences such as the area of the rectangle.

14. THE ALGEBRAIC VERSUS THE ARITHMETICAL APPROACH TO ALGEBRA

In the primary mathematics education of Western countries no strong tendencies can be felt towards a geometrical interpretation of operations and computing laws, and none towards an algebraical interpretation. On the contrary, never have arithmetic antidigmatic methods been flourishing as they are now in algebra, fractions included. In the Soviet Union, the algebraisation of arithmetic instruction has been tackled. These investigations (from the circle of V.V. Davydov) are hardly known in Western countries. In my view, rather than unfamiliarity with the Russian language, the reason for this ignorance is that at first sight they do not seem to promise much. I have given a closer look at them*. The investigations concern experiments in the 1st to 4th grades (7–11-year-olds), which were carried out in the second half of the sixties. Because of endless repetitions and stylistic clumsiness it is boring reading matter; another seemingly forbidding feature is its strong dependence upon such teaching methods and subject matter as prevail in Soviet education. Those disadvantages and many others are more than outweighed by what seems to me an unusual quality in principle: a sound pedagogic-psychological idea behind these experiments, their design and their analysis.

The investigations** are concerned with teaching a topic which is

* I translated part of it for private use and published a reasoned summary as 'Soviet Research on Teaching Algebra at the Lower Grades of the Elementary School', *Educational Studies in Mathematics* 5 (1974), 391–412.

** V.V. Davydov (ed.), *Psihologičeskie vozmožnosti mladših škol'nikov v usvoenij matematiki*, Moscow, Izd. Prosveščenie, the contributions of G.G. Mikulina, G.I. Minskaja and F.G. Bodanskij.

characteristic of Soviet instruction from the first grade onwards: *word problems*. A few patterns may evoke some idea of what this topic means.

1st grade: In the morning . . . tractors worked on the land. In the course of the day some more joined them. Then there were . . . of them working. How many more had joined them?

Kolja had a number of books. Dad gave him . . . more and Mum . . . more. Then he had . . . books. How many did he have originally?

2nd grade: A department store got . . . tons of vegetables and later . . . tons more. They sold a . . . part of it. How much did they sell?

A bed was planted first with . . . plants, then with . . . times more and finally with . . . more than the first planting. How many were planted?

3rd grade: At a building site . . . labourers worked. Among them there were . . . bricklayers and of the remainder there were as many carpenters as painters. How many carpenters worked there?

In a workshop, pillow slips were sewn from three pieces of linen. The first piece was . . . meters long, the second . . . meters longer than the first, the third . . . times shorter than the first. After sewing . . . meters were left. How many meters of linen were used for the slips?

4th grade: The Moskva 407 car weighs 480 kg more than the Volga and 970 kg less than the Čaĭka, but the Čaĭka weighs 490 kg less than the Moskva 407 and Volga together. Find the weight of each car.

In one basin there were 190 l of water, and in another 750 l. The first fills with a speed of 40 l a minute, and the second empties with a speed of 30 l a minute. After how many minutes is there an equal amount of water in each basin?

This is a kind of problem which for the last half a century has been of declining importance in Western Europe and probably has now been eclipsed (in the Netherlands for about 30 years); in the mathematical instruction of the Soviet elementary school it has been further developed and its didactics – arithmetical rather than algebraical – have been brought to great prosperity. As early as the end of the thirties, A.Ja. Hinčin (Khintchin) sharply criticised this arithmetical method, which he called tasteless and of which he stated, after an inquiry among teachers that it is learned by very few pupils only. In later years B.V. Gnedenko and A.I. Markušievič assailed this method anew. These charges were continued and strongly intensified by V.V. Davydov and his school. It is highly remarkable what Davydov opposes to it. The sound pedagogical-psychological idea behind the experiments is that – in many cases – abstraction and generality are not attained by an approach using a large number of concrete and special cases. They rather require (if no paradigmatic example is available, a circumstance we considered in our discussion too) a straightforward abstract and general approach.

This consists in early letter arithmetic, or so they call it, which at least in word problems even precedes numerical arithmetic in time. The children are shown quantities of water, blocks, grits, and so on, which are indicated by letters. It is concretely shown that a is part of b, that a water together with b water yields $a + b$ water, that $a - b$ water is left if b water is taken away from a water; and the same is symbolised in drawings, expressed verbally, and formulated by means of an abridged symbolic language. The ease with which pupils understand, assimilate and apply such equivalences as $a + x = b$, $x = b - a$, $a = b - x$ is operationally decisive. They are protected against all mistakes that are invited by the numerical approach. Indeed with numbers it is so comfortable to know that if it is subtraction, it is the smaller that is subtracted from the larger one, that divisions do not leave a remainder, and so on. But apart from this, it is obvious that the letter approach offers many advantages.

It is a pity that it does not lead further than literal arithmetic. No genuine algebra arises. If Kolya reads a pages today and b tomorrow, it is $a + b$ together, and $b + a$ is marked as wrong. If a machine weighs p kg, k machines weigh pk kg and certainly not kp kg. Distance must be written as speed times time, and not the other way round. The literal expressions are process descriptions rather than names of magnitudes. They are not properly used for calculations: if it happens, it is the procedures of the arithmetical tradition that are relied upon.

It is to be regretted that these remarkable ideas have not been realised more consistently. Nevertheless I cannot but express the highest praise for the well designed didactics and the method of reporting – I know nothing like this in the Western literature. The statistical evaluation of this method proves its superiority convincingly compared with the old arithmetical method. The pupils instructed by means of literal arithmetic approach a 100% score in solving the final test problems, while control classes, even of higher grades, do not succeed by more than 50–60%.

It is, however, surprising that even for the control classes this percentage is far above Hinčin's data mentioned above. Has didactics meanwhile improved to such a degree, or do the control classes belong to better schools?

These questions are idle. I can imagine that Hinčin would not have accepted these experiments as a counterproof of his statements. Though those authors again and again assert that in the course of their experiments the children learn to solve new problems self-reliantly, it appears that they always think within the narrow frame of a small number of patterns of problems, which I believe Hinčin and the other critics would hardly have accepted. I am convinced the butt of their criticism was not only the arithmetical method, but also the choice of artificial problems, contrived in order to exercise this method. What the experiments achieved is to show that by means of literal arithmetic the performance of pupils in solving this special kind of word problem can be improved. But as algebra these problems are meaningless; algebra is better exercised in full swing rather than as literal arithmetic.

The authors may have known this, though they may have argued that arithmetical methods have to be defeated first of all on their own battleground. Indeed, this may be good tactics; although it is certainly wrong strategy. Opportunism can be dangerous policy. Teaching problems must be solved fundamentally.

After this criticism I once more emphasise the fundamental value of these investigations: abstraction and generality not according to the sprinkler method but as a principle, from the start onwards. The experiments show convincingly that this is possible and they make it probable that algebra can start better – and perhaps earlier – than now.

15. LEVELS OF LANGUAGE

Earlier I gave utterance to my amazement that hardly anything seems to be known about the learning processes of the mother language. No doubt much goes on there continuously and unobtrusively. Yet everybody knows, from observation in the family environment, sudden linguistic acquisitions – pronouncing other people's names or one's own name (or what is interpreted by the adult as the child's naming himself in the process of learning his language), the sudden success with the pronounciation of resistant phonemes or words, the first sentence, the first composite sentence. Some of these sudden acquisitions are spontaneously and consciously lived through by the child learning his language; others are stressed by the adults.

I will not occupy myself with the phonetic learning process though it need not be unimportant for learning mathematics – for instance one of my sons and one of my grandsons had such troubles with the Dutch word for two, 'twee', that for a long time they refused to pronounce it or replaced it with other numerals.

The process of learning vocabulary will also be disregarded, though such an essential development as acquiring the categories of the adult seems closely connected to the acquisition of the stock of words.

I attach more importance to syntactical acquisitions. It is reasonably known in which order they are acquired, but it is unknown *how* it happens. One may be surprised that the causal structures are so late since the child's actions betray the doubtless operational mastery of – logical and factual – causalities. I guess it is functional flaws in the query and answer game of child and adults that is responsible for the delay of the active linguistic use of causal structure. If the child or the father asks 'Why are there no apples today?', the mother is not likely to answer 'because the greengrocer did not get them' (and certainly not 'we do not have apples because there were none at the greengrocer's'), but the answer will probably be 'the greengrocer had no apples'. And if the mother asks the child 'why are your hands that dirty', she does not insist on an answer that begins with 'because'. So there are quite good reasons why after the 'why' the 'because' is so much delayed.

We will soon see that the syntactic structures that are mathematically interesting, and suggested by mathematics, are of another kind. But before entering this field, a remark of principle.

We all know that most of us understand more language than we can speak. The maxim of an experiment in foreign language instruction in the 5th–6th grade I recently read – "we cannot demand that all pupils are equally far in speaking, but we do absolutely demand that they are equally far in understanding" – is quite plausible to me, and as long as it does not express defeatism, I can even approve of it. Yet I ask myself how thoroughly the fact of general understanding and restricted speaking has already been studied in its didactical consequences, not only for language education but for all education where language is the vehicle. One of these consequences indeed is the division of the members of a social system into groups of those who can formulate proposals, plans, commissions, decisions, and those who can understand, and carry them out – a division which at school need not coincide with that into teacher and pupils. I dealt with the consequences of this linguistic gradient on p. 52, and it is clear that I would like to understand, and if possible, to conquer them. The following, however abstractly formulated, might prove to be a contribution to it.

If I distinguish levels of language it need not be levels in the learning processes, though structurally they can be quite similar. This should be stressed to avoid misunderstandings. On the other hand I should say that I discovered them as levels in learning processes.

I start with an example that is already known, though it is purely linguistic and lacks any mathematical touch.

I take a walk with Bastiaan (3; 5). We are passed by a wheelchair with a woman in it pushed by a nurse. The lady in the chair says something to the nurse. Bastiaan asks: "What did the lady say to the lady that pushed the wheelchair?"* After the second 'lady' he hesitated, before he, hurriedly, ejaculated the relative clause. Obviously he had noticed that something was wrong with the double use of the word 'lady'; the relative clause was a conscious addition, recognised as necessary.

Bastiaan's construction is hybrid: 'the lady' is ostensive the first time; the second time – with the clause added – relative. An entirely ostensive construction would be 'what did the lady say to the lady?' and an entirely relative one 'what did the lady in the chair say to the lady that pushed?' Bastiaan used formally relative constructions very early; the striking feature in the reported event is the conscious experience of the necessity of relative constructions – a symptom of a higher level in the learning process.

In the first grade of a primary school (6–7 years) we had the children discovering mirror symmetries; among others they had to complete half a figure, for instance half a leaf of a tree. There were failures; sometimes children are misled into interchanging not only right and left but also 'above' and 'below', which delivers a central rather than an axial symmetry – adults too frequently err by explaining oblique parallelograms as mirror symmetric. Describing symmetry and asymmetry goes on in an ostensive language 'if there is a spot here, such a spot must be there too', and in this ostensive language it is discussed with the children what is wrong, and explained why. Children at this age can hardly be led on the level of the use of relative language in this context, and even with older ones it requires long preparations. One is

* Dutch: "Wat zei de mevrouw tegen de mevrouw die het wagentje duwde?" It is not easy translating colloquial language.

confronted with a complex of constructions which is not easy to describe, and before being described must be organised mathematically – a beautiful example of mathematisation. An auxiliary mathematical concept is badly needed, that of reflecting, or mirror image, together with its linguistic expression; concrete mirrors are of course a useful device in developing it. With 'mirror image' it becomes easy to describe seemingly complicated situations; in a plain and concise language it can now be told why the completed leaf must, or must not, have a spot here or there. One cannot expect pupils to invent this auxiliary notion; aimful guidance is indispensable. A similar experiment in a fifth grade (11–12 years) shows pupils able to find on a Mercator map of the Earth the antipode of a given point, but unable to describe this process, not to speak of explaining it. Because of the lack of instruments as description by coordinates this is hardly possible.

Let us come back to symmetry! The concept of mirror image can reasonably be handled while the children cannot yet describe what it is, not even how it is properly constructed. 'Mirror image' can be an undefined concept which translates the 'here-there' relation mentioned earlier into relative language: 'to every spot there belongs its mirror image', 'these are mirror images of each other'. What a mirror image is, however, is explained ostensively, where the demonstration can be an action, such as the construction of the mirror image with a ruler and compasses. The real action can already have been replaced with an action that is only described. 'What is the mirror image of P with respect to l?' can be rendered as 'How can we find the mirror image?' and answered with 'I drop the perpendicular from P upon the straight line l and extend it as much behind l as P is before.' At a higher linguistic level the definition of 'mirror image' and the description of its construction can be given in relative language, for instance 'A point is a mirror image of another if it is at a right angle as far behind the mirror as the other is before', or with more sophistication, 'Two points are mirror images of each other if, being on opposite sides of the mirror, they are as far away from the mirror at the same point'. These are complicated constructions which require a considerable linguistic ability; in fact the describer will mostly prefer description by an activity. The mathematical language, however, knows other, more efficient, devices: introducing *conventional symbols for variables*. As the reality of everyday life is mathematised by such auxiliary concepts as 'reflection', so is everyday language by conventional symbols for variables. In the present case this might be: 'The points P, P' are called mirror images of each other with respect to a straight line l if PP' is perpendicular to l and divided into equal parts by l', or shorter 'if l is the perpendicular bisector of PP'.'

Likewise properties of the perpendicular bisector can be formulated at various linguistic levels. Two points are given on the paper without naming them – though in order to communicate with you, I call them P, P' – a few more points are indicated, again with no names – though on your behalf I call them $Q_1, Q_2, Q_3, \ldots$ – such that always according to their lengths $PQ_1 = P'Q_1, PQ_2 = P'Q_2, PQ_3 = P'Q_3$ and so on, where pairs of identical symbols in these line segments show those which are meant to be of equal length, and this activity is accompanied by statements such as 'this is as long as that', 'this is as long as that', and so on. The new points are situated upon this straight line – which I show – perpendicular to the line joining the first two points, a fact that is again described in ostensive language.

With such ostensive methods children can very early progress very far in geometry; the reason why, in the traditional school programme, geometry comes rather late is that traditionally it is taught in a language that would not suit very young children – this is a point I will deal with more circumstantially later on.

It depends on the linguistic skills of the pupils at which moment – possibly pushed by a gentle impulse – they will pass to partially or entirely relative methods. Again the most expressive language is that by conventional variables such as I used to communicate with the reader, and which would produce constructions like the following:

> Q lies on the perpendicular bisector of PP' if and only if $PQ = P'Q$,

or further symbolised,

$$Q \text{ on the perpendicular bisector of } PP' \leftrightarrow PQ = P'Q.$$

In a first approach I distinguished three levels (but this will soon be refined): the ostensive language where showing with the index finger or mentally is accompanied by words like 'this' and 'that'; the relative language where objects are described by their relations to other objects; the introduction of conventional variables, which makes the relative language function more smoothly. Along with this I made another distinction: whether the description regards a state of affairs or an activity – for instance, 'the first street to the left of the third street to the right beyond the traffic light' versus 'go straight to the traffic light, then take the third street right, and of this the first street to the left.' The only ostensive element common to both expressions is 'the traffic light'; the language is mostly relative, once as a description of a state of affairs, and in the other case as a description of an activity, which, however, includes words such as 'then' with a temporal ostensive touch.

Algebra too can provide us with examples. I choose that of the square root. A description like

$3^2 = 9$ so 3 is the square root of 9,

$5^2 = 25$ so 5 is the square root of 25 and so on

is exemplary and therefore as it were ostensive. If the following is said:

> the square root of a number is found by looking for a number that squared gives the original number

the description is relative by means of activities; on the contrary:

> the square root of a number is that number, the square of which is the original number

gives a description of a state of affairs with uncomfortable variables of everyday language such as 'the number', 'the original number'. In

$$x = \sqrt{a} \leftrightarrow x^2 = a$$

conventional variables are used, but it can be done even better with a new auxiliary concept,

> taking the square root is the inverse of squaring,

a functional description, which is made possible by introducing a suitable function, that is by raising 'taking the square root' to the rank of a function.

Admittedly much in mathematics – even genuine mathematics – can take place at the ostensive level. I am going to tell of a most significant episode I witnessed at a four days' conference for inspectors and other responsible people of our lower vocational education – for this quite extensive but neglected branch of our secondary educational system we had drafted, not a curriculum, but a source of teaching subjects, and we intended to explain to the participants what we had in mind for mathematics in lower vocational education. In the course of our activities we have developed the habit of showing such things by means of practical exercises rather than lectures. The participants were no mathematicians; most of them were people who had not kept in mind much of the mathematics learned after primary school. A whole afternoon they had been busy with exericses, which, as for contents, were close to lower vocational instruction though of course they took place at a higher level.

The sequence of exercises I am going to describe deal with probability. In groups of two to four the participants worked on instruction sheets. Again and again the Pascal triangle emerged in their exercises (with the orientation of the Galton board: head = down to the left; tail = down to the right); it played an important though not formalised part. While I observed the participants, one of them addressed me: "I feel as though I were among the deaf and dumb". When he saw my stupid face, he went on: "Like computers that do something and do not know what". I analysed my observations and it dawned on me what I would say at the evening meeting of the conference where I had to give a talk. I repeat the main points of this talk in an edited version:

You have solved probability problems; and in order to solve them you have developed, calculated, and considered a kind of triangle which is named after Pascal (Fig. 12). You have reasoned in a concrete way with these triangles. You have explained and recalled to your neighbour and yourself the

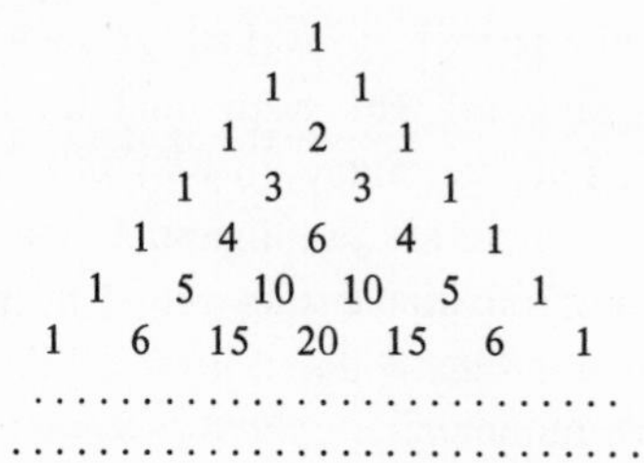

Fig. 12. Pascal's Triangle.

definition of the Pascal triangle while accompanying certain movements of your index finger on the paper by phrases like 'this here plus this there is that' ('this here' with the finger on the 4, 'this there' with the finger on the 6, and 'that' with the finger on the 10); you have proved propositions while your fingers glided along an oblique line and you have mouthed words like 'the sum of those is that' $(1 + 3 + 6 + 10 = 20)$. With your index finger you climbed up and down in the Pascal triangle while you were proving a particular statement. I assure you this is top quality mathematics. The greatest mathematicians might act like this, in particular if they are exploring a new domain. It is, however, certainly not the most recommendable method of communicating mathematics and of incorporating it into one's memory. Language obviously has more efficient tools. How can we find them?

The language you used this afternoon is characterised by its demonstratives. It is a general language but it is chock-full of demonstratives like 'this', 'that', 'these', 'those' which require index finger movements to be understood. It is a primitive language. Try now to get free from the use of the index finger while still preserving the proving power of showing.

You must get rid of the demonstratives. (I tried it several times with other people: the proposals indicate partial steps.) 'This plus this at the right is that', '. . . is that below', 'this plus that is the neighbour below', 'two neighbours together make up the neighbour below', 'every number is the sum of both of its neighbours above'.

This then is the final formulation of the first stage. It is an interesting feature that the perspective must be changed – that one must look from below to above to find the simplest formulation.

Well, I continued, but what do 'neighbour' and 'upper' mean. Try to tell it to a blind man or over the phone.

One must eliminate the triangle, too. How can such geometrical structures be eliminated? By coordinates! The horizontal layers are numbered from above. I propose, as is the fashion today, to start with 0. In the 0-th line there is one figure 1, in the 1st there are two figures 1, and so on. Within the lines the places are numbered from the left to the right, again starting with the number 0. This is the coordinate description of the Pascal triangle. Now comes its filling up with numbers: . . . the 4th member of the 7th line is the sum of the 3rd and 4th member of the 6th line . . . the $(k + 1)$-th member of the $(n + 1)$-th line is the sum of the k-th and $(k + 1)$-th member of the n-th line. Eventually I propose the mathematical notation: the k-th member of the n-th line is denoted by $\binom{n}{k}$, and this then for all natural numbers k, n. Thus

$$\binom{n+1}{k+1} = \binom{n}{k} + \binom{n}{k+1}$$

is the formula for the binomial coefficients. Then we can also write down the formulae which arise if the index finger glides along an oblique track:

$$\binom{1}{1} + \binom{2}{1} + \binom{3}{1} + \ldots + \binom{q}{1} = \binom{q+1}{2}$$

$$\binom{2}{2} + \binom{3}{2} + \binom{4}{2} + \ldots + \binom{q}{2} = \binom{q+1}{3}$$

$$\cdots\cdots\cdots\cdots\cdots\cdots\cdots\cdots\cdots\cdots\cdots\cdots$$

$$\binom{p}{p} + \binom{p+1}{p} + \binom{p+2}{p} + \ldots + \binom{q}{p} = \binom{q+1}{p+1}.$$

By the way, think about how to prove it formally!

I did not expound this in order to teach you a piece of formalised mathematics but to accompany you in a learning process and to make the learning process conscious to you (which at the same time represents a learning process for myself). Its content is not so much the mathematics of the Pascal triangle but the cognition of what formalising and algorithmising mean in mathematics. The mathematical language is neither an arbitrary invention nor a jargon detached from any content. It develops in an entirely natural way in phases of abstraction or rather formalisation. First the primitive demonstratives of everyday language were thrown out in order to get rid of the accompanying index movements, and this happened by replacing them with relations of a graphic or geometric character like 'neighbour' and 'upper'. Then the graphical tools were eliminated and replaced with ordering tools of a more abstract character such as numbering by natural numbers, while 'upper' was replaced with the transition from the $(n + 1)$-th to the n-th line and 'neighbour' by the transition from the $(k + 1)$-th to the k-th and $(k + 1)$-th member. The conventional variables emerged.

Then a third step follows where relics of everyday language as 'k-th member of the n-th line' and 'sum' are replaced with mathematical symbols, a fourth where 'and so on' is replaced with a new variable (indicated by p in the above formula), and a fifth where the three dots are relieved from duty by the Σ sign:

$$\sum_{n=p}^{q} \binom{n}{p} = \binom{q+1}{p+1}.$$

These are linguistic levels according to which the mathematical language evolves: in the same way I do it before your eyes, evolving rather than serving up. This then is what should be required from learning processes: getting the pupil to ascend the levels of his language rather than serving up ready made linguistic forms.

16. CHANGE OF PERSPECTIVE

16.1. *Grasping the Context*

In the course of a comparative study one of our collaborators* taught one and the same subject to two first forms of secondary instruction (7th grade, 13–14 years), denoted in the sequel by A and B, both having 25 pupils. Class A belonged to a school type that is leading to university and higher vocational studies, class B belonged to lower vocational instruction (trade and domestic economy school); A was co-educational, whereas almost all pupils of B were girls. The school of A was situated in a small university town, the school of B in a small industrial agricultural town. In both of them the subject was dealt with in two lessons, but it required 70 minutes in A, 130 minutes in B.

It started with the query: "How many children does the average Dutch family have?" The estimations matched in A and B reasonably what is the factual situation in the corresponding social groups. "How can we check this?" In class A the children go straight up to what we call samples, in class B the first answers are like 'Let us get information at the town hall'.

One settles on samples. Following a suggestion of the experimenter the children take an inventory in the class, calculate averages, draw histograms. In A a pupil spontaneously remarks that the sample is not good (her argument is that there are no families with 0 children in the sample included, and

* Mr. W. Kremers.

the others react intelligently upon this remark. In group B where the histogram shows 0 families with 0, 1, 9, 10 children (one with 11) it is difficult to convince the children that, in view of the method of sampling, 0 families with 0 children is not due to chance, as 0 families with 1 child is likely to be. The children do not understand properly what is wrong with the sample.

After some discussion the experimenter proposes another method of sampling: each girl notes down five families with which she is acquainted giving the respective numbers of children. This is followed by calculations, and qualitative discussions on the importance of size and the representativity of samples. In the second lesson a similar subject is dealt with according to the same principles: the frequency of wearing glasses among 20–65 year-olds. The experiment was concluded by a test that aimed at ascertaining whether the girls had understood the importance of size and representativity of samples in a qualitative sense. I give a translation of the test items:

Which of the following investigations do you judge to be right, and which not? Explain the answer.

1. In order to investigate how often a week on the average Dutch students go to the movies, one investigator called up three students in each of the university cities (Amsterdam, Utrecht, Groningen, Leyden, Nimeguen, Rotterdam, Tilburg, Twente, Delft and Eindhoven) and asked them how many films a week they see on the average.

Right/wrong. Explanation.

2. In order to investigate how many people watch a certain television programme, the N.O.S. arbitrarily chose 1500 people to fill out each day on a form which programme they had watched that day.

Right/wrong. Explanation.

3. In order to investigate how young people in the Netherlands spend their leisure hours, a group of investigators chose a town at random from the register of an atlas and asked all 10–18 year-olds of this town how they spend their leisure hours.

Right/wrong. Explanation.

4*. In order to investigate how often a month on average the Dutch housewife does shopping in the market, one researcher asked 200 house-wives in each of 60 arbitrarily chosen markets how often they do their shopping in the market.

* Question 4 was only asked in class B.

Right/wrong. Explanation.

How did you like these two lessons? Have you learned anything? If so, what?

In class A the answers to questions 1–3 were predominantly satisfactory; at any rate the children had grasped what was at stake. This understanding was lacking with 22 among the 25 pupils of class B. I translate, as far as possible, the answers of five of these girls to the four questions:

1. Right, then they need not decrease the number of films.
Wrong, there is only one film a week on the average.
Right, as the people may go to many films, and the students must know how much money they contribute.
Right, since they may also go to the movies once in a while.
Wrong, for they can go every day a few times to the movies, and this I find wrong for the students because indeed they are students.

2. Wrong, because the people can know themselves which programme they like to watch.
Wrong, I find it ridiculous to do this.
Wrong, it is not normal, it only costs the people postage.
Wrong, I think it is not their business, the people must know themselves which TV programmes they want to watch.
Wrong, because it is none of their business which programmes they watched that day.

3. Right, for now they think for once about young people [struck out and replaced with:] Wrong, this only costs time; it is a waste of time.
Wrong, they do not have to tell everybody everything, and they can know themselves what they do.
Right, because now and then they go elsewhere.
Right. Properly speaking it is wrong and right, because I find that something is always going on, a country fayre, or something.
Right, because then you can see the difference in the use of leisure time.

4. Right, then they need not abolish the markets.
Wrong, because there is a market at least once a month. And they can also go elsewhere.
Wrong. It is not really their business.
Wrong, because some people go thrice a week to the market and others once a week, and those who do so thrice a week will certainly need it.
Wrong, the housewives may go to the market whenever they want to.

I mention this unpretentious though most revealing study here rather than in the section on probability because the main result, not at all intended or foreseen, has a wider scope than that of a special mathematical domain. It is a paragon of – catastrophic – failure to grasp the context – I mean the context which was of course intended, the mathematical context. The 22 pupils who failed did see a context – the social one. They could not free themselves from it, they could not achieve the required change of perspective. Was this so silly? The longer I think about it, the more I become prone to answer the query in the negative and to ask a counter query: Which screw was loose with the pupils of group A (and the three girls of group B who did it well) that they obeyed the crooked wishes of the mathematician, obediently disregarded the social context, and had no problems in accepting the mathematical context? The way I formulated my counter question indicates that I value the behaviour of the 'good' pupils not only in a positive sense. I estimate the refusal of the 'poor' pupils as high as the willingness of the 'good' ones. In a more thoroughly mixed group both would neatly complement each other. The 'good' would have learned from the 'poor' that there exists something like a social context, and that they are obliged to provide arguments if they insist on eliminating it, and the eyes of the 'poor' would have been opened to the mathematical context in such a discussion.

I answered the query by a counter query but I cannot offer even a trace of an answer to the counter query. Yet I believe that the observation I reported here is the most important I have been confronted with for quite a while, and I am sure that the questions it gives rise to are the most urgent we are expected to answer. Recently I saw a French investigation: about 60 girls of the same age and level as the previous group B were asked a few questions, like "what do you think of when you hear about the transitivity of a relation?" and at the end "what do you think is the use of mathematics?" All but one of the sixty showed convincingly that they had not got the slightest idea of the subject matter that had been instilled into them for more than a year and that they could not classify mathematics otherwise than as useless or as a torment. The B-pupils of our experiment at least knew a context to which they could cling and moderately enjoyed the lessons. The sixty lacked even this; there was not any context from which they could have changed to mathematics. In their eyes mathematics is due to remain a sealed book.

And this, we know well enough all over the world, is the fate of mathematics in the eyes of many – the majority? – who must learn it. As a mathematician one meets now and then people who tell you that up to this or that grade they had understood absolutely nothing of mathematics, when all of a sudden the scales fell from their eyes – there follows a strange and unintelligible story about the event that marked the turn. This was their entering into the context of mathematics, but do not count those who never succeed, even if they obediently repeat all problems the teacher shows them.

Hesitatingly I will add a few remarks on our experiment – there have not up to now been new experiments to check my interpretations, or rather, to get an answer to what in fact are mere queries. Didn't the B-pupils stick to the social context because it had not been dealt with in the lessons? Were their hearts not simply in their mouths when they completed the tests? Shouldn't it have been our first task to do justice – not only on behalf of the 'poor' pupils – to the social context and its great wealth? It started with the query: How many children does the average Dutch family have? 'Children', 'Dutch', 'family' stand in the social context, and to a certain degree this even holds for 'average', but the query itself is far away from it, though it can also be understood within this context. This the pupils could not know, the 'good' pupils included.

There are indications in this story which might be of practical value – I mean all kinds of opportunities and traps one has to know if teaching matter is to be created which is related to reality. Moreover it involves a general warning 'always ask yourself whether the pupil possibly did not grasp the context.' And finally it is a challenge to a more profound quest into 'grasping the context'. Later on, in probability and geometry, I will touch on this problem anew.

16.2. *A Logical Problematic*

The reader certainly knows that I have the strange habit of understanding by logic the same thing which everybody calls logic (even a formal logician when he does not pursue formal logic). Lewis Carroll's *Alice in Wonderland* involves more, and more profound, logic than his recently republished horrors entitled *Symbolic Logic* and *The Game of Logic*. Linguistic analysis such as pursued in Section 15 belongs to logic as I see it. And of course I consider it as logic if I observe and analyse the thought of children and my own thought. Everybody knows how difficult it is to observe thought processes. Does it help having the other person think aloud? It is quite probable that then he only recites a scheme or a formalism he has learned. Developments of thinking, discontinuities in learning processes will rarely happen aloud; one should recognise them by symptoms.

There is however a type of negative symptom which is more conspicuous, quite frequent, and yet informative: blocking, malfunctioning, non-functioning, bad functioning of formalisms, schemes, tactics, strategies. One kind I have many times observed and I shall deal with now, is related to what I have called change of perspective – it is a blocked, or wrong, or insufficient change of perspective.

Let us take an example. The first graders (6–7 years) are busy with the map of a fairy island. At cross-roads they place qualitative sign-posts on which remarkable goals are indicated by pictures – later on also quantitative ones (that is with kilometers indicated) – along a nonbranched road, for instance a road from the tower to the mill (10 km long), where sign-posts are to be placed at intermediate points. It is an unproblematic task. Now the problem is inverted – the change of perspective. The sign-post with the pictorial or numerical data is given; place it where it should be. It takes trouble with the qualitative ones; with the quantitative ones only a few pupils succeed – I stress once more, it is a linear problem, a rectilinear road from the tower to the mill. The same difficulty is observed in the first year of lower vocational training (7th grade, 13–14 years) with quantitative sign-posts in the two-dimensional landscape; the pupils just manage a sign-post 'Baarn 5 km' but not one with 'Baarn 5 km, Zeist 7 km'. An even more astonishing fact: A group of good fifthgraders – who without any trouble have understood that an angular height of the sun of 45° means the equal length of a vertical ruler and its shadow; who can explain this by drawings and transfer it to similar questions – are unanimously frustrated by the problem "where should I stand to see the front of a 20 m high house from an angle of 45°". It takes time and trouble until it dawns upon the first of them. Putting together a puzzle after a model makes no difficulty in a first grade; but cutting a picture into puzzle pieces according to a model is much too difficult – they do not have the slightest idea how to do it.

I can go on in this way, and I will do so. I accumulate the examples not because it would bring us closer to the solution of a problem, but in order to make clear that there is a problem to it, a didactical problem, which would deserve – I do not say, to be solved, but – to be recognised. Indeed I believe it would didactically pay at least to discover the common element in the problems of change of perspective, to have the learner experience and operationally use this common element, to pursue exercises of change of perspective aimfully, systematically, and early, in order not to be surprised by blockings which were never foreseen.

Exercises of change of perspective are not unusual in traditional arithmetic teaching: 'How much should I add to 7 to get 11?' or formalised '7 + . . . = 11'. More difficult: 'To what should I add 7 to get 11', which does not conserve its greater difficulty in the formalisation. 'What should I subtract from 11 to get 7' is of course easier than 'From what should I subtract 4 to get 7?' which suggests a subtraction rather than the addition that is required. Even if similar questions reappear with multiplication and division, the repertoire is restricted and hardly paradigmatic. The change of perspective is indeed facilitated by the availability of a known operation that schematises the change of perspective.

A well-known catastrophe of wrong change of perspective is exemplified by problems I take from arithmetic teaching. The pupil has filled in a 5 in

$$7 + \ldots = 11.$$

It is now

$$7 + 5 = 11$$

with a red pencil mark in the margin. The 'correction' is

$$7 + 5 = 12$$

with a new red mark. The reader is asked to imagine how it goes further, and to complete the story. One can write complete theatrical dialogues on this theme. They have, as a matter of fact, been written. They need not deal with 7 + . . . = 11 or any other arithmetical problem. They exist in many variations on all themes, the most beautiful being those between husband and wife where of course the husband is the one who puts the red marks.

'$-15°$C cold', $-15°$ Southern latitude, the pipe was shortened by -15 cm: try discussing it. Finally it is: You know that below zero 15 is the same as -15, or don't you? Or: 'the pipe was 100 cm and is now 85 cm, which is minus 15'.

This game can be played without numbers and the catastrophes can touch more vital complexes than measurements. This means that what is here done or neglected in arithmetic and mathematics teaching may be of more than local significance.

The second graders were busy in the 'practice corner' with a problem I had not attached any importance to. It was something like the following 'addition table' (Table I) with the instruction: Put a circle into the squares where the sum is 20, and a cross into the squares where the sum is 30.

TABLE I

+	6	12	18	11	22	16	8	21
8								
14								
24								
12								
18								
2								
9								
19								

After less than a quarter of an hour all children had finished expect one who had done nothing and still aimlessly moved his finger over the pattern; as he did not even count on his fingers, I thought he was very poor in arithmetic. Eventually I intervened, put my finger beneath the first column and asked him whether some circle might be put in this column. He immediately put a circle into the correct square and in less than a minute completed the problem. He was excellent in arithmetic, he did not count on his fingers. Obviously he had been seriously blocked. For some mysterious reason he could not perform the change of perspective which consists in reducing an equation with two unknowns to the disjunction of equations with one unknown by substituting values for the other unknown, in other words transforming the problem

$$(?\ulcorner x, y \urcorner) F(x, y)$$

into the problems

$$(?x)F(x,y),$$

an important and indispensable strategy. I am ashamed I underestimated this problem and entirely neglected to observe the strategies of the other children, and whether some had had difficulties similar to those of the blocked boy, though sooner overcome. I only remember that some children noticed that in every column and every line there could be at most one circle and one cross. I find it alarming that one pupil – and probably a good one – can be blocked by almost nothing, and that a very small impulse suffices to raise him over a seemingly high but factually ridiculous threshold. How often will it happen at school that children lag behind because of mere futilities?

A currently quite popular type of exercise is presented by the following pattern (Figure 13):

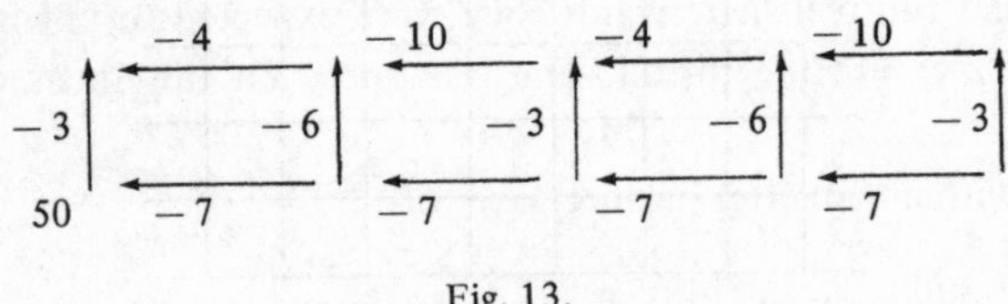

Fig. 13.

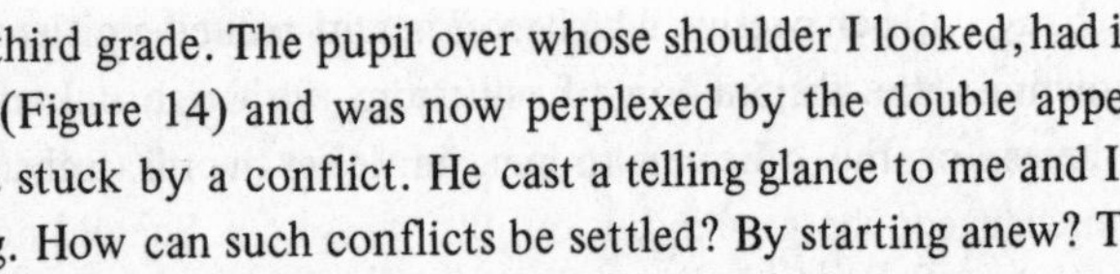

47 −4 −10 −4 71 −10 81
−3 −6 −3 −6 −3
50 −7 57 −7 64 −7 71 −7 78

Fig. 14.

It was in a third grade. The pupil over whose shoulder I looked, had it partially completed (Figure 14) and was now perplexed by the double appearance of 71. He was stuck by a conflict. He cast a telling glance to me and I answered by nodding. How can such conflicts be settled? By starting anew? This would be a method, though an uncertain one. And if the *problem* was wrong? He did not consider the possibility. He decided to change his perspective. He started with the 71 above and ran back. At the 78 below he drew the eraser, changed it into 84 and run further back until I stopped him. What to do now? I could have given him a new sheet and had him start anew, but this would have been too cheap an escape. I wanted to base the help on a more profound foundation. A discussion developed, neighbours intervened. It was like a dramatic scene. I looked for help but the teacher was too busy in another corner. Eventually I was saved by the bell. Among my readers there will be quite a few with much wider didactical experience than I have. How should one act in such a situation? How can one explain to a pupil what is wrong there? How can one give another person insight into his change of perspective conflict and how should one help him out of the swamp? This indeed matters: not whether on a new sheet he may solve the problem correctly.

In a fifth grade (11–12 years) a group of four pupils worked on an instruction sheet with the following problem. They were given three cotton reels, a full, a half full and an empty one; the full one was said to contain 200 m thread*. They had to weigh the three reels in order to determine how much was on the half full reel. Afterwards they were expected to unwind the half full reel and measure the thread. The last query on this sheet was: "Is it right?"

Weighing with a bad letter balance gave for

full	48.5 g
half full	26.0 g
empty	23.5 g

(I substitute arbitrary numbers since I do not remember the actual data.) With some help the group found the right approach and calculated decently; that is to say, they left the calculating to a willing and assiduous girl who made long divisions with lightening-speed. After the query "how much thread is there on the half full reel?" 20 m was filled in; that is, the girl did this while the others, who had left, were busy in the corridor unwinding and measuring. They came back with the result 24.50 m. The girl picked up the eraser and started correcting. She wanted to go back up to the weights. I tried to talk her round. It cost me much trouble to have her leave the measured and calculated data unchanged; she gave in but only to please me. She did not sacrifice the answer 'yes' after the last query, however. In school, right it must be. As

* In fact the thin thread had been replaced by thicker material.

a matter of fact I would not be astonished to hear that at home she had corrected the whole according to her own ideas.

Of course there is more behind this story than a wrong change of perspective. Settling conflicts must go further back – what matters here is the didactics of measuring and processing data. Nevertheless I would like to know what a more skilled didactician would have done here. She was a very intelligent girl, I would have wished I could have convinced her. But the problems at stake here are not local ones. One should start at greater depth. But where?

I have told this story at many opportunities, and every time there is someone who reacts: 'This is the future physics student in the laboratory – as the twig is bent', and so on. It is right; no, it is wrong. The student in the physics laboratory who acts this way, is cheating, but she was not. I would rather say: the future mathematician.

17. THE FIELD OF TENSION BETWEEN GLOBAL AND LOCAL PERSPECTIVES

I am fed up with one contrast cultivated in mathematical didactics – that of 'concrete' and 'abstract'. These words are not frequently found in my publications. I use 'concretising' and 'abstracting' though not properly as opposites, and certainly not so that I tie up mathematics to abstraction: in a short while I will deal with this more thoroughly. A pair of opposites the reader will meet more frequently in my publications is 'general' and 'particular', but not so that the general is identified with the abstract and the particular with the concrete, and certainly not to raise the question of life and death whether it is right to proceed from the general to the particular or the other way round. I considered it more appropriate to elucidate the didactical relation between the general and the particular by means of comprehension and apprehension and by means of the 'paradigm'. If opposites are wanted, I expect more from 'global and local perspectives'* – we will meet here anew problems of change of perspective such as considered in the Section 16.

An area where the tension between global and local perspectives is certainly most familiar, is reading instruction. The child is expected to recognise each

* Global and local organisation as dealt with repeatedly in *Mathematics as an Educational Task*, is only an extreme case, at quite high a level, of what I mean here by global and local perspective.

word, each letter and at the same time to overview the whole sentence, the whole story, and this is somehow a serious contradiction. Reading tests contain items that aim at global understanding, and others that ask for details. In a reading speed test the subject may have overlooked details or be stuck on details and never have reached the end which may be indispensable for the global perspective. I learned reading – German – by phonetic spelling, where first each single letter is read, then the whole word and after a sequence of words once more the whole sentence. During the same period the usual method in the Netherlands was moderately global. I always thought that in languages with a spelling like that of English, reading must necessarily be taught at least in a word global setting, but this assumption seems to be wrong as I infer from accusations uttered in the U.S. against the global method as responsible for an alleged decline of reading achievements.

I need not meddle with the struggle on reading instruction, at least at the elementary level; at a higher level reading achievements certainly influence mathematics instruction; only in purely numerical problems can reading skill be disregarded.

Earlier on in another context I mentioned a theme for the first class of our lower vocational school (7th grade, 13–14 years), a detective story with a modest mathematical content which was intended to motivate ill-motivated pupils. At the end of the first page of the story the question is asked where the inmate who escaped at 7 o'clock from the prison at Groningen with a car that goes at 150 km an hour would be found at 8 o'clock. The majority of the pupils had no idea how to answer this query; they were not able to combine the three data 7 o'clock, 8 o'clock, 150 km with each other, probably they had not even noticed them. The text was only globally read, in fact it tempted them to do so. On the other hand after a few – local – instructions on computations, listings, drawings, they do not know anymore what is the global subject they are busy with; it is advisable to build into such a text periodic questions that aim at the global connection in order to be sure that it does not escape the users.

I chose this example out of many. People often think that little children are inclined to a global perspective and then are amazed that they notice details that easily escape adults, and extol the little ones' power of observation. In fact, little children focus differently, and as they do not yet know what they, according to the adult experience, should pay attention to, they do so on other things than adults, which influences their global impression too. Yet the tension between global and local perspective is permanently felt. The wrong achievement, according to the adult view, in many Piagetian experiments, is caused by a global perspective where the local perspective would have been relevant. Conversely if one has children of grades 1–2 (6–8 years) compare two drawn chains of pearls or mosaics with each other, the comparing happens stepwise locally while one finger runs over the one and another over the other object; it is then difficult to induce children to look globally for striking differences. Children who are given a picture to be divided up into puzzle pieces following a divided-up model on a different scale, are able to find local bearings, for instance a few key points of the cut line, in particular at the border of the paper, but they do not grasp at all the course of the cut line between the key points; they even behave as though this did not matter.

An even less assuming didactical subject is the localisation of numbers in the 'field of a hundred', that is to say, of the numbers from 1 to 100 within an empty lattice of 10 by 10 squares. Observations of strategies in a second grade may be a source of interesting ideas, if they are organised by means of the categories of local and global perspective. There are children who use the tenfolds as local bearings from which they proceed by forward and backward counting; others who extend this sytem of local bearings with positions they have meanwhile ascertained, and finally those who structure the field of a hundred globally by means of the tens as indicators of the rows and of the units as indicators of the columns. If geometrical structures are shown on the field of a hundred, say a diagonal, many children recognise certain local regularities in the corresponding arithmetical structures, whereas a few grasp the regularity globally, say as an arithmetical sequence. Some are able to grasp and describe the logical connection between the geometrical and the arithmetical structure locally, though a global grasp and description of this connection seems too difficult at this age level: as a whole a profusion of exciting variants in an unassuming subject matter.

In curriculum development and instruction one should seriously consider the tension between global and local perspectives. Everybody grasps and experiences globally the linear order on the number line or in magnitudes – probably the linear order in magnitudes is constituted thanks to the suggestion of isomorphism with the number system or with the geometrical ray. For millenia mankind and even mathematicians have been content with the global grasp of linear order, and for the great majority this has not even changed today. Mathematicians, of course, know that this globally given order can be locally grasped by the law of transitivity and a few others, and can be axiomatically described. From this cognition many didacticians draw the conclusion that the linear order would and should be constituted starting with transitivity. This explains exercises where 6–7-year-olds are instructed to complete arrow diagrams according to the law of transitivity. No doubt this functions quite nicely as an algorithmic activity, but beyond this it is utterly worthless. The logical construction of the law of transitivity – a definition with an implication within the definiens – is far beyond the grasp of even 8-year-olds; but even concretisations like 'you race harder than you, and you harder than you, how is it with you and you?' (of course accompanied by suitable movements of the index finger) – these are simply not understood. On the contrary it is quite easy with drawn seesaws: 'A above against B below, C below against B above, what about A and C?' or even 'A with B above against C with D below, and A below against C above, what can we conclude now?' In a mathematical system the law of transitivity might be at the basis of linear order; developmentally transitivity is a consequence of linear order, and the axiomatic view is one of those inversions I called antididactic. The mathematician is right to be proud that by the local grasp of the linear order he makes the extension possible to partial order, but didactically this is entirely irrelevant. I pass over the distressing fact that pupils are deluded with the false idea that transitivity includes a total description of their intuitive idea of linear order.

I think it is worthwhile repeating in the present context an example from my earlier book*, the most drastic example of this attitude, though at a higher level than the preceding one. It is the Archimedean property of linear order. One deals with a magnitude, say length, chooses a 'unit' e, and forms its rational multiples, that is the set $\mathbf{Q} \cdot e$. The Archimedean property simply says

> there is no a smaller than all of $\mathbf{Q} \cdot e$, and no b larger than all of $\mathbf{Q} \cdot e$,

a quite reasonable property, and exactly what is needed in work with

* *Mathematics as an Educational Task*, p. 200.

Archimedean magnitudes. It is the global grasp of the Archimedean property. Well, two millenia ago it was discovered that this postulate can be derived from the much more modest

to any a, b there is an $n \in \mathbf{N}$ such that $na > b$.

Indulging in the passion to manage it with the most modest means, is a typically mathematical attitude. As a matter of fact introductions to mathematics are not the most appropriate places to display such habits, and among students the only ones who would like to be educated by such examples to accept a similar attitude, will be the future mathematicians. By anti-didactical inversion the global definition of the Archimedean property can be replaced with a local one. Yet in modern mathematics global definitions are much preferred above local ones provided they are as exact. So if one would start today from scratch, each mathematician would choose the global definition and at most mention the second definition as a cheaper one, but it seems that even in mathematics a thousand-year-old tradition is not easy to break.

I passed from the tension between global and local perspectives in spontaneous learning processes to that in organised processes. It is the tension in the attitude of the teacher, or of the designer of teaching matter, which in the main I shall deal with now. If as a teacher one does not trust one's intuitions but subjects the 'what' and 'how' of his teaching to conscious analysis, one should also be conscious of the danger that the result of this analysis might be promoted to the rank of teaching matter and method. Earlier on I quoted terrifying examples of instructional atomism. The teaching matter is dissolved into concepts and statements on concepts and the instruction is organised according to such relations between these statements as are determined by common subjects or predicates. Any global perspective is avoided, and it is to be feared that it is even made impossible.

I have rejected this view of instruction as contrary to my picture of man, in which instruction is seen as a means of acquiring culture. But beyond this I would propose to investigate learning processes – spontaneous and guided ones – with a view to the parts global and local perspectives play in these processes. My isolated examples – much less than for comprehension and apprehension – provide little information. Throwing a learner into a swimming pool and commenting on his movements is no method to teach swimming. But neither is it done today, as far as I know, by explaining to him the singular swimming movements and body carriages in the different phases of the swimming process and waiting to see whether he is able to integrate them into one activity. A good swimming teacher knows where between these extremes swimming is taught the most expeditiously, and if he is able to do so, he should communicate it to others, even though this is not easy. It is another question whether beyond this empirical approach a more profound scientific one would make much sense.

It depends on many circumstances how the parts of global and local perspectives should be cut out. Foreign language instruction diluted over four or eight academic years with a few lessons a week requires another strategy than one condensed into 8 hours a day during 6 consecutive weeks. Teaching matter and method in general, class environment and age of the pupils are quite influential. Nevertheless in mathematics I would stress the global perspective since it is the more difficult one and therefore easily neglected. If I prepare some teaching matter, I am inclined to start globally, for instance with a complex situation that still needs structuring, or a great and not directly solvable problem, which in the sequel remains visible as a bearing amidst the wealth of local approaches, or is regularly being made visible; the summit and finish of the exploration may be the exhausting of the situation (or part of it) and the solving of the problem.

But this is only a proposal, which admits many interpretations. One may try to test and to compare them, guided by one's good genius – or the evil one of criticism – but it would be healthier if one could build upon more fundamental insight. Not insights from which recipes could be derived, but paradigmatic material. Examples of the relation between local and global perspective in learning processes or in steering learning processes might mean great progress. It is a big problem how to find them.

18. THE FIELD OF TENSION BETWEEN QUANTITATIVE AND QUALITATIVE PERSPECTIVES

The word global is often used as an opposite to 'quantified' or 'with quantitative precision'. I did not mean it this way though in fact the opposites 'local–global' and 'quantitative–qualitative' have much in common, which, however, I do not want to stress. A formal difference between both is that in the tension field 'quantitative–qualitative' certain systems of synthesis are pre-established, and this might make it easier to handle this opposition in a didactical-phenomenological respect, provided that it does not lead to careless anticipations of this synthesis.

If one states that common salt is composed of sodium and chlorine, it is a qualitative statement which turns quantitative as soon as one adds the ratio of the components. From stating the coldness of a particular winter day to giving the precise temperature, there are many shades of meaning (for instance such as used in weather forecasts), and it depends on the actual context what is then called qualitative or quantitative. Ordering a set of objects or events linearly according to some magnitude criterion can be interpreted as qualitative or quantitative according to the particular viewpoint. One can quantify with more or less precision, and at the various degrees of precision quantitative coarseness versus refinement can appear as quality versus quantity.

These are transitions between opposites rather than the system of synthesis I alluded to earlier on. It will depend on the required final result – which can indeed be entirely qualitative – with which precision quantification is performed. Statements on the goodness of quantification can be *absolutely qualitative* or *comparatively qualitative* or *more or less sharply quantified*. There we are amidst the theory of errors in the mathematical sense. But it should be borne in mind that this mathematisation, as indeed any whatsoever, is arrived at by a process that is itself mathematically relevant. It is this field of awareness about the precision of quantifications that I meant when I alluded to the system of synthesis in the tension field of 'quantitative–qualitative'.

From this exposition I now draw the connecting lines to instruction, and I do so in a multiple way: the tension between the quantitative and qualitative perspectives of the pupil, the teacher, the designer of subject matter. Indeed, changes of perspective such as dealt with earlier on, are, at least operationally, familiar to teachers and textbook authors even if they have not understood them as a didactic problem; on the contrary the tension between quantitative and qualitative perspectives has the peculiarity that it is not bridged even by people who are well acquainted with mathematical instruction. I will demonstrate this soon by examples.

Quantification as an aim in itself is widespread and virtually no more opposed today – in the computer era nobody dares to doubt this aim lest he be considered old-fashioned. Earlier on I described professional number hunters hoping that from the profusion of numerical material, if only it is subjected to mathematical sophistication, eventually some knowledgeable facts will arise; the range of collecting can go as far as closing the eyes to the dreary origin of these numbers. Even if these are excesses – with authoritative credentials indeed – they are only offshoots of a widespread inclination to quantification. It augurs ill for efforts to explore such an important field as that of the tension between quantitative and qualitative perspectives, if in pursuing an alleged science of education people ignore this tension, if they are at all aware of it. But in spite of this attitude the tension between quantitative and qualitative sight is an essential ingredient of learning mathematics and of the learning process in any field where qualities are to be quantified and quantitative results are to be evaluated qualitatively.

In the first chapter* I told of 19th century philologists who made efforts to find out which stadion Eratosthenes could have meant in the 3rd century B.C. when he assessed the circumference of the Earth as 250 000 stadia; Eratosthenes' assessment was based on the measurement – or was it a mere estimation? – of the distance Alexandria–Syene, which in fact was determined as 5000 stadia, a round number, which indicates a recognised or unrecognised error of 10% and condemns any sophisticated distinction of different stadia to irrelevance. Numerical precision is one of the weakest points in all quantitative understanding, as appears whenever numerical data are uncritically taken over or transferred from one system of measures into another. Wind velocities when specified because of their record character by press, radio or television, are always something like 162 km per hour, or 180, or 144. If ever one doubts how and to what purpose wind velocities could or might be measured with such a precision, one will notice that all of these data are multiples of nine. One would guess that they are measured in the number system with basis 9, but this is not the reason; they have been translated from the meter-per-second language of the Meteorological Institute into the kilometer-per-hour language of the automobilist, from round numbers into their precise equivalents rather than into rounded off numbers. In a Dutch encyclopedia I found for the length of a lion 2.40–3.30 m and for its weight 180–225 kg – data that betray their origin in feet and pounds. An American plane pirate was reported to have asked a ransom of 2 653 000 florins; it is not

* p. 4.

explained what he would do with so many florins since in fact it was a million dollars converted into florins according to the current exchange, as velocities of satellites are converted from km/sec via miles/hour into km/hour. If decimalisation progresses far enough, the inch in Shakespeare's "every inch a king" will eventually be converted into centimeters.

Can we expect anything else from the type of arithmetic teaching that drills children to experience numbers detached from any context? Of course the judicious understand which context is meant. They succeed in displacing themselves from the world where $10^{10} - 1$ is miles away from 10^{10} because the one is divisible by 9 and the other is not, into the different world where a one more or less does not matter. But does the pupil acquire this judgment which the textbook author shows he is lacking, at least as a textbook author, if in his work he juxtaposes such problems deprived of any context? Both worlds may rightly claim reality, the world where precision is a virtue, and the other where it is a vice, and in order to be at home in both of them one should have learned to distinguish them consciously.

Not long ago* I told the story of the girl – fun-makers said "the future experimental physics student", I said "the born mathematician" – who would not accept that a measurement might fail to confirm a calculation, and performed a wrong change of perspective in order to make the wrong thing right. I did not succeed in convincing her of what was wrong in her activity. Of course not. It was locally impossible indeed. With this one example I would not succeed. The misunderstanding was more deeply rooted. I ought to have begun more fundamentally and earlier in order to correct or to prevent the mistake. But where are the roots with which to start?

Another example, from the second grade (7–8 years). The teacher has drawn a circle around a wheel on the blackboard. If it is rolled off, where does it arrive after one turn? All estimates are much too short. After a few proposals the periphery is measured with a string, which is stretched on the blackboard. Now, if the wheel is turned twice, thrice, where does it come then? The children are well acquainted with the technique of transferring line segments, and on their sheets they use paper strips to practise it. Then two wheels come into play with diameters which are as 2 to 3. Where will they together have performed a number of turns? It is tried on the sheets, it is

* p. 252.

repeated with various ratios, and sooner or later the children grasp what is behind it. Write a 'problem' for each construction, it is said, which means

$$3 \times 2 = 6, \quad 2 \times 3 = 6,$$
$$6 \times 2 = 12, \quad 4 \times 3 = 12,$$

and so on. Then the type of problem is complicated by using three wheels, with diameters 2:3:5. Again the same questions. Some children have got it, they still transfer line segments, and write the 'problems'

$$15 \times 2 = 30, \quad 10 \times 3 = 30, \quad 6 \times 5 = 30,$$

even if the sequence does not match the drawing because of transfer errors. Others stick to the drawing and write 'problems' like

$$14 \times 2 = 28, \quad 10 \times 3 = 30, \quad 15 \times 2 = 30$$

because this is the way the three numbers stand below each other on the three number lines.

How to act here? It would be an excellent starting point to discuss precision and measuring errors. Unfortunately the bell was just too early.

There are more number concepts between Heaven and Earth than I distinguished in my analysis*, and somehow they must be acquired. There I mentioned the measuring number, and the real number as its apotheosis. But previously to its apotheosis the measuring number enjoys an earthly existence which must be taken very seriously. As a matter of fact the number concept of the essentially inaccurate number is not born in the 5th grade with decimal numbers and such and such a decimal figure – the million dollars, when translated into florins, also acquires a mistaken accuracy. What accuracy of numbers means can only be understood in a context. Certainly one can elaborate numerical data by precision data (3.461 ± 0.002); one can enrich arithmetic with error theory. But these are advanced phases, which should be preceded by more fundamental and more elementary ones. In fact with the explicit error data the accuracy is detached from its context, but to reach this point one must have first understood it within this context.

If at the beginning of the present chapter I viewed the pre-established syntheses in the tension field 'quantitative–qualitative' as facilitating and at

* *Mathematics as an Educational Task*, Chapter 11.

the same time jeopardising the didactical phenomenological analysis, I just meant what I have now expounded in more detail. At any rate it is instruction itself, which is in jeopardy by the mere existence of these syntheses and which invites one to inflict or anticipate them rather than to cause the results of these syntheses to be experienced by the learner as genuine syntheses. Estimating is taught sometimes as an extra to measuring, sometimes as a preparatory exercise, and perhaps also as an introduction to systematic error theory, but too often this happens in too meagre a context, if there is any context at all. Estimating, however, is an activity we practise incessantly, and much more frequently than measuring; overlooking this fact in arithmetic shows a poor sense of reality. Could arithmetic teaching be improved by providing experiences in estimating? It is indeed a hard thing to make explicit habits that have become our *second* nature; but if this is true, how did we succeed in doing so in the natural sciences? Well, we, that is mankind, did succeed there, because there we started – it is the old story – by making the *first* nature explicit; yet as far as education is concerned *this* science is still due to make its first steps.

Meanwhile it is just here, in exploring the tension between quantitative and qualitative perspectives that a method presents itself which I have so often proposed that people may be tired of reading it again: a didactical phenomenological analysis as a preparation for constructing rich, lavishly rich, teaching matter; and while offering it one should make an intelligent observation of the learning processes of learners as well as of teachers, in order to improve, refine, more profoundly anchor, the didactical phenomenology and arrive at a revision of the teaching matter.

I repeat the sketch of this strategy here because nowhere does it impose itself so urgently. In the view of many, mathematisation means quantification; and undoubtedly quantification is one of the most striking aspects of mathematisation – seizing upon a crude matter numerically is just the step from quality to quantity. But this is not the end of mathematising, nor is it its beginning. The qualitative seizure itself requires a learning process as does the return to the qualitative view, and as does even more the continuous interplay between quantitative and qualitative; it requires the learning of schemes the mathematical character of which is no less cogent while it remains in our unconscious.

Rather than indulging in a theory, I shall illustrate this by an example: I have to go shopping downtown; I have to have finished by precisely half past ten, because then somebody can pick me up in front of the department store (no parking!) in order to go with me to another place. I have to do shopping here and there, so many minutes for this, so many for that. I must buy two cans of this because tomorrow night I will get twice as many guests (is there enough money left in my bank account?). I shall walk, as the bus is not dependable. How long does the walk take? Up to this or that point it is always 17 minutes, to the department store it is longer by half; let us say 25 minutes. So I will leave my place then or then – let us have a margin. With a little detour I can be 90% sure that I will meet the postman in the sidestreet and be able to take the mail with me. Indeed I expect an answer from America to a letter that – so many days one way and so many the other – might just be delayed by the weekend by two days.

Let this be sufficient. I could continue this example as long as you like. I think in many features it justifies what I tried to express more theoretically. One of these features is how numerically uncertain data can be reconciled with sharp data, in order to attain entirely qualitative objectives; and the other is estimating on the strength of more or less certain proportionalities. The passage also included a quantitatively specified probability: 90% sure. Or is this 90% really a quantitative specification rather than a non-obligatory phrase? Only a context can show what it is. Did the postman come nine days out of ten at this time? Or was it ninety days out of a hundred, and what is the difference?

19. GRASPING THE CONTEXT – CHANCES

For a long time I have hesitated whether I should resume the thread of probability from my earlier book. It was difficult to make up my mind since this book must be completed somehow, but after the last sentence I cannot escape probability any more.

When I wrote my previous book, I had wider didactical experience with probability than with any other topic – experience gained teaching university freshmen. I could not then take A. Engel and T. Varga into account, except for a brief mention. A course by our institute for 11th–12th grades (17–19 years) had still to be written and nobody had thought of experiments in primary schools. Since then I have experienced much in this field, and even published something of a more theoretical character. I still hesitated. There is no point where I am as much hindered by the prefatorial character of my knowledge as here. Nowhere do I feel more intensely the need for a didactical phenomenology, at least as an organisation scheme. I lack, however, not only the strength – this would not be the worst – but also the courage to write it. I admire courageous people and sometimes feel myself like Hamlet,

> Thus conscience does make cowards of us all;
> And thus the native hue of resolution
> Is sicklied o'er with the pale cast of thought.

How courageous are those textbook, film and television authors who succeed after half an hour or an hour in having 8-year-olds or 11-year-olds, or 14-year-olds calculate the probability of a double-six with a pair of dice, and after a week solve statistical decision problems. Can they boast experience different from mine? Or am I a coward, and does the world belong to the courageous? This question can frequently be asked, when innovators present their material – group theory for Kindergarten, linear algebra for 8–9-year-olds, foundations of analysis for 11-year-olds – but probability is a very special case. Indeed it is up to one's discretion what one means to convey in school by group theory, linear algebra, or foundations of analysis at such and such an age. Probability, however, is somehow fraught with relations to reality. Probability is something rather like common sense and elementary arithmetic, by means of which one can add not only 3 and 2 but also three eggs and two eggs, and in a similar way the understanding of probability can be tested.

I recounted a story about pupils of the 2nd grade who were convinced that a throw of a six is more difficult to obtain than of a one and that it is easier for the teacher than for pupils, though after an hour of not too skillful cutting, sticking, and painting they were converted to the contrary conviction. It was a detour that could have been avoided. As a matter of fact one could have told the children from the start that the six faces were equiprobable, with no influence exerted by the player. Which method would have been better? Are there tools to decide such questions in the arsenal of the present statistical techniques of instructional research? One can teach two groups of children according to different methods, and at the end evaluate the teaching results more or less quantitatively. Then one would have stated and compared local successes or failures; but what does this mean? Will the groups of pupils be tested once more within three months after the last lesson? Perhaps they will. But a year later? Where could one find them? And in parentheses: the results are to be published sometime. Could it not affect the total attitude of the learner and his behaviour when confronted with other problems, whether he has had impressed upon him the equality and constancy of the probabilities by definition, or whether he has experienced them in his own activity, by the work of his hands, the sight of his eyes and the wit of his mind? But how can one test this by local means? And where are the efficient tools that would allow it? Evaluating instruction and pupils by local means creates paths of least resistance, the variety of which prevents the search for a path that leads to the right goal. Meanwhile philosophy is evoked to decide whether the equality and constancy of the probabilities of the dice are to be impressed upon the pupils or to flow from their own activity.

What is the pupils' own activity worth? How casually they converted themselves! Are all dice really so nicely cut out, glued together, and painted, so symmetric that the chances are equal and not subjected to influencing? Of course it is not so, and it is thoughtlessness to assume it – pleasing thoughtlessness because it was neither the time nor the opportunity to have the pupils experience something else, some greater truth. Of course it is easy enough to cure the pupils of this thoughtlessness, or at least of the symptoms of this particular thoughtlessness. One can also educate them to be critical; this, however, lasts longer, also in its consequences. One does not convince them with the self-made cardboard dice that probabilities can be different, but with examples where blind empiricism takes lame sophistry upon its shoulders. What, if anything, can be learned from self-made cardboard dice? It is agreed upon and readily conceded that in actual dice throwing the sides are not equally frequent; one knows that much should be left and credited to fortune. The equality of chances is deduced from symmetry. Are the dice really that symmetrical? How could it be? They have been arbitrarily painted. Though not the individual die, this may help all taken together to equiprobability. But at which level could this conclusion be made conscious?

At any rate the pupil now knows that all probabilities are equal. He does not yet know that this is not true. A cogent example must convince him. 11–12-year-olds are asked whether certain games are fair.* Every game the

* Television programme 'Kijk op Kans'.

results of which are guided by accident and cannot be influenced, is considered as fair – that is the general attitude. Obviously one has not yet experienced anything that would contradict this belief, or one does not know how to decide such a question; fairness and fortune are still too vague to be delimited from each other.

A game with two coins is proposed to three children: the first is to win with head-head, the second with tail-tail, the third with a mixed result. Very few children have second thoughts on fairness but as soon as they are asked to argue them, they hesitate. Some say it cannot be decided because all is accident. The three children are asked to try it out. The pile of mixed results towers above the two others. Is it fair? Yes, it is just chance, there is nothing to say about it. Do their doubts gain weight with the increasing length of the trial? Yes. And the need to decide the question, does it get more forceful? I am not sure. And if so, do they then take cognisance of what happens here, that the increasing tower of mixed results is no wonder at which to be struck dumb, that one way or another one should be able to find out what is wrong?

Obviously if in the life of an 11–12-year-old this is the first time that he explores such a problem, the didactic observer who asks these questions somehow comes either too early or too late. As an observer he is too rash with a question that seems already pregnant with a conclusion; as a didactician he should have proposed such a game much earlier. Of course there exist things like wonders, for instance that elephants have trunks and camels have humps, but for a long time the child has been broken of the habit to ask "Why?" in such cases. There are, however, things that one can try to find out – why the cycle-tyre got flat, why the dog barked, or whether it was not by accident. Does it need an explanation why the mixed results surpassed the head-heads and tail-tails? Experience can tell you what needs an explanation, and what not – strictly individual experience. There is a stage where the query why wood burns and stone does not is as idle as that about the trunks and humps, and it remains idle as long as it is asked within the context of everyday experience. Not until it is put into the context of chemistry, with terms like oxygen and oxidation, does it become meaningful. No learner can be expected to invent the context of chemistry, nor to appreciate it if it is imposed upon him. Indeed there is one thing that he does not learn in this way, that is, which questions fit into this context; asking the right questions at the right opportunity is an art and a burden that others cannot take off one's shoulders.

If I wander away in my arguments to other disciplines, it is due to the contrast between probability and other mathematical concepts which makes probability seem more akin to the natural sciences. If mathematics is expected to contribute to solving a problem, the problem should be raised to and then within its mathematical context, but in the case of probability this context looks far away. Accident, yes, this is a familiar idea, but most often accident and probability are separated by a ravine, and intelligent experience must show where the ravine is only a big step wide. A chemist is far from considering the chemical context as self-evident in the learning process – wasn't he once introduced into this context quite explicitly? If I may judge from the majority of textbooks, the context of probability is considered as self-evident, and so far it is indeed different from natural science contexts. The different attitude towards probability is comprehensible and not unwarranted. The context of probability belongs to the domain of common sense, but for most of the contexts of natural sciences common sense alone would not suffice. Sure, in mathematics all is self-evident, but it is just this peculiarity that makes mathematics the least self-evident of all. Logical and psychological self-evidence are often confused with each other – or to put it better – one confuses self-evidences of different levels.

For 11–12-year-olds it is a *tour de force* to recognise the probabilistic context in the problem of the two coins, to grasp that the predominance of mixed results needs and allows an explanation. (In fact the age does not matter here; it does matter whether the learner ever experienced being introduced to mathematisable contexts.) But this game is only one approach, and perhaps not even the best, not even a paradigmatic one. How does a child that experienced the probability context, say in our television programme, react outside this programme? A girl that had been exposed to it, had – accidentally – got to participate in a game where one keeps a number from 1 to 100 in mind and the other must guess it by asking as few as possible yes-no-questions. The girl put the game into a probabilistic context, maybe because it was a game, maybe because choosing a number, or guessing a number, is a chance act. This wrong tendency diverted her at every turn from the necessity of developing a strategy of questioning towards technical aspects of probabilistic calculations; the familiarity with probabilities was only a confusing element though it would not have been so had this familiarity been more fundamental and less technical. What matters here is developing a strategy, but this context was less familiar to the girl or hidden under the probabilistic context. The strategy required by this problem can be unstochastical, at least in the first approximation, and therefore ignorance with regard to probabilistic ideas can make it easier to find a strategy. In fact in the next approximation a stochastic strategy is to be preferred, but this is too sophisticated. We have used the same game in experiments with heterogeneous learning groups. Guessers start with the halving method but do not pursue it after the first or second step; they too seem to be hampered by probabilistic afterthought. The suggestion that the one who keeps the number in mind may cheat in order to have the game prolonged may then be helpful, probably because it eliminates probabilistic diversions.

I have adduced this example not because it yields much information, but because it might lead to informative observations. In the case of the girl just mentioned the picture is even more confused by a subsequent experience. When she had to play the same game with a draught board (with 100 squares), she did not have the slightest difficulty finding the right strategy. Why did this work go much better? Because it was geometry? Because geometry neutralised the diversion to probability? Because it reminded her of some seeking games?

I am not sure whether the approach "Is it fair?" of our television programme was the right one. It is an old tradition to start probability with games, and this is not too bad, but it is perhaps one-sided. What if we were to ask the question of accident or not and of equiprobability while considering all kinds of geometrical patterns – fishes in water swimming stochastically or following a certain trend, iron filings unordered or in a magnetic field, books mixed up on a shelf or arranged according to some system, rain drops on a pavement? Wherever numbers are involved, as they are in many games, a certain mathematisation already takes place, whereas geometry is a more original context. This idea dawned on me anew after the experience of the last paragraph.

I guess it is now clear why I adduce all these experiences and why I hesitated to open the present section. As far as probability is concerned, I still hope to collect more experience, and at the background of this experience to try didactic phenomenological analyses. At this moment I lack such experience – I mean experience related to acquiring, recognising, delimiting probability contexts. At this point rather than at the elaboration of didactic details I locate the most urgent task in the quest for understanding learning processes in probability.

In order to understand whether a game is fair, and what fairness means, one is obliged to quantify the consequences of accidents. Experience shows that at this point the quantifying attitude is not at all self-evident for 11–12-year-olds. In everyday language probability terms are most often of a qualitative character: quantitative clauses ('90% certain', 'I bet 1 to a 100') are actually not meant in a quantitative sense. But once ideas of quantifying a probability have started, the seeming obligation to quantify can produce an inclination to do so and lead to premature associations. I recall the two problems of Chevalier de Méré that led Pascal to the theory of probability. The pre-Pascal solutions show the noxious influence of number practice. In 'at least one six in four throws with one die', and 'at least one double-six in 24 throws with two dice', and in the 'problème des partis' the presence of numerical data seduces one to apply the schemes which are conventional in the world of numbers, with the consequence that the first problem is insufficiently, and the second not at all, put into the probabilistic context. Pascal corrected it, and thus far the problems are paradigmatic, in a definite way. As far as relations between theory and reality are concerned, the history of probability has been a history of the discovery of probabilistic contexts, which may appear trivial with hindsight, though they were not so in history nor are so for the individuals even if their learning process reflects in no way that of mankind.

I am going to enumerate a few examples of such certainly non-trivial contexts that deserve to be discovered: the law of large numbers, that is the idea of mathematising the track leading from mass phenomena to constituting the probability concept and seizing upon probability numerically, afterwards in the inverse direction, from the autonomously defined probability as a new starting point; the idea of interpreting observation errors stochastically; ever new ideas for recognising natural phenomena and processes as randomly conditioned and stochastically seizable, culminating in the ideas of statistical mechanics; the idea of accepting stochastically conditioned experience as such – mathematical statistics; and the idea of designing strategies of action consciously according to a stochastic scheme, in particular with the intention of withholding information sources from playing opponents.

I gave a somewhat abstract summary, and I did so in an approximately historical order, that is the order in which the particular historically paradigmatic problems were solved, rather than posed. It is conceivable right here that we must have the individual deviate from the learning process of mankind; in solving problems from the early days of statistics we can render the learner assistance made possible by the later learning processes of mankind. I will illustrate this statement with a more circumstantial exposition of the last example of the preceding paragraph.

Early in the history of probability and repeatedly later on people were confronted with game situations that looked paradoxical. As these games were quite complicated and would require lengthy calculations (for instance the game Le Her*) I refrain from expanding them and instead replace them with a simpler one, which I am going to copy from my previous book**: *A* chooses one of the numbers 1, 2, 3, 4, 5. If *B* guesses it, he gets from *A* as many florins as the chosen (and guessed) number indicates; if he misses it, he gets nothing. Of course, *B* must put up a stake in the game but the main question at this stage concerns the strategies that *A* and *B* should employ. If *A* writes down numbers 1, 2, 3, 4, 5 at random and with equal probabilities, it would be *B*'s strategy to guess only fives which yield him, as soon as he wins, the highest gain: if he wins at all, he would prefer, of course, to win as high a pay-out as possible. In order to cut *B*'s gain, *A* will choose fives less frequently. If he goes as far as to choose no fives at all, *B* will restrict himself to guessing 1, 2, 3, 4 only, which increases his gain prospects. So *A* must observe the rule: not too many but also not to few fives. For *B* it is quite similar; if *B* guesses too many fives, *A* punishes him by means of abstention in choosing fives; if *B* chooses not enough fives, *A* judiciously evades choosing 1, 2, 3, 4. And in a similar fashion it happens with choices other than five. Reflections on such problems were, and still are, even more confused by a seemingly infinite seesaw. *A* says: If I do not choose enough fives, *B* guesses less fives, but he knows that I know this and that I want to cause him to choose more fives and so he will not choose too few fives; but he also knows that I know that he knows this, and so on.

Formulated more briefly: *C* must inform *D* about the state of a system

* Cf. *Grundzüge der Mathematik*, H. Behnke (ed.), IV, pp. 157–158 (1966).

** *Mathematics as an Educational Task*, p. 609. Cf. H. Freudenthal, *Probability and Statistics*, Amsterdam, 1965, Elsevier, pp. 105–106.

with states X and Y. The actual state is X but this must be kept secret from D. Lying involves the risk that D who knows his customers, discovers the truth, by mistrusting me, C says to himself, so I will speak up the truth. D, however, can draw the same conclusion and say to himself that I try to mislead him by speaking the truth, so it is more advantageous to lie, but this reflection too can be made by D, and so on. (A shorter variant: He says X in order to make me believe it is Y; yet X it is, so why does he lie?)

Problems like this one, which for centuries were discussed unsuccessfully, are now being solved by J. v. Neumann's minimax strategy. Both A and B have to make up their minds to choose a stochastic strategy, which means for A choices of probabilities $p_1, \ldots, p_5$ in choosing the numbers $1, \ldots, 5$, respectively, and for B choices of probabilities $q_1, \ldots, q_5$ for guessing $1, \ldots, 5$ respectively. To every choice of these p and q belongs a gain expectance $L(p, q) = \sum_i p_i q_i$ for B. Now if B knows A's choice of p, he will fix his q such that $L(p, q)$ becomes maximal. Conversely A, if knowing B's choice of q, will determine his p such that $L(p, q)$ becomes minimal. None of them knows the choice of the other, and both of them seem to be caught in a vicious circle. This circle is broken by the minimax principle: A considers all choices q possibly made by B, calculates their consequence for every choice of p he himself can make, and then decides in favour of that choice of p for which the maximally possible loss is as low as possible, that is he determines p^0 such, that

$$\max_q L(p^0, q) = \min_p \max_q L(p, q).$$

B acts similarly: he chooses q^0 in such a way that his gain, minimalised by A's efforts, becomes as large as possible,

$$\min_p L(p, q^0) = \max_q \min_p L(p, q).$$

(It appears afterwards – as a mathematical fact – that

$$\min_p \max_q L(p, q) = \max_q \min_p L(p, q) = L(p^0, q^0).)$$

I refrain from explaining procedures to find solutions p^0, q^0 – the minimax strategies – they can be found at the places cited.

I stress once more that until J. v. Neumann's solution one felt quite helpless when confronted with such problems. I have never tried them at a low level, nor as an approach to probability, though I have various reasons to venture the conjecture that it would pay to try them. It is true that psychologists have investigated the stochastical behaviour of subjects in playing against chance instruments or against another player, as well as their learning behaviour, depending on a number of parameters, but this is not what I meant by the investigations I would welcome. I should like to employ such strategy games in learning mathematics and in observing mathematical learning processes, or rather I would suggest this be done; and after what I said earlier I would prefer to start with geometrical games. I am convinced this can be an instrument of investigation that on the one hand would lead us to develop instructional techniques and on the other hand might prepare for fundamental knowledge. The learner is put into a situation where he must act in one way or another; his actions are not only observed, but the learner is also led to act in a deliberate way and to argue his decisions; one tries to have the learner embed his actions in an unconscious strategy that might be reviewed afterwards more consciously. This would be mathematics emerging in a unique way from action, first unreasoned, and in the course of the learning process, more profoundly understood. It certainly remains vague what I promise myself from this theme, as I have not tried it out; but in spite of its vagueness, it will be well understood within the frame of my philosophy of education.

At which level could this start? I think as soon as the children have grasped the purport of stochastic games. I know very well that much then must remain implicit though we can seize upon it by mathematics – similar features will later on be noticed in geometry. At this level we can renounce the mastery of combinatorial artifices; but in the domain of probability it is just an advantage that one can avail oneself of the expedient of games which are understood by playing them correctly – I often wondered why certain games of cards are played so well by people who can hardly tell why they play them the way they do rather than otherwise. It is what I called the lowest level in the learning process, thus indispensable as a first step; if the learning process is well planned and guided, this base must guarantee that concepts are operationally available in the domain of action before they are made explicit.

In the field of probability, simulation is a most powerful tool at the lowest level; in the approach sketched earlier, as in any other, it will play a preeminent part. The significance of simulating for instruction in probability was first recognised by A. Engel; it is a serious shortcoming in my previous book that I did not pay attention to simulating in the chapter on probability. Since then I, and our institute, have availed ourselves of this tool and collected data. The isomorphism of a lot of instruments, which it is suggested simulate certain probability distributions, is understood by the learner with no discussion involved; it is accepted, and in no way doubted, that roulette wheels with six equal sectors are equivalent to dice; and that with the last digits in the telephone directory equal probabilities can be simulated. The question why it is so cannot be answered as long as only positive evidence is available. The learner should intentionally be misguided in order to provoke erroneous simulations, which may shed new light upon the positive evidence. It is entirely justified to start with geometric simulations; but perhaps it would be better not to pass from the geometrical to the combinatorial simulation without raising problems as we did in our television programme; the pupil ought at least to know that something new is coming up. The clearest transition is offered by the die where the geometrical sides are made to correspond to the numbers 1, 2, 3, 4, 5, 6. In the case of the die, the equiprobability was concluded from its geometry, in an intuitive and nonformulated way. The geometrical group of the die, which interchanges its corners, edges and faces became as it were the group of *throwing* dice; it was transformed into the activity of throwing dice. By arithmetising the die the same group becomes a certain permutation group of the numbers 1, 2, 3, 4, 5, 6; the geometrical symmetry is translated into one of this system of permutands. All this can remain unconscious or vaguely conscious though non-explicit, at least for a while. Wouldn't it pay to make this conscious in the course of learning processes, at higher levels? The connection between geometry and probability is not far-fetched. In former times people were afraid of geometrical probabilities, and sharply opposed them since they doubted the right of admitting *a priori* probabilities. There is a connection between both attitudes. I think the concept of geometry was too narrowly taken and the structuring power of groups underrated. Elsewhere* I stressed that many probability fields which spring from forming models of reality are in fact more richly structured than they might appear. Often they bear a group of automorphisms – called symmetries – which sometimes suffice to settle the probabilities, or at least subject them to narrowing conditions. The same right and the same duty that

* *See* Bibliography [39].

are appropriate to crystal and quantum theoreticians to take full account of the symmetries of their systems extend to everybody who practises probability theory, at least if it is done bearing in mind the relations to the real world.

Once more, I set this forth not because I believe that it should be somehow fitted into instruction; not because groups should somehow be made useful; and not because this would be a way to place them into a suitable context; but because it sheds light upon the position of the theory of probability with regard to reality in a way that complements the numerical approach meaningfully. The pupil – though not only he – accepts too easily that the faces of the die, and congruent sectors of the roulette, are equivalent in a probabilistic sense. At a higher level it is worthwhile rendering this more difficult to him (and to oneself) in order to break him of the habit of thoughtlessness. It is a non-trivial justification of what was thoughtlessly accepted to notice that the rotating die imitates the rotation group of the cube as does the rotating roulette the rotation group of the circle. Where does this belong? A renewed didactical interpretation of probability should find out.

I indeed think that what looks revolutionary in A. Engel's and T. Varga's approaches is only a first beginning. In probability we are attached to a tradition which is so durable because it is so good. Probability has been taught nearer to the reality than any other mathematical domain. The menace of a quasimodernism that overcame traditional arithmetic and mathematics teaching in many places did not hit probability teaching seriously. Fears I expressed several times* were not confirmed by the textbooks. It is true that all of them join in a badly understood show of set theory axiomatics, but this is restricted to the first chapter, or to the first two. After this obligatory kotow towards modernism it continues briskly with such probability theory as had its roots three centuries ago, in the style in which it had always been taught and in which the author himself learned it.**

So far the good side of faith in the tradition of probability instruction. Until a few years ago probability was at most taught in the highest grades of secondary education or even only at university; instruction in mathematical statistics is a quite recent phenomenon. The justifiable efforts to start earlier

* For instance, *Mathematics as an Educational Task*, p. 613.

** I exposed this in more detail in *Educational Studies in Mathematics* **5** (1974), 261–277.

with probability – much earlier – have resulted in a parallel transport of subject matter as it were – if I now disregard Engel and Varga. Psychological research about probability such as Piaget's and Fischbein's is also traditionally tied up. As matters stand at present, I stressed I consider this as a virtue. Today's virtue may be tomorrow's vice provided new virtues are recognised. I make efforts to understand anew the contexts of probability and their interplay – the present section was to prove it. I want to be radical, but where are the roots? I would like to observe learning processes, but what should I teach to be able to do so? I could continue with such interrogative sentences, but how could I write a last sentence of this section without an interrogation mark?

20. I SEE IT SO

The title of the present section has been translated from the Dutch "Ik zie het zo". It is what children answer after they have solved a mathematical problem if you ask them: 'Why?' 'How do you know?' Since the first time this answer became conscious and problematic to me – it was the solution of a difficult arithmetical problem by a 9-year-old* – it has perplexed me many times. One thing I now know for sure: the answer is no subterfuge, it is simply true. It is no symptom of guessing nor is it an acknowledgement of impotence of verbal expression. On the contrary: seeing the solution prevents the child from making verbal efforts.

If somebody asks you 'how do you know that this is Mr. Johnson?', and if Mr. Johnson is standing before you, you will isolate from his face, his body, his countenance, his gesticulations, his language, some features that are peculiar to Mr. Johnson, though it is another question whether together they characterise Mr. Johnson. If, however, Mr. Johnson, or his picture, is not before your eyes, but only in your imagination, it bcomes much more difficult to indicate some peculiar features, unless Mr. Johnson distinguishes himself from his fellow-men in a very striking way, for instance by a collossal beard combined with total baldness of his head, or by a wooden leg, or by a thunderous voice.

* *Mathematics as an Educational Task*, p. 129. There I translated the answer by "I just felt it", but this would not fit well here.

But why should I describe Mr. Johnson at all? In order to recognise him? I know exactly what he looks like; he is before the eye of my mind. In order to explain to somebody else what the gentleman looks like whom he is expected to meet at the railroad station? But then I would say: 'He will exhibit a copy of a well-known series of mathematical books'. This is simpler and more reliable.

Since much of what we have experienced as subject matter has been served up in a carefully analysed state in order to be synthesised by us we are amazed about such a primary phenomenon as global recognition and construct the problem how we manage to integrate the profusion of isolated impressions into one total stream. Yet in fact the total impression is the primary datum and – conscious or unconscious – analysis is *a posteriori*; it is a new direction of perception that requires effort and attention. We should not be amazed about children's seeing it so, but rather about ourselves who do not see it so, or who judge that seeing-it-so is not enough, or believe it to be a miracle.

Ourselves – this means adults. But the borderline is to be drawn at an earlier age. About 11–12 years. Then something changes, children do not see any more what they saw before. Do they not dare? Do they become more critical? Is it because the developing verbal abilities suppress intuition? Has reading laid such a claim on the visual faculty that less room is left for optical imagination not tied to language? Does traditional geometry instruction start at the age of 11–12 years because then one may be sure that the geometry of the 'I see it so' has disappeared? The traditional phasing of subject matter indeed rests on experience.

This section with its strange title will deal with geometry. I discussed traditional geometry instruction and its mere recent evolution in a long chapter of my often mentioned book*. Two tendencies were clearly distinguished: One quarter that considered geometry as an excellent opportunity to show that linear algebra was of some use, and another where people believed themselves to be able and obliged to 'save' geometry by replacing instruction in geometry by instruction in some foundations of geometry. This I contrasted with my own philosophy: geometry as experience and interpretation of the space in which we live, breathe, and move. And this fitted

* *Mathematics as an Educational Task*, Chap. XVI.

very well into my philosophy of mathematical education in general: mathematising spatial experiences and experiments as an example of mathematising in general. Has much changed meanwhile on the market of geometry instruction? I do not think so. Recently at a conference on geometry instruction the views and opinions were about the same as when I wrote that book. After a paragon of genuine, intuitive, locally organising geometry instruction – but then for university students as today these young people do not know any geometry any more – somebody asked why genuine geometry should be banned from school and only allowed at university. The answer was: "It's that the university students also get linear algebra and foundations of geometry."

When I wrote my previous book my view was directed from this basic philosophy upwards. Speaking more concretely, I imagined a course of geometry instruction starting at Grade 7 (our first year of secondary education) which, depending on the ability and bent of the pupil, moves more quickly or more slowly, or stays exclusively at the lowest level, possibly proceeding to local, or even global, organising, and which for a few may end with an incorporation of geometry into a system of mathematics.

There is nothing I would retract from this, but there are essentials I would add to it now, notably first of all and as a principle a change of perspective of my own. It is not that I have discovered new land: rather, I have discovered its importance, a relevance that is greater than I then presumed, perhaps a decisive relevance. I owe this discovery to the children at primary school and of pre-school age with whom I worked. Few, but nevertheless conclusive, observations showed me the way. With the main conclusion I opened this section. Geometry starts earlier than the 7th grade and geometry instruction should take this fact into account. Geometry starts earlier and in another way: about the 7th grade age something indeed happens with the children: geometry ends – I mean the geometry of "I see it so". And then geometry *instruction* starts. It does so for some good reason, since geometry is expected to be more than "I see it so". Quite a few concluded from this demand that "I see it so" must be eliminated, forbidden. But how can geometry instruction even include more than "I see it so" if it does not even include this? Again and again in the course of the centuries innovators hit upon the idea of starting geometry with the "I see it so". Yes, at the age of 11–12 years, which could mean: too late. Might we not be missing a chance, an opportunity that never returns, if we do not lead children at primary school age to geometry? This was a question which I affirmed the more positively the more children I observed. In the curriculum development of IOWO I insisted upon geometry. Of course this is more easily said than done. Proposing brand new, totally untested subject matter involves a serious responsibility. A responsibility, in particular, towards the teachers, who are asked to move into unexplored territories, and who are cruelly deprived of all the safety they are accustomed to in leading a class. It is an adventure to try out new things in the classroom. Courage is rewarded if it succeeds. Well, did you ever observe a teacher (or yourself) after such an adventurous lesson? Discouraged he is, since he does not have the class at his fingertips as he is used to having; it does not run like clockwork as it usually does. Then he needs somebody who observed the class to encourage him. Not to console him, but to tell him honestly that it was excellent: better, in its vitality, than all that is had at one's fingertips and that runs like clockwork.

Geometry in a primary school – it must be well prepared, as must all things, or else they go wrong. But preparing does not just mean carefully elaborating all details; geometry stands or falls with improvisation. Preparing means opening oneself to geometry, recognising and seizing upon geometry whenever it emerges, asking again and again the questions: Is this geometry? What is geometry?

Indeed, what is geometry? Often enough I have argued that geometry does not start as late as formulating definitions and theorems. Geometry starts as early as organising the spatial experiences which lead to these definitions and propositions. Likewise putting something into a geometrical context is geometry – perhaps I did not stress this strongly enough in my former discussions on geometry, so after my commentary on grasping the context it is worthwhile making up for it.

Let us assume that after the usual chapter on the geometry of the circle the teacher would like to illustrate the well-known theorem on the square of the length of the tangent. He asks the question how far one can see from a tower or mountain of given height, or where the horizon lies, or how far a television transmitter reaches. What has the question to do with geometry? Well, we mathematicians know it very well. But now take somebody whose mind has not yet been tainted by a profusion of geometry. He will answer: it depends on the weather, on meteorological conditions; and he is right! One must be a mathematician, mathematically adjusted, mathematically instructed, to get the mere idea that these questions have something to do with geometry, that these questions are to be understood in a mathematical context. To be sure, if this question is raised in the geometry lesson, after the chapter on lines related to the circle, the context is marked with a red pencil, and the only thing one has to do is look for the right theorem to match the situation. But in the open country the mathematical concept or theorem that is appropriate to the situation is not delineated and printed with big letters and figures. It takes trouble to recognise the mathematical symbols in the great book which is Nature, according to Galileo. I stressed this earlier; but I repeat it now because it is our everlasting didactical foolishness as mathematicians to offer reality in a form which according to our prejudice might be raw material but in fact is already mathematised. The problem of scope of vision or of television transmitters is better placed before the theory of the circle than afterwards as a so-called application; the tangent from a point outside the circle is more meaningfully motivated by the optics of the horizon than the other way round.

But let me make this remark in parentheses: I have promised to go to greater depth, not staying at the level where pupils have already got an intimation of the geometrical context (though for some it can come harder or easier to put something into a geometrical context), but reaching down to the level where geometrical contexts have still to be formed or to be made explicit, to the developmental phase where the geometrical seizure of reality is not yet supported by a verbal conceptual apparatus and its handling, where in efficiency visualisation is still the peer or even superior to verbalisation.

"What is geometry?", I asked a few paragraphs ago. Geometry at the primary school age is what, seen through the attitude of the primary school child, is characterised by the answer "I see it so" to the query "Why?" In the chapter on geometry of my previous book I had geometry start where efforts are, and should be, made to get another answer from the learner than adducing a mental visual experience. It is not that I would not have taken this more primitive answer seriously. I already stressed: if the child declares "I see it so", one should believe it and not question it. Many times have I witnessed children at primary school age seeing things adults do not see, with an immediateness we do not know. I think that this gift – is it not a gift? – is lost about the age of 11–12 under the influence of the developing verbal abilities, or at least weakened or suppressed.

As a teacher, however, one need not be at all content with the answer "I see it so". Earlier on I discussed what I called condensation kernels, devices to make internal vision externally visible. One of these condensation kernels is asking, when a group of children are taught, that the child who 'sees it so' should explain it to the others who do not see it; in the change from being asked questions to teaching others the child may acquire appropriate means of expression. Another condensation kernel might be to ask the child: 'Draw (or model or show) what you see'. Children who are given that kind of assignment get accustomed to illustrating their answer, and also their attempts at finding the solution, by such visible arguments.

Nevertheless, often enough one does not get more than the global, uncondensed answer "I see it so" which is indeed typical for geometry at the primary school age. Geometry instruction at this age might offer condensation kernels to "I see it so", but should not be delimited by the availability of condensations. All that can be attained in geometry instruction as regards ability of verbal expression is so much gain, but verbal expression cannot be the goal. As a matter of fact I stressed this formerly with respect to initial geometry instruction at secondary school. For too long people have tried in geometry instruction to teach the *verbal expression* of geometry rather than geometry itself and notably to children many of whom were not susceptible to this kind of expression. It should be the leading objective of geometry instruction in the primary school that it teaches *geometry*. It must be left to the delicacy of the teacher, who rightly likes the children's courses of thought to be precipitated in clean formulations, to estimate how far he can go in this way. If "I see it so" is replaced by stammering on the part of the pupil or imposed explanations on the part of the teacher, one has not made any didactical progress. Everybody who practises teaching is able to test for himself how difficult it can be to argue verbally what one sees clearly and distinctly. It is another story that it may be useful to try it, but this can only be motivated by proceeding systematically to doubt intuition.

Thus far my philosophy of primary school and pre-school instruction in geometry! From this viewpoint I would like to recommend as learning processes to be analysed those which I came across in the course of my observations, though here too the lack of a didactical phenomenology hinders me. It does not hinder me as seriously as elsewhere. If only I open my eyes, the examples of geometry in the primary school pour in. To all those who make great efforts to prepare traditional geometry somehow to make it fit for primary school, I would propose that they should for once discover and put in relief the geometry implicit to the teaching matter of the primary school such as it has been and is being developed right now. It costs a great deal of effort to conquer prejudices such as are imposed by the traditional subject matter, but it is worth the trouble if ingenuousness opens new horizons. Much of what I shall adduce here will appear to many not as geometry – perhaps not even as subject matter worthy of a learning process. Against this view I believe that we have to put aside traditional value systems and to open our receptors to all impulses however petty they might look at first sight.

I repeat the example of Bastiaan (4; 3) with the red currants: At the rectangular table he is sitting opposite his sister, his father opposite his mother, his grandfather opposite his grandmother, when suddenly at the dessert he lifts his spoon in the greatest agitation and ejaculates: "So many are we!"* Indeed it was six. I asked him "Why?" and he answered "I see it so", and then "two children, two adults, two grandpa and grandma". Possibly the six currants lay on the spoon in the same configuration of six as we occupied around the table, but this I could not see. At that time Bastiaan was still quite unsure with numbers and obstinately refused to count. There was some substitute for the number concept and this was, as in this observation, of a geometrical character – this may be normal at this age. Our set theory prejudices prescribe us to interpret the relation made by Bastiaan between currants and people as a one-to-one mapping; it is, however, more global, not atomised into elements but structured into groupings. Am I right to call this geometry?

Bastiaan plays with Bauersfeld's game of cubes. He puts them into the box in such a way that only red faces appear on the surface. The game includes 31 cubes with red faces; three rows of eight with one of seven elicit him the exclamation "There is one missing". Is this geometry?

He builds the fence of a farm from fence pieces. "This must be as long as this" he says and means opposite sides of a (somewhat crooked) rectangle. Is this geometry?

* *Zoveel zijn wij.*

Fig. 15.

Fig. 16.

Fig. 17.

Fig. 18.

Such questions can be answered more confidently if we proceed to higher ages. Part of the first grade of our design school is filled by the project 'Waterland'*. It is a fairy island; its picture hangs against the front wall of the classroom. On the island there are towers, mills, bridges, intricate buildings, landing places, a town with a square lattice like a net of streets and avenues, and outside the town roads and signposts. What should be shown on the arms of a signpost standing at this particular place; or, if the signpost with the pictures on its arms is given, where should it stand? Tell somebody who asks you how to go from the landing to the mill. How far is it from here to there? Where between the mill and the tower should a signpost with certain numerical data stand? What do you see around you if you are at these cros-roads? Where does the river come from? How can you climb that strange building in the right-hand corner? Furthermore there are a large number of sheets with puzzles: the island cut into pieces – though on another scale – which must be put together again; and conversely tasks of cutting the picture according to a given pattern. As a preparatory exercise to finding the shortest paths in the net of streets and avenues, a child must play a postman who delivers mail to addresses in the classroom. How can one find the shortest paths in the lattice? And what does it mean, if anything, 'a shortest path'? Calculations are made with lattice distances – children are liable to count touched squares rather than edges. How should one describe a lattice path? We will come back to this particular activity.

Some of the matter I just mentioned has already been touched upon in Section 16 'Change of Perspective': from "What is on this road sign?" to "Place this road sign"; from "What do you see when you are standing here" to "Where do you stand if you see this?" The pictures we used in trying this change of perspective were not easy, but they were not too difficult either for the children who know the island from beginning to end. As a variant on this theme, from an environment the children were equally well acquainted with, here are some pictures of the school building and its fore- and background. "Where was the photographer standing?" it is asked; "How far away from the school?" Look at the photographs (Figures 15–18). How is this settled? Of course for Figure 15 the camera was very near; for Figure 16 a bit farther away, but what about Figures 17 and 18? Of course, the height at which the background skyscraper towers above the schoolbuilding is monotonically related to the distance of the camera from the school front. If people had

*Cf. 'Five Years IOWO', *Educ. Studies in Mathematics* 7 (1976), No. 3.

considered in good time this use of the pictures, they would have asked the photographer to take the four pictures, or even some more, on one and the same line (preferably a vertical line to the front of the school). Or just conversely, one would have had it photographed at the same distance from different angles. Or one would have had him turn the camera at a fixed place round a horizontal axis in order to get more or less foreground in the picture. The designer of the project did not bother about so much systematics at the first approach. Should one adopt it in the revision? Should such material for 6–7-year-olds be already so heavily structured and schematised that all three parameters are nicely separated? This is to start a question for principles as to how heavily structured the material should be which is offered: I am inclined to offer younger children phenomenologically richer material, which as to explicit structure is poorer, and even with older children to start with this kind of material; for this reason I do not like logic blocks and would not expel the children in the foreground on the playground even if they persuaded the other pupils to look first not for geometrical structures but for friends in the picture. The farther one progresses, the sharper the geometrical structures may be put into relief. And this theme offers wide prospects for progress. It is a theme that can be developed vertically from kindergarten to the highest grade of mathematics instruction. From the qualitative separation of the three parameters to dealing with the pure case where only one parameter is variable, from merely qualitative estimations of distance and angle of vision to recognising and formulating the monotonic character of the relation, from reading the quantitative relation in a drawing or model to inverting this relation and the inference, from the experimental approach of making drawings to the geometrical approach, up to the use of trigonometric functions and survey methods – such a profusion of problems clearly indicates sequences of levels in the learning process. It is a very promising theme of vertical curriculum development of which, however, up to now nothing has been tried let alone designed. We did not even think about what could be decisive steps in such learning processes and at what age they could take place. Take for instance something like the idea of the rectilinear propagation of light, or more concretely, the technique of objectifying the relation between the observer and the observed object in a drawing where the eye of the observer and the observed thing are rectilinearly joined, and mutual positions of the joining straight lines are subjected to analysis: when in a learning process could this become operational? When conscious? When accessible to formulation? The fact that such a question can only be asked rhetorically shows how much fundamental observation is still to be made of geometry instruction.

From this theme I turn to another that has been satisfactorily tried out in 3rd grades (9–10 years) though it would fit into the 2nd grade (8–9 years) as well: geometry in the lattice, shortest paths in the lattice, lattice distances – I have already mentioned the mistake that pupils count squares rather than edges! Distances occur not only in a direct setting (the distance between A and B), but also with change of perspective: Find the points at a given distance from A. One observes the pupils working on such problems, how they discover the one earlier, the other later, and derive the symmetries of the solution from the symmetries of the lattice. How easily it is accepted that the solution is composed of parts lying on straight lines, and that the figures corresponding to different distances are 'similar'!

This theme can also be developed vertically. When and how can the pupil explain why the solutions must look the way they do ('if one is subtracted vertically, it must be added horizontally'), and that solutions for increasing distances can be inductively derived from each other?

My first experiences with geometry at the primary school age are related to calculations of areas of plane figures. In my previous book* I recounted the story of one of my sons who had posed himself the problem of doubling the square, made famous by Plato's dialogue 'Meno', and had solved it in his own way. With a grand-daughter of 8 years, and afterwards with many more children, I did it differently. I posed her the problem of replacing the drawn square by one of twice its area; after about half an hour when she had not yet succeeded, I comforted her: "It is still too difficult for you, but at some time in the future I will show you how to solve it." A fortnight later, I brought a geoboard with me, had her calculate rectangles with sides parallel to those of the geoboard (delimited by rubber strings), and delineate herself figures of a given area (for 10 she took a 3-by-3 square with a 'balcony'). Then I delimited an 'oblique' square (with the diagonal of the unit square as a side), and she jumped to her feet and said: "This is two, and it solves the problem of a fortnight ago". This discovery was followed by a sequence of similar problems some of which she posed by herself. An alarmed adult who

* *Mathematics as an Educational Task*, pp. 144–145.

Fig. 19.

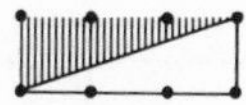

Fig. 20.

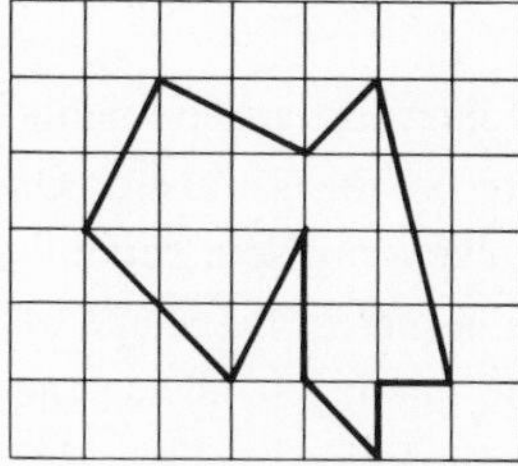

Fig. 21.

had observed us, exclaimed: "What are you doing with the child? She does not even know Pythagoras's theorem – or does she?" I am afraid by the time she has to learn Pythagoras's theorem, she will have lost her pleasure with geometry.*

Calculations of areas were also the subject of a theme for 8-year-olds: Re-allotment. A rectangle covered with a square lattice was divided by straight lines between lattice corners into whimsical, even non-connected pieces of land. This division had to be improved by reparcelling such that eventually each farmer would get the same area as he had had before. Three levels of operations could be observed with the children. First, that of cutting and sticking (Figure 19; the hatched triangle is added above in the right corner); second, local supplementing (Figure 20; the given triangle is supplemented by the hatched one to become a rectangle twice as big). At these two levels a given polygon (Figure 21) is dissected into triangles and trapezoids, which are dealt with by cutting and sticking or by local supplementing; the third level is that of global supplementation, that is fitting the given figure into a rectangle from which the superfluous parts are subtracted – in one

*Meanwhile I found an even better approach. Start with halving a square. Have a handkerchief or paper square folded such as to produce half a square.

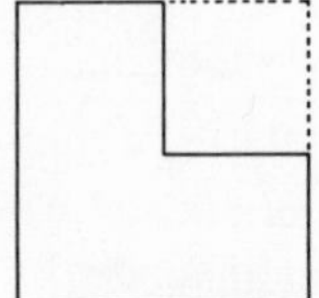

Fig. 22.

third grade class only one pupil reached – spontaneously – this level of treatment.

I now return to the geometrical achievements of the girl who recognised the doubling of the square on the geoboard. Once I gave her an L-shaped figure and asked her to solve a problem certainly familiar to many readers: the problem arises when a corner in the shape of a quarter of a square is cut away from the square, and one has to divide the result into four congruent pieces (Figure 22). She immediately drew the solution, which took her mother half an hour to find; whereas her grandmother did not succeed in discovering it at all.

Another time I brought with me a chessboard and a die, the sides of which matched the squares of the chessboard in size. When the die was repeatedly turned over upon the chessboard, the problem was whether it would reach each wanted position on each prescribed square. Whenever I gave a path to be covered by the die, the girl predicted the final position faster than I could check it experimentally. Since she saw everything, it was impossible to put her upon such a track of reasoning as an adult mathematician would follow to solve the problem.

I did quite a lot of geometry with this girl (who was not good at arithmetic at school!). The most surprising event was something that happened once when I visited my children, and, as usual, the girl (then 10; 3) asked me to give her a problem. I was tired, and as I had no better idea, I gave her a type of problem I do not like: Two friends are sitting in a pub where you may stay as long as you like after midnight to consume what you have bought before midnight; nothing, however, is sold after midnight. There they are: *A* with 5 bottles of beer; *B* with 3 bottles. A few minutes after midnight friend *C* drops in. Since he can get nothing, he suggests to the others that they should all share the provisions in equal parts, which is accepted. When the bottles are all emptied, they settle up – that is, *C* deposits 80 cents on the table, and the others divide it between them. How did they divide the 80 cents?

The girl wrote 3 into 8 and started a long division only to exclaim indignantly: "This does not divide – or does it? Why do you give me problems that do not go?" I answered: "But they shared the beer honestly – or didn't they?" For one moment she was dumbfounded. Then she drew eight rectangles she called bottles and divided each by two horizontal strokes into three parts she called quarters*. In each of these "little" bottles she wrote who had emptied it, A, B, or C; this included marking with C 7 "little bottles" from A and 1 from B. She also drew eight 10 cent pieces and gave 7 to A and 1 to B.

After this 'success' I had the audacity to propose her a 'tap problem': one tap filling a bath in ten minutes, the other doing it in 5 minutes, how about both together? She drew a bath, a big and a little tap, divided the bath in two thirds filled by the big tap and one third filled by the small tap, but eventually went astray in the fractions she was not familiar with.

'Is this geometry?' I ask once more. Certainly it is mathematics, and if people tell you mathematics consists of abstractions, I show them this example. Just concretising can be mathematics; and often mathematics is concretising rather than abstracting. It is a terrifying experience to see educationalists, who lack affinity to actual instruction, lost in investigations on a kind of teaching of word problems which develops around a linguistic analysis rather than the concretisation of the given texts – a hopeless method. The concretisations actually required will most often be of a geometrical nature, as was the case with the beerbottle problem. Is there any need after solutions like the one the girl gave, to ask 'why?' She 'saw' it and showed me lucidly, by the drawing, what she had seen – in fact this has become her habit.

"A birthday party with 10 children, boys and girls; when half of the boys had left, 6 children remained. How many boys and girls were there at the party?" She 'saw' the answer, and the explanation she gave her younger sister confirmed it. "A full milk can weighs 10 kg; when half of the milk is poured out, it still weighs 6 kg; how much did the milk weigh and how much the can?" She had big difficulties with the problem – it was about half a year before the beerbottle problem. Her cousin – a boy, somewhat younger – had

* Dutch *kwart*, obviously confused with *part*; she had not yet learned fractions.

difficulties with the first and then without any difficulty, solved the second. I should add, however, that with the boy I had discussed weight half a year earlier, whereas with the girl I had not even tested whether she knew what weight means.

Though 3rd graders may be familiar with length measurement, the geometrical interpretation of weight is something they still have to become acquainted with. This interpretation is then readily accepted: they are taught to compare objects with the balance (no use of weights) and arrange them linearly according to the results*. The linearity of order, obvious for length, is without ado transferred to weight, whereas questions aiming at transitivity are not even understood. The global geometrical idea of linear order is didactically much superior to the local logical one of transitivity – I refer the reader to what I said about this phenomenon earlier on**. What matters didactically is mathematising real situations by means of the linear order.

This is not at all self-evident. In the case of teaching weight to 8–9-year-olds it requires a learning process, and this is even true – you would not believe it – with time. To many of them the differentiation of the past is not a conscious idea. Our IOWO theme 'Time, Length and Graphs' started with a differentiation of the past, concretised by pictures of a sequence of generations (great-great-great-grandmother, great-great-grandmother, great-grandmother, grandmother, mother); this led to the technique of the time axis, upon which macro- and micro-courses were represented. The first graph was that of the growth of a baby according to its height – a quite natural example as the baby in its stages of development can be placed, as it were, upon the time axis on the blackboard, the tops forming the graphic representation of the growth. The steepness of the graph is readily interpreted as a – qualitative – measure of the speed of growth. An incidental mistake in the drawing (one interval on the time axis which is too small and which evokes the false impression of faster growth) is discovered as such and explained. It followed the story of a complicated journey which is translated from the geographical map into a graph, which conversely gives the opportunity to read characteristic features of the journey. The usual mistake of pupils, that in time-path graphs they consider the graph as a trace of the motion, is virtually excluded by this approach.

* Meanwhile the spring balance has proved to be an excellent didactic tool, even with younger children. Cf. Bibliography [73].
** p. 255.

Is this geometry? Yes, but in another function – not as up to now where the gist has been grasping space. It is, rather, interpreting space not for the purpose of understanding it but in order to use it as a tool to understand conceptual ideas that are less accessible to a direct grasp. It is geometry not for geometry's sake but, as people say today, as a model: the curve as a model of the function; the straight line as a model of the linear function.

Ratios and proportions rather than linear functions were the usual terms in former times, but the expressions themselves are still seasonable although the global approach suggested by the linear function matches better the development of the child and of the subject matter. I have made a closer didactic phenomenological study of ratio*. It is a subject that invites vertical curriculum development; we have not yet worked enough at it**. How closely it is related to geometry is shown by a trick that surprises people at every level. I put a coin on the projection table of the overhead projector. "What is it?" "A circle". "It is a coin. Which one?" . . . No answer. I put another coin beside the first and tell you it is a silver dollar. What is the first? . . . "And this is a dime" . . . "And this a cent". "Yes, then it is a nickel."

How many times does the projector enlarge? I put a pencil on the table of the overhead projector. Look at the screen. This is the same kind of pencil. How can the pencil be compared with its projection? By putting the second beside the first? No, then they are the same on the screen. Yes, but how many times does the projector enlarge?

It is so obvious that the geometric approach to proportion is more efficient than the numerical one that nobody will dare to deny it. But is it geometry? This too cannot be denied though it lacks the wealth of genuine geometry which we mathematicians appreciate in the classical subject matter.

Of course I have made enough propaganda, and often enough, for geometrical mappings, starting with reflections, in the primary school; once we even experimented with it, but it fitted badly into the frame in which we then worked, so we left the work unfinished. We will certainly resume it. IOWO people were, and still are, afraid the concept of mapping would not catch on with teachers and pupils. I do not share their fear, but I do share their prudence.

For the 6th grade (12–13 years) we have developed a subject matter that

* p. 292.

** Meanwhile it has been scrutinised more closely. Cf. for instance: J. v.d. Brink and L. Streefland, 'Young children (6–8) – ratio and proportion', *Educ. Studies in Mathematics* **10** (1979), 403–420.

looks more like what is usually called geometry than the above mentioned subjects. Its title is 'Time, Distance and Velocity on Our Earth'; its final goal and summit is an explanation of the 'gain' or 'loss' of a day a traveller incurs when he tours around the Earth*. The booklet starts with the circles on the Earth and the antipodal points; maps are shown, and the antipodes are established on a Mercator map. The altitude of the Sun is determined; which leads to practical angle measurement. How can the height of the Sun be obtained by means of the shadow of a vertical ruler? How do the height of the Sun and the shadow behave in the course of the day? Local time, time zones, and the date-line are dealt with. Train movements according to one page of the railway timetable, and meeting and overtaking on railroad and racetracks are graphically represented. How fast does the Earth turn at various latitudes? How does the length of the day depend on latitude and season? The race of the hands on the face of a clock and their overtaking, the position of the hands as functions of time, all these are graphically represented. And finally, similarly, the race between the Sun and the traveller around the Earth in the same and in the opposite sense, which, graphically represented, answers the problem of the gain or loss of one day.

There is no profound wisdom contained in the present section on geometry. Experiments on geometry at the primary level are certainly made in many places. It is my suggestion that we should not look for sophisticated, definitely mathematised subject matter, but first discover geometry as it presents itself. A further step towards a scientific approach would be to observe the reactions of pupils to such subject matter and to analyse them according to levels; a still further step would be to find points of attack where the limits of the geometry of 'I see it so' can be transgressed, where the pupils become capable of detaching geometry from its intuitive context. This is not in order to urge them to leave this context, but to teach them rational methods of grasping what they see.

21. AN EXAMPLE OF DIDACTICAL PHENOMENOLOGY – RATIO AND PROPORTION

21.1. *Preparation*

This analysis starts on a higher level, as to form and content, than didactical phenomenology: globally orienting, introducing concepts, settling on

* Cf. 'Five Years IOWO', *Educ. Studies in Mathematics* 7 (1976), No. 3.

terminology. However, in order not to overburden the exposition, formalisation will be rather loose; for instance, we will speak of equal magnitudes if *objects* of equal magnitude are intended (equal lengths if line segments of equal length are intended, and so on). Sometimes we will speak of the ratio of two objects if it should be the ratio of certain magnitudes of these objects (for instance, the ratio of two metals in an alloy rather than of their masses).

We proceed from a heavily mathematised example: uniform motion. 'In equal times, equal distances are covered' is a popular definition; and this is, if continuity is tacitly assumed – as it should be – equivalent to the formally stronger statement 'distances are in proportion to times'. There are two magnitudes* concerned: time and length; and a function that assigns a length to a time, namely the *length* of the path covered during the *time* interval. The ratios considered here are those of pairs of one and the same system (time *or* length); the ratios in one system are required to equal the corresponding ones in the other – this is the postulate of the uniformity of motion. We designate ratios formed with a system as *internal* to distinguish them from the *external* ones that will be discussed a bit later. For a long time natural laws used to be formulated in terms of internal ratios – good examples of this habit are Kepler's second and third laws; in equal times the radius vector from the Sun to a planet sweeps equal areas; the squares of the times of revolution are in the same ratio as the cubes of the long axes of the orbits. In the course of the algebraisation of the natural laws the emphasis in the formulation shifted to the external ratios.

If now in the above example, instead of the ratios of distances and the ratios of times, one considers the ratio of distance and time, one gets a ratio that is again a magnitude, namely velocity. This is an example of an *external ratio*. So internal ratios are 'abstract' numbers, whereas external ratios are in general 'concrete' numbers. The habit of formulating natural laws in internal ratios, which prevailed for so long, was rooted in the Greek tradition, which allowed algebraic relations only in a complicated geometrical setting, where ratios were only admitted between magnitudes of the same kind. This tradition pervaded the theoretical sciences longer than commercial and technical mathematics, where direct, non-geometrised operations and external ratios

* Concerning magnitudes, cf. *Mathematics as an Educational Task*, p. 199.

were earlier admitted; even today pure mathematicians often show little understanding for the meaning and practical value of these techniques.

Uniform motion can also be defined by the constancy of velocity, that is of an external ratio. The equivalence of both definitions of uniformity – internal and external – is an important non-trivial cognition. If formalised, it is expressed as the equivalence of

$$s_1 : s_2 = t_1 : t_2$$

(paths are in the same – internal – ratio as times), and

$$s_1 : t_1 = s_2 : t_2$$

or, for short

$$s : t = \text{const.}$$

(the ratio path : time is constant). Interchanging the middle terms in a proportion is so familiar to us that we can hardly realise the width of this mental jump.* Older arithmetic instruction was quite conscious of this jump; rather than bridging the gulf, one invented two kinds of division. Together with this twin monster the awareness with regard to this problem vanished, and since today nobody is aware of this mental jump, nobody raises the question whether it could not be too big for the learner.

I used the uniform motion as a paradigm. The concept of internal ratio for arbitrary magnitudes is obvious; it is equally obvious what one means by saying one magnitude is mapped upon another with conservation of the internal ratios. This then is a *linear mapping*, or with an older terminology, *proportion*. Yet the linear mappings of one magnitude upon another are also obtained by forming the quotient magnitude and postulating its constancy, that is the constancy of the external ratio. So there are two ways of defining linear mappings:

by the equality of corresponding internal ratios;
by the constancy of the external ratio of corresponding values.

The definition by internal ratio is analogous to the implicit (postulatory)

* It is a drawback of Greek geometry that, because of the lack of external ratio, interchanging the middle terms must be circumvented by means of complicated procedures.

definition of linear function; the definition by external ratio is analogous to the explicit (algorithmic) definition of linear function.

This preparation, however, is not yet sufficient. Ratio must be viewed in a broader context than that of relations within and between magnitudes. We want to include such disparate objects as

> a set of animal species with their average weights (or other quantitative characteristics),
> the set of flight connections with their prices (or distances),
> a set of countries with their numbers of inhabitants (or their areas),
> a set of articles with prices (or weights),
> the set of components of an alloy with their masses,
> the set of age classes of a population with their numbers,
> the set of use categories of the soil of a nation with the corresponding areas,
> the set of diseases with the number of cases for each one,
> the set of pairs of points of a plane figure with their mutual distances.

The common feature in these examples is a set (in general indicated by Ω, Ω', and so on in the sequel), and a function (denoted by w, w', and so on), which accepts values of a certain magnitude. The difference between the first four and the following four is striking: in the first case Ω has quite concrete elements and is defined by the common traits of its elements, and the function w describes internal properties of the elements – we will call such an object, quite arbitrarily, an *exposition*. In the second case the set Ω has as its elements classes which have been formed out of a universe according to certain critieria important for that universe; the function w describes the size of the class (not necessarily a whole number – see the fifth example). We call such an object a *composition*. The ninth example, a not unimportant one, is wholly different from the preceding ones.

The examples also differ in the way they are used. A typical use of the first kind: $\Omega =$ set of articles, w the price function, w' the weight function. The functions are compared with each other – they prove to be linearly dependent for 'equal' articles. A typical use of the second kind: One considers two alloys with the 'same' components and their mass functions; the sets Ω and Ω' are related by identification of the 'same' components; the mass functions w, w' are correspondingly related and compared; it is the 'same' alloy if the functions w, w' are linearly dependent. A typical use of the last example: Two planar figures are mapped one-to-one upon each other; this induces a mapping of the pairs of points and connects the distance functions with each other; if the mapping conserves ratios of distances, the two functions are linearly dependent.

The common feature of these examples of use is the following: Ω is mapped on Ω', which induces a connection between w and w'; the possible linearity of this connection is a point of interest.

I apologise for this highbrow abstract discussion; rather than a didactic phenomenological analysis it is a preparation in order to settle beforehand certain concepts and terms and avoid disorientating digressions.

21.2. *Elaboration*

Prior to *ratio* we have to discuss *equality of ratio* or *ratio preservation*, as we will call it. If this order sounds strange in the ears of non-mathematicians, it does, however, fit into a whole complex of ideas that mathematicians – or at least the younger ones among us – imbibed with their mother's milk – I mean of the *alma mater* university. To the same degree 'equally heavy', 'equally long', 'equally good', are prior to 'weight', 'length', 'goodness'. It does not explain here how the posterior is constituted from the prior.

Preservation of ratio is a property of mappings of planar or spatial figures that emerges early in a child's development – witness the understanding of a copy of a painting, or a model of a building. Preservation and non-preservation are stated by comparing the map with what is mapped – actually the thing being mapped may itself be an image. The things being compared can be somewhat gross parts of the original and the image – 'the head is much too big', namely as compared with the trunk – or global dimensions – 'much too long', namely as compared with the width – or distances of pairs of points can systematically be related to each other – 'all ratios of distances are conserved in mapping'. All these examples regard the invariance of internal ratios, though more sophisticated parameters can be involved – 'this is a right angle, so the one in the image must be a right angle as well'.

According to general principles one may expect such levels as:

recognising preservation or non-preservation of ratio by mappings;
constructing ratio preserving mappings;
resolving conflicts in the construction of ratio preserving mappings;
handling criteria for the preservation of ratio;
formulating criteria for the preservation of ratio;
deciding about the necessity or sufficiency of such criteria.

Term and concept 'relatively' (or comparatively) are rooted independently of ratio and proportion. The concept 'relatively', if not the term, is reasonably constituted at the end of preschool age. 'This chocolate is sweeter, because it contains – relatively – more sugar'. 'A flea can jump relatively higher than a man'. 'A journey to America is relatively more expensive than one within Europe.' 'In the Netherlands there are relatively more bikes than in Germany'.

The terms 'relatively more, as much, less' can be given various shades of meaning from qualitative to precisely quantitative. In particular to establish 'more' and 'less', estimations may suffice, though they can be refined by additives like 'much', 'somewhat', 'very much'.

'Relatively' can be made more precise by 'in relation to . . .' ('comparatively' by 'if compared with . . .'). For instance in our last example: If compared with the number of inhabitants, there are more bikes in the Netherlands than in Germany.

According to general principles one may expect such levels as:

understanding that what matters in certain orders is comparative order;
understanding 'relatively' in the sense of 'in relation to . . .', with the criterion of comparison filled in in the blank space;
completing 'relatively' and 'in relation to' in a context;
knowing what 'relatively' and 'in relation to' mean in general;
explaining what 'relatively' and 'in relation to . . .' mean in general.

The preceding is parallelled by a concretisation of the concept of ratio, which may be intended as an illustration but can lead to greater depth. 'Expositions' can be illustrated by histograms and pictorial statistics;

'compositions' by sector diagrams or other divisions of planar figures. For instance: the EEC countries are visually represented by rectangles with equal bases, and heights proportional to the areas, which are placed beside each other as in a histogram; the numbers of inhabitants are visually represented by rows of human figures, where, for instance, one figure is worth one million inhabitants; both can be combined into one by placing the human figures into the rectangles, in order to show the different densities of population (ratio of number of inhabitants to area). An example of a 'composition' could be a circle divided into sectors, the areas of which are in relative correspondence to the categories of the use of the soil by the nation; a series of such diagrams for several countries can be used to visually represent differences such as the more or less agricultural use of the soil.

Such illustrations are again a kind of ratio conserving mapping, with ratios other than those of the distances of pairs of points under consideration – in the last examples the relative area, the relative number of inhabitants, the relative area of the use categories.

According to general principles one may expect levels such as:

> understanding histograms, pictorial statistics, division of areas and similar visual representations as ratio conserving mappings of expositions and compositions;
> constructing such visual representations;
> deciding conflicts in constructing them;
> understanding the principles of such visual representations; and describing them;
> recognising conservation of ratio as the common principle in these visual representations; and
> describing it.

Furthermore, as regards comparing two or more expositions and compositions:

> deciding questions on 'relatively more, as much, less' by means of those visual representations;
> making such decisions possible by manipulating the material;
> understanding the principles of such decisions; and
> describing them.

The algorithmic counterpart of the visual representation of the concept of 'relatively' is the following numerical technique of processing. Verifying preservation of ratio under a mapping f is simplified by the remark that

$$w(A):w(B) = w'(f(A)):w'(f(B))$$

need not be examined for all pairs A, B of Ω; indeed the validity for A, B and B, C implies the validity for A, C – a property that might be called the *transitivity of ratio comparison*. As far as mappings conserving ratio of distances are concerned, the procedure of verifying the preservation of ratio undergoes further simplifications based on geometrical facts (in the plane it suffices to examine the preservation of the ratio for distances from two fixed points; the remainder is then guaranteed by congruence theorems).

It is less trivial to grasp that preservation of ratio can be described by the existence of a constant scale factor, that is, the external ratio. Further things to be grasped are related to the behaviour of the preservation or ratio and of scale factors if mappings are carried out in succession. In the case of magnitudes it is important to notice that the preservation of ratio is essentially recognisable as an isomorphism with respect to comparison and addition within the magnitude.

According to general principles one may expect such levels as:

simplifying the verification of the ratio preserving property by the use of the

- transitivity of ratio comparison,
- geometric congruence properties,
- external ratio, and scale factor,
- isomorphism with respect to comparison and addition within magnitudes,
- behaviour under compositions of mappings;

simplifying the construction of ratio conserving mappings by these devices;
deciding conflicts in applying these devices;
understanding these devices; and
describing them;
understanding relations between these devices; and
describing them.

In the course of algorithmisation this is complemented by:

understanding ratios in the context of the arithmetic of fractions; and
describing this relation;
understanding properties of ratios as properties of fractions; and describing this relation;
understanding the ratio conserving property of mappings as linearity; and
describing it in this way;
understanding the properties of ratio conserving mappings as properties of linear mappings; and
describing them in this way.

Though in a didactical phenomenology they would properly belong to a chapter on fractions we mention here the converse of the preceding group:

understanding fractions in the sense of ratio; and
describing this relation;
understanding the properties of fractions as properties of ratio; and describing this relation;
understanding linearity in the number domain as the property of preserving ratio; and
describing it this way;
understanding the properties of linear mappings in the number domain as properties of ratio preserving mappings; and describing them this way.

Ratio conserving mappings serve not only in visual representations; they have their own cognitive function, as is shown by our first example, the uniform motion as a ratio conserving mapping of the magnitude time in the magnitude length. The ratio conserving mappings themselves are illustrated

graphically (the straight line as an image of the linear function),
nomographically,
by means of the slide rule,

and algorithmised by

proportionality tables (proportionality matrices),
formulae for linear functions.

According to general principles one may expect here such levels as:

reading;
constructing;
understanding of the principles;
describing the principles; isolated and
in their mutual connection.

Recognising whether, and predicting that, a mapping preserves ratios requires principles that are more profoundly rooted and less accessible. They can hardly be cleared up without a previous didactic phenomenology of the concept of magnitude. The following discussion tries no more than to sketch a way in which this can take place.

I start with an exemplary list of adjectives, the meaning of which will soon become clear:

many, big, long, wide, high, thick, much, full, long-lasting, heavy, fast;
strong, old, sharp, blunt, soft, dense;
bright, warm, red, loud, wet, high;
sweet, beautiful, painful;
clever, interesting, sleepy, difficult;
valuable, expensive, rich.

Some of these words have various meanings (such as 'bright'). The adjective 'high' stands twice in this list; in the first place it may mean a property of mountains, in the second a property of sounds, but this does not matter here.

One can ask the questions:

Which properties admit comparatives?
Which properties admit doubling?

('Doubling' stands here as a paradigm; more general would be 'multiplying', maybe also halving, dividing, finally also adding.)

How to check comparatives?
How to check doubling?

How to make comparatives?
How to make doubles?

These are questions on factualities though with a considerable logical or linguistically analytical touch.

The central question is that of doubling. The means of doubling is taking two equals together. This is the way to transform a tower into one of double the height, namely by putting an 'equal' tower on its top. Temperature shows that it is not always that easy; the temperature of a liquid is not doubled by adding a liquid of the same temperature; likewise the speed of a rolling ball is not doubled by uniting it with one of the same speed. Parameters that, when taken together, behave additively are called *extensive*: number, length, area, volume, weight, energy, brightness (of a light source), electrical charge all have this property; others like temperature, colour and sweetness are called *intensive*. Yet, even parameters like temperature, or rather temperature difference, can be interpreted as extensive parameters, though of a process rather than of a state. So what are taken together are not the states but the processes. As to temperature, for instance, a difference of temperatures, which is obtained by means of heating with a source of heat W during a time t, is doubled, if the 'same' process is repeated (actually this holds only within certain limits). In the case of – vectorial – velocities, this taken together with the aim of doubling looks again different; if A with respect to B and B with respect to C have the same velocity, A has double the velocity with respect to C.

The principle by which the preservation of the ratio of mapping is explained and predicted can now be formulated as follows:

> *Two parameters of the same object, each of which is extensive under the operation of taking together, are linearly related.*

I do not claim that this digging has brought profound wisdom to the surface. The result, is in a wealthy wording, the criterion to which each able teacher will appeal more or less consciously if he wants to convince his pupils where they may use the 'rule of three' and where not. 'He who works double the time, gets double the money' he says, for instance; and perhaps the teacher puts twice the same amount of money under two equal intervals on the time axis. Or 'in double the time, double the distance' with a similar illustration. It is clear why one cannot draw any inference from the number of wives of Henry VIII to that of Henry IV, since the rank number of kings of equal name can with no kind of taking together be explained as an extensive parameter. It is shown that the rule of three is not applicable to the problem 'if a man covers a distance in 3 hours and his son does so in 2 hours, how long do they need if they walk together?', by the argument that going together, for instance of people who are equally fast, is no taking together such that it doubles the speed. Yet also in the problem of the working men who do certain work first individually and then together, the central question is: does the required time double if two equals work together? No, it halves, so the reciprocal time emerges as an extensive parameter.

According to general principles one may expect such levels as:

> deciding on the ratio conserving property of mappings in factual contexts and problem situations;
> recasting factual contexts and problem situations in such a way that ratio conserving properties come into prominence;
> deciding conflicts under these circumstances;
> describing principles of such constructions and decisions.

In these activities auxiliary activities are required in which, according to general principles, such levels may be expected as are:

> on behalf of orientation about ratio preservation:
>> viewing parameters which are extensive under the same taking together; and
>> looking for them;
>
> grasping the importance of such parameter systems for ratio preservation; and
> explaining it.

In the auxiliary activities required for the last items, one may expect according to general principles such levels as:

> deciding with respect to states and processes whether they are extensive according to a given way of taking together;
> finding extensive parameters for given ways of taking together;
> finding ways of taking together that make given parameters extensive;

finding parameters and ways of taking together that fit with each other;
understanding what extensive parameters are; and
describing it.

21.3. *Final remark*

This section has been an exemplary attempt at didactical phenomenology. Though developed on the basis of general didactical experiences it is a desk design. Only at one point, though an important one, has it been meanwhile corrected as a consequence of classroom experience. I did not pay enough attention to two phenomena, which in the definitive version will be accounted for by references to other sections of the didactic phenomenology: first the part played by estimations in the development of ratio and ratio preservation; second the diverging meaning of ratio in frequency statements of probabilistic character, where for instance 1 out of 10 does not mean the same as 10 out of 100.

With such lists of didactical phenomenology in one's hands (or in one's mind) one should observe the reactions in the field – pupils, teachers, counsellors, parents – to the integrated theme or project 'Ratios', and analyse them, in order to arrive at an *a posteriori* list of objectives of instruction. I expect that this didactical phenomenology will need correction, that superfluous elements will have to be cancelled, and that there are gaps to be bridged, in a way that the beautiful system and the linear order will be decisively encroached upon.

I do not know whether this approach can be more than a challenge for subjects other than mathematics: but the subject of mathematics offers its own opportunities and knows its own requirements.

EPILOGUE

The present book was virtually written between midsummer 1973 and autumn 1974 – a few sections are of earlier or later date. The original is German; it has been translated into English by the author himself.

Its philosophy and its instrumental ideas have since then been vastly put to the test in the educational development carried out by the IOWO – which does not mean that they have been corroborated nor that they have served as a handbook or guidelines in the developmental work. Nevertheless I may mention – because it was not my merit – a new system of formulating educational objectives that has been designed and intensely applied. Much has been attempted in the development of methods of observing the learning processes of pupils, teachers, and education students; and a vast amount of material has been collected. Pieces of didactical phenomenology have also been created. All this has been done in the everyday course of developing mathematical education of all kinds. But even now I would not dare to write more than a preface to a science of mathematical education.

The work that has been done is witnessed to by a large amount of informal – internal and external – publications. A small part of it has been translated into English and part of that has been or will be published. A broader stream of publications will follow, provided the IOWO survives and in good health overcomes its present struggle for life. But whatever happens, I proffer my thanks to all who contributed efforts and ideas to this work.

27 September 1977 HANS FREUDENTHAL

BIBLIOGRAPHY
OF PUBLICATIONS BY HANS FREUDENTHAL
ON MATHEMATICAL EDUCATION

1. 'De algebraische en de analytische visie op het getalbegrip in de elementaire wiskunde', *Euclides* **24** (1948), 106–121.
2. 'Kan het wiskundeonderwijs tot de opvoeding van het denkvermogen bijdragen. Discussie tussen T. Ehrenfest-Afanassjewa en H. Freudenthal' (Publicatie Wiskunde Werkgroep van de V.W.O.), Purmerend 1951.

2a. 'Erziehung des Denkvermögens' (Diskussionsbeitrag), *Archimedes* Heft 6 (1954), 87–89. (This is a translated extract from 2.)

3. 'De begrippen axioma en axiomatiek in de Wis- en Natuurkunde', *Simon Stevin* **39** (1955), 156–175.

3a. 'Axiom und Axiomatik', *Mathem. Phys. Semesterberichte* **5** (1956), 4–19.

4. 'Initiation into Geometry', *The Mathematics Student* **24** (1956), 83–97.
5. 'Relations entre l'enseignement secondaire et l'enseignement universitaire en Hollande', *Enseignement mathématique* **2** (1956), 238–249.
6. 'De Leraarsopleiding', *Vernieuwing* **133** (1956), 173–180.
7. 'Traditie en Opvoeding', *Rekenschap* **4** (1957), 95–103.
8. 'Report on Methods of Initiation into Geometry', ed. H. Freudenthal, (Publ. Nederl. Onderwijscommissie voor Wiskunde), Groningen, 1958.
9. 'Einige Züge aus der Entwicklung des mathematischen Formalismus, I, *Nieuw Archief v. Wiskunde* **3** (1959), 1–19.
10. 'Report on a Comparative Study of Methods of Initiation into Geometry', *Euclides* **34** (1959), 289–306.

10a. 'A Comparative Study of Methods of Initiation into Geometry', *Enseignement mathématique* **2**, 5 (1959), 119–139.

11. 'Logica als Methode en als Onderwerp', *Euclides* **35** (1960), 241–255.

11a. 'Logik als Gegenstand und als Methode', *Der Mathematikunterricht* **13** (1967), 7–22.

12. 'Trends in Modern Mathematics', *ICSU Review* **4** (1962), 54–61.

12a. 'Tendenzen in der modernen Mathematik', *Der math. und naturw. Unterricht* **16** (1963), 301–306.

13. 'Report on the Relations between Arithmetic and Algebra', ed. H. Freudenthal (Publ. Nederl. Onderwijscommissie voor Wiskunde), Groningen, 1962.
14. 'Enseignement des mathématiques modernes ou enseignement moderne des mathématiques?' *Enseignement Mathématique* **2** (1963), 28–44.
15. 'Was ist Axiomatik, und welchen Bildungswert kann sie haben?' *Der Mathematikunterricht* **9**, 4 (1963), 5–19.
16. 'The Role of Geometrical Intuition in Modern Mathematics', *ICSU Review* **6** (1964), 206–209.
16a. 'Die Geometrie in der modernen Mathematik', *Physikalische Blätter* **20** (1964), 352–356.
17. 'Bemerkungen zur axiomatischen Methode im Unterricht', *Der Mathematikunterricht* **12**, 3 (1966), 61–65.
18. 'Functies en functie-notaties', *Euclides* **41** (1966), 299–304.
19. 'Why to Teach Mathematics so as to Be Useful?' *Educational Studies in Mathematics* **1** (1968), 3–8.
20. Paneldiscussion, *Educational Studies in Mathematics* **1** (1968), 61–93.
21. 'L'intégration après coup ou à la source', *Educational Studies in Mathematics* **1** (1968–1969), 327–337.
22. 'The Concept of Integration at the Varna Congress', *Educational Studies in Mathematics* **1** (1968–1969), 338–339.
23. 'Braces and Venn Diagrams', *Educational Studies in Mathematics* **1** (1968–1969), 408–414.
24. 'Further Training of Mathematics Teachers in the Netherlands', *Educational Studies in Mathematics* **1** (1968–1969), 484–492.
25. 'A Teachers Course Colloquium on Sets and Logic', *Educational Studies in Mathematics* **2** (1969–1970), 32–58.
26. 'ICMI Report on Mathematical Contests in Secondary Education (Olympiads)', ed. H. Freudenthal, *Educational Studies in Mathematics* **2** (1969–1970), 80–114.
27. 'Allocution au Premier Congrès International de l'Enseignement Mathématique, Lyon 24–31 août 1969', *Educational Studies in Mathematics* **2** (1969–1970), 135–138.
28. 'Les tendances nouvelles de l'enseignement mathématique', *Revue de l'enseignement supérieur* **46–47** (1969), 23–29.
29. 'Verzamelingen in het onderwijs', *Euclides* **45** (1970), 321–326.

30. 'The Aims of Teaching Probability', in L. Råde (ed.), *The Teaching of Probability & Statistics*, Almqvist & Wiksell, Stockholm, 1970, pp. 151–167.
31. 'Introduction', *New Trends in Mathematics Teaching*, Vol. II, Unesco, 1970.
32. 'Un cours de géométrie', *New Trends in Mathematics Teaching*, Vol. II, Unesco, 1970, pp. 309–314.
33. 'Le langage mathématique. Premier Sém. Intern. E. Galion, Royaumont 13–20 août 1970', OCDL, Paris, 1971.
34. 'Geometry between the Devil and the Deep Sea', *Educational Studies in Mathematics* **3** (1971), 413–435.
35. 'Kanttekeningen bij de nomenclatuur', *Euclides* **47** (1971), 138–140.
36. 'Nog eens nomenclatuur', *Euclides* **47** (1972), 181–192.
37. 'Strategie der Unterrichtserneuerung in der Mathematik', *Beiträge z. Mathematikunterricht*, Schroedel, 1972, 41–45.
38. 'The Empirical Law of Large Numbers, or the Stability of Frequencies', *Educational Studies in Mathematics* **4** (1972), 484–490.
39. 'What Groups Mean in Mathematics and What They Should Mean in Mathematical Education', in *Developments in Mathematical Education, Proceedings of the Second International Congress on Mathematical Education* 1973, pp. 101–114.
40. *Mathematics as an Educational Task*, Reidel, Dordrecht, 1973.
40a. *Mathematik als pädagogische Aufgabe*, Band 1, 2, Klett Stuttgart, 1973.
40b. *Mathematik als pädagogische Aufgabe*, Band 1, 2, Klett Stuttgart, 2. Aufl. 1977, 1979.
41. 'Mathematik in der Grundschule', *Didaktik der Mathematik* **1** (1973), 2–11.
42. 'Nomenclatuur en geen einde', *Euclides* **49** (1973), 53–58.
43. 'Les niveaux de l'apprentissage des concepts de limite et de continuité', Accademia Nazionale dei Lincei, 1973, Quaderno N.184, 109–115.
44. 'De Middenschool', *Rekenschap* **20** (1973), 157–165.
45. 'Waarschijnlijkheid en Statistiek op school', *Euclides* **49** (1974), 245–246.
46. 'Die Stufen im Lernprozess und die heterogene Lerngruppe im Hinblick auf die Middenschool', *Neue Sammlung* **14** (1974), 161–172.
47. 'The Crux of Course Design in Probability', *Educational Studies in*

Mathematics **5** (1974), 261–277.

47a. 'Die Crux im Lehrgangentwurf zur Wahrscheinlichkeitstheorie'. In: *Didaktik der Mathematik*, ed. Steiner, Wiss. Buchgesellschaft, Darmstadt, 1978.

48. 'Mammoetonderwijsonderzoek wekt wantrouwen', University Newspaper "U", State University of Utrecht, June 1974.

49. 'Mathematische Erziehung oder Mathematik im Dienste der Erziehung', Address 21 June 1974, University Week, Innsbruck.

50. 'Kennst Du Deinen Vater?' *Der Mathematikunterricht* **5** (1974), 7–18.

51. 'Lernzielfindung im Mathematikunterricht', *Zeitschrift f. Pädagogik* **20** (1974), 719–738; *Der Mathematikunterricht* **23** (1977), 26–45.

52. 'Sinn und Bedeutung der Didaktik der Mathematik', *Zentralblatt für Didaktik der Mathematik* **74**, 3 (1974), 122–124.

53. 'Soviet Research on Teaching Algebra at the Lower Grades of the Elementary School, *Educational Studies in Mathematics* **5** (1974), 391–412.

54. 'Een internationaal vergelijkend onderzoek over wiskundige studieprestaties', *Pedagogische Studiën* **52** (1975), 43–55.

55. 'Wat is meetkunde? *Euclides* **50** (1974–1975), 151–160.

56. 'Een internationaal vergelijkend onderzoek over tekstbegrip van scholieren', *Levende Talen*, deel 311 (1975), 117–130.

57. 'Der Wahrscheinlichkeitsbegriff als angewandte Mathematik', *Les applications nouvelles des mathématiques et l'enseignement secondaire*, C.I.E.M. Conference, Echternach, June 1973 (1975), 15–27.

58. 'Wandelingen met Bastiaan', *Pedomorfose* 7, No. 25 (1975), 51–64.

59. 'Compte rendu du débat du samedi 12 avril 1975 entre Mme Krygowska et M. Freudenthal', *Chantiers de péd. math.*, June 1975, Issue 33 (Bulletin bimestriel de la Régionale Parisienne), 12–27.

60. 'Pupils' Achievements Internationally Compared – the I.E.A.' *Educational Studies in Mathematics* **6** (1975), 127–186.

60a. 'Schülerleistungen im internationalen Vergleich', *Zeitschrift für Pädagogie* **21** (1975), 889–910. (This is a translated extract from 60.)

61. 'Leerlingenprestaties in de natuurwetenschappen internationaal vergeleken', *Faraday* **45** (1975), 58–63.

62. 'Des problèmes didactiques liés au langage', pp. 1–3; 'L'origine de la topologie moderne d'après des papiers inédits de L.E.J. Brouwer', pp.

9–16. Lectures delivered at the University, Paris VII, in April 1975 (offset). (With Krygowska).

63. 'Variabelen (opmerkingen bij het stuk van T. S. de Groot', *Euclides* **51**, 154–155), *Euclides* **51** (1975–1976), 349–350.
64. 'Bastiaan's Lab', *Pedomorfose* 8, No. 30 (1976), 35–54.
65. 'De wereld van de toetsen', *Rekenschap* **23** (1976), 60–72.
66. 'De C.M.L.-Wiskunde', interview, *Euclides* **52** (1976–1977), 100–107.
67. 'Valsheid in geschrifte of in gecijfer?' *Rekenschap* **23** (1976), 141–143.
68. 'Studieprestaties – Hoe worden ze door school en leerkracht beinvloed? Enkele kritische kanttekeningen n.a.v. het Colemanreport', *Pedagogische Studiën* **53** (1976), 465–468.
69. 'Rejoinder', *Educational Studies in Mathematics* **7** (1976), 529–533.
70. 'Wiskunde-Onderwijs anno 2000. Afscheidsrede IOWO 14 Augustus 1976', *Euclides* **52** (1976–1977), 290–295.
71. 'Annotaties bij annotaties, Vragen bij vragen', *Onderwijs in Natuurwetenschap* **2** (1977), 21–22.
72. 'Creativity', *Educational Studies in Mathematics* **8** (1977), 1.
73. 'Bastiaan's Experiment on Archimedes' Principle', *Educational Studies in Mathematics* **8** (1977), 3–16. (This is a translated extract from 64.)
74. 'Fragmente', *Der Mathematikunterricht* **23** (1977), 5–25.
75. 'Didaktische Phänomenologie, Länge', *Der Mathematikunterricht* **23** (1977), 46–73.
76. Review: 'The Psychology of Mathematical Abilities in Schoolchildren', by V. A. Kruteskii, *Proceedings Nat. Acad. Educ.* **4** (1977), 235–277. (With J. van Bruggen.)
77. Review: 'Soviet Studies in the Psychology of Learning and Teaching Mathematics', (6 vol.), ed. by J. Kilpatrick and I. Wirszup, *Proceedings Nat. Acad. Educ.* **4** (1977), 201–234.
78. 'Brokjes semantiek', *Pedagogische Studiën* **54** (1977), 461–464.
79. 'Cognitieve Ontwikkeling – kinderen geobserveerd'. *Verslag 199e Alg. Verg. Prov. Utr. Genootschap*, 1977.
80. 'Teacher Training – An Experimental Philosophy', *Educational Studies in Mathematics* 8 (1977), 369–376.
81. 'Bastiaan meet zijn wereld', *Pedomorfose* **10**, No. 37 (1977), 62–68.
82. 'Address to the First Conference of IGPME', *Educational Studies in Mathematics* **9** (1978), 1–5.

83. Modern Wiskunde Onderwijs? Goed wiskunde-onderwijs? Intermediair, 28 april 1978.

84. *Weeding and Sowing,* D. Reidel Publ. Co., Dordrecht, Holland, 1978.

84a. *Vorrede zu einer Wissenschaft vom Mathematikunterricht.* Oldenbourg, München 1978.

85. 'Change in Mathematics Education Since the Late 1950's – Ideas and Realisation, an ICMI Report', *Educational Studies in Mathematics* **9** (1978), 143–145.

85a. 'Change... The Netherlands', *Educational Studies in Mathematics* **9** (1978), 261–270.

86. 'Soll der Mathematiklehrer etwas von der Geschichte der Mathematik wissen?' *Zentralblatt Didaktik d. Math.* **10** (1978), 75–78.

87. 'Nacherfindung unter Führung'. In: *Kritische Stichwörter,* ed. D. Volk, Fink Verlag 1979, 185–194.

88. 'Rings and String', *Educational Studies in Mathematics* **10** (1979), 67–70.

89. 'Lessen van Sovjetrekenkunde', *Pedagogische Studiën* **56** (1979), 17–24.

90. 'Structuur der wiskunde en wiskundige structuren; een onderwijskundige analyse', *Pedagogische Studiën* **56** (1979), 51–60.

91. 'Onderwijs voor de kleuterschool – cognitief, wiskundig', *De Wereld van het Jonge Kind,* 1979, pp. 143–147, 168–172.

92. 'Introductory Talk', Congresso Internazionale, L'Insegnamento integrato delle scienze nella scriola primaria, Roma 7–15 gennaio 1976. *Acad. N. Lincei* **326** (1979), 15–32.

93. 'Konstruieren, Reflektieren, Beweisen in phänomenologischer Sicht'. *Schriftenreihe Didaktik d. Math. Klagenfurt* **2** (1979), 183–200.

94. 'Ways to Report on Empirical Research in Education', *Educational Studies in Mathematics* **10** (1979), 275–303.

INDEX